ESSAYS IN RUSSIAN AND EAST EUROPEAN HISTORY

Festschrift in Honor of Edward C. Thaden

Edited

by

Leo Schelbert and Nick Ceh

EAST EUROPEAN MONOGRAPHS, BOULDER
DISTRIBUTED BY COLUMBIA UNIVERSITY PRESS, NEW YORK
1995

EAST EUROPEAN MONOGRAPHS, NO. CDXXV

DJK
40
E87
1995

PREFATORY NOTE

This Festschrift was initiated by James Fisher and Nick Ceh, students of Edward C. Thaden, and they also solicited the manuscripts from the contributors. George Huppert, John Kulczycki, and Zdenko Zlatar served on the editorial board, and several of the contributors reviewed manuscripts and offered helpful suggestions. Leo Schelbert and Nick Ceh prepared the final manuscript in cooperation with Catherine Prygrocki, Natalie Hector and Tim Northrup.

The essays have been divided into three parts which reflect Edward C. Thaden's main scholarly concerns: Imperial Russia, Eastern Europe (especially its Russian borderlands), and Historiography. Within each part the essays follow in chronological order and, as a whole, reflect Thaden's multifaceted and wide–ranging scholarly orientation. Transcriptions of names, Slavic transliterations, and style of footnotes are presented as each author offered them in order to minimize editorial intrusion.

We are grateful to Melvin Holli, former Chair of the Department of History, for making its resources available; to Stephen Fischer–Galati for agreeing to publish the volume in the East European Monograph series; and to Gene Ruoff, Director of the Humanities Institute at the University of Illinois at Chicago, for a generous contribution towards the cost of preparing the final manuscript.

Nick Ceh
Leo Schelbert

Prologue

EDWARD C. THADEN: AN ESSAY IN APPRECIATION

Zdenko Zlatar

I first met Edward C. Thaden in 1969 when I started my Ph.D. program at the University of Illinois at Chicago (at that time it was still Chicago Circle). I remember very well as a young student going to see a scholar whose reputation had preceded his coming to Chicago Circle and who had been announced to us as a great expert in Russian and East European history— precisely the areas I was thinking of switching to, but had not yet made up my mind about. It was thus with some hesitation, not to say trepidation, that I went to see Ed Thaden, not quite sure what to expect from such a well – known authority in the field. I remember Ed smoking his pipe—its aromatic flavor leaving an indelible impression upon me (I seem to think it was Danish tobacco)—and looking very impressive and just what I expected a scholar to look like. From the very beginning what I liked about Ed Thaden was his great charm: his ability to relate to other people in very courteous and yet very warm and human terms, his ability to act as a gentleman in the true tradition of a gentleman–scholar, and yet to show an interest in and keen appreciation of other people's concerns and problems. I was struck by his willingness to spend a lot of time (I probably spent three hours with him during our first meeting) with prospective students, to share his great wealth of knowledge with remarkable precision, yet admirable lightness, and to suggest topics and approaches with a touch of a master. During our first meeting Ed suggested to me more books in Russian and East European history, each important in its own right, than I have probably had time to read in the last quarter of a century since – but I have always been richly rewarded by his suggested reading and confirmed in my opinion of him as one of few authorities in the field who has been able to keep abreast of an enormous amount of publications, both in Russian and in several other East European languages, in addition to those in English, French, and German, that has kept pouring forth from the presses. It is indeed a singular achievement, and truly a mark of a remarkable scholar.

I always found Ed Thaden as a teacher at his very best in a seminar where he could bring to bear upon a subject a vast erudition with a lightness of touch which still amazes me. I always remember his ability to roam over the vast distances of Russian and East European historiographies, and yet summarize such complex issues in a very concise, one is tempted to say, elegant way. It was when commenting upon the participants' papers and presentations that Ed often gave an example of how one should critique without being acrimonious or partisan, of how one should be thorough without seeming petty, of how one should give pointers without sounding overbearing. I have never seen Ed Thaden lose his self–control: temper had no place in his dealings with students. But I have seen him share his experiences in the Soviet Union with his students in an engaging, often rather jesting way, which made us realize that we are dealing not just with a fine scholar, but with a very perceptive and sensitive human being as well. For his seminars I attended revealed Ed Thaden's profound sense of humanity in addition to his display of scholarship.

In the life of every scholar books, especially monographs, are so many signposts on the long road of his (or her) career: they bear witness not just to what one has digested, critiqued, and interpreted, but what one has used as stepping stones to other, future projects. Ed Thaden has always impressed me both as a fine connoisseur of Russia's internal policies, above all Russification, and her foreign policy, in particular in regard to the Balkans. Yet, it is in the area of Russian intellectual history that Thaden wrote what will remain a classic in its field for a very long time to come: his *Conservative Nationalism in Nineteenth Century Russia* surveyed a very disparate, and difficult field in a relatively brief compass. Almost every sentence in this monograph summarizes a book or an article: its mastery of compression is unequalled in its field. It is a book which in its coverage and interpretation claims the whole field as one's own and achieves it in an assured, yet modest tone. Thaden's *Russia since 1801* is in my opinion the best textbook on 19th-century Imperial Russia available not just in English, but in any language, including Russian. It is a great pity that by being out of print for quite some time it has not been available for purchase by students.

As a scholar training future scholars, as a writer of internationally acclaimed studies, and as a professor teaching students Russian and East European history, Ed Thaden set such standards which some of us, his former students and present friends and colleagues, can hope to emulate, but not really surpass. He has set us an example of what a scholar can be, of what a scholar should be. It is an example that I, speaking for myself, find constantly moved to aspire to. That is why I dedicated my second book, *Our Kingdom Come,* to Ed Thaden with the only words I could come across that would do justice to him: *tu duca, tu signore, e tu maestro.*

Contents

Part Three: Historiography

Part One
Imperial Russia

Chapter 1

TATISHCHEV'S NOBLE PLAN

Rudolph Daniels

With the creation of the Commonwealth of Independent States in 1991, Russia has entered into a new era of its history. It is a process of undoing of more than seven decades of Marxist ideology and rule by the Communist party. At the same time Russia has once again sought ideological and to some degree economic unity with Western Europe. These changes are often compared with those of the Petrine era, and along with the political and economic reform, these are sure to be a new set of values and an attendant culture.

While the changes in the current Commonwealth were in part caused by dissatisfaction with communism and generated by the people themselves, during Peter the Great's time, he had to force his ideas on an unwilling Russian population. In the early 1700's Peter tried to transform Russia into a modern, western–style state. He, therefore, modernized Russian commerce and industry, the administration of the Orthodox church and the government structure as a whole, and required the nobility to adopt western European customs, culture and attire.

Peter's administrative reforms strongly affected the nobility as a class. While he created nine bureaucratic colleges to oversee and to regulate everything from the navy to mining, he changed the meaning of the Russian aristocracy. Peter abolished the traditional system of *mestnichestvo* whereby a member of a noble's family had to receive an equivalent or higher rank than his most prominent ancestor. In its place Peter created a Table of Ranks. Each of the Table's fourteen ranks determined the individual's responsibility and authority in the Petrine administrative system. When reaching the eighth rank, an official achieved the status of hereditary nobility for himself and for his family.

More than streamlining the government bureaucracy, with the Table of Ranks Peter actually transformed the old Muscovite nobility into a new Petrine service class. He forced the nobleman to make greater sacrifices for the state. Peter the Great's generation of nobility had to adjust to the new demands and role: they had to learn Western ways and become an elite corps of this new expertise. Soon many noblemen identified themselves with the responsibility of continuing to bring Western culture to Russia. In short the Russian nobleman became a *Kulturträger.*[1]

One of the more famous of these new noblemen was Vasilii Nikitich Tatishchev who at one point personally served Peter the Great and quickly identified himself with his role within the new Petrine requirements.[2] Tatishchev distinguished himself in foreign service, and in 1730 he was instrumental in restoring Empress Anne to full authority following an attempt to limit her power.

He later developed state mining enterprises in the Ural Mountains and, as leader of the Orenburg Expedition, brought new areas in the south under Russian rule. During his whole life he searched constantly for primary sources on Russian history and wrote a multi–volume *Russian History* as well as a *Geography* and other important works. Some are still consulted today as they contain information not available in other sources.

During two periods of his life Tatishchev turned his pen to more literary projects. In the early 1730's he wrote *Conversation of Two Friends on the Use of Knowledge and Education* and in 1740, he wrote his *Testament.* Both these works demonstrate that Tatishchev had thoroughly absorbed the Petrine attitude toward the nobility and the state, and he wished to influence others to follow accordingly.

The *Conversation of Two Friends* was based upon a discussion held among Princes S.G. Dolgorukii and A.D. Kantemir, Archbishop Theofan Prokopovich and several members of the newly established Academy of Sciences.[3] Tatishchev was close friends with the Princes, and associated

---

1. For a complete study of the eighteenth century Russian nobility see Marc Raeff, *Origins of the Russian Intelligentsia.* New York: Harcourt, Brace & World, Inc., 1966. The role of cultural leadership is mentioned specifically on p. 87.

2. For a general biography of Tatishchev, see A.I. Iukht, *Gosudarstvennaia deiatel'nost' V.N. Tatishcheva,* Moscow: Nauka, 1985, and Rudolph Daniels, *V.N. Tatishchev, Guardian of the Petrine Revolution.* Philadelphia: Franklin, 1973.

3. V.N. Tatishchev, "Razgovor dvukh priatelei o pol'ze nauk i uchilishch," N.A. Popov, ed., in *Chteniia v imperatorskom obshchestve istorii i drevnostei rossiskikh pri moskovskom universitete,* I (1887), pp. 1–121.

frequently with the members of the Academy. The *Conversation* is in the form of a dialogue consisting of one–hundred and twenty questions and answers.

Along with mentioning major themes in Western European philosophy, Tatishchev argued that all knowledge derives from human nature and, therefore, "the proper study of man is man." Everyone must have a degree of self–knowledge to choose good and avoid evil, and he argued that the human's intellectual powers reside in the soul. He reasoned that when the mind reflects upon something, and it makes a selection, reflection is completed. The will, which ultimately makes choices, is influenced by honor, lust, and religious precepts.

The balance of these influences change with age. A young person tends to material things and the "desires of the flesh." When an adult, one chooses an honorable or dishonorable life. And with age one tends to be more religious and acquires an inner peace.

Using the analogy of ageing, Tatishchev explained that mankind increases its knowledge as does the individual. In human history writing was the first important stage of development, and the second was the birth of Christ. In more recent times he praised printing, since it increased the spread of knowledge. Books could then be made available to a wider audience less expensively.

Tatishchev's list of recommended readings included both ancients and moderns. Among the classical philosophers he cited Aristotle, Plato, Draco, Tertulian, Seneca and Tacitus. Among the moderns he suggested Descartes, Copernicus, Galileo, Pufendorf and Hugo Grotius. He also recommended reading theologians including Pope Gregory the Great, John Wycliff and St. Ignatius.

Since education, above all, should be practical, Tatishchev divided subject matter into five categories: 1. necessary, 2. useful, 3. amusing, 4. curious, and 5. harmful. For those entering state service, he recommended special emphasis on writing, geography and history, rhetoric, and foreign languages. He considered the arts "foppish," because they were cultivated by courtiers, and he believed alchemy and astrology were a waste of time.

Tatishchev used the second half of his *Conversation* to argue for a comprehensive system of education for Russia. Even though the St. Petersburg Academy served the need at one end of the spectrum, Russia lacked an elementary and intermediate system of education. Teachers had to be trained and schools established in each town. He recommended the curriculum of the Moscow Slavic–Greek–Latin Academy, with the addition of the study of mathematics and modern science.

Tatishchev stressed the nobility's need for education. By studying geography, history and foreign languages, the nobility would become an elite and spread Western ideas and culture throughout Russia. They would thereby continue Peter's work of westernizing the country. He thereby gave them the task of enlightening Russia and strengthening the monarchy. As for political education Tatishchev strongly supported monarchy as the only means of modernizing Russia. Moreover, he believed it to be the only form of government suitable for such a large landmass. At the same time he called for the writing of a new law code and the continuance of the reforms of Peter the Great.

From 1739 to 1741, Tatishchev remained in St. Petersburg and was held in prison on charges of embezzlement. He spent most of his time working on his *Geography*. Being in ill health and believing that his end was near, he wrote a *Testament* for his son which had implications for the Russian nobility. In fact, there is every indication that Tatishchev had a wider audience in mind.

Sometime in 1740, Tatishchev willed all his possessions to his son Evgraf and elaborated his ideas for the nobility.[4] He wanted the nobility to retain its dignity and honor as a class and, again, support the continuation of the Petrine reforms.

Tatishchev first reiterated the type of education he suggested in the Conversation, then recommended the military for the nobleman. Civil administration, however, was the highest form of service a nobleman could offer, since it took the greater knowledge and skill. Moreover, without a smoothly functioning state apparatus, nothing could be properly maintained. Young noblemen should "apprentice" in several of the administrative colleges to learn how the system functioned.

The nobility, according to Tatishchev, should identify imperial administrative interests with their own. They must always uphold and preserve the absolute authority of the monarch. Along with being impartial in every legal procedure, he admonished that the civil servant should "never refuse anything or ask for anything from superiors."

Along with their administrative duties, members of the nobility could still make distinct contributions at the imperial court. Their presence enhances the court, and they could be helpful in an advisory capacity. They must, however, refrain from hypocrisy, intrigue and personal gain. They should use their time at court to improve Russia's culture and help create a more cultured image for Russia.

---

4. V.N. Tatishchev, *Dukhovnaia tainago sovetnika, i astrakhanskago gubernatora Vasiliia Nikiticha Tatishcheva*. St. Petersburg, 1773.

Even retirement did not release the nobleman from his duties. He then should manage his estate efficiently. By looking after those in his charge on the estate, the nobleman would continue to render service to the state. In both the *Conversation* and in the *Testament*, Tatishchev gave direction to the Petrine Service nobility to become an elite with an important purpose. This new identity could be achieved through education and state service. Some would be most fortunate to even advise the monarch. The main task was to protect the authority of the sovereign and to serve the new Petrine Russian state.

While the *Conversation* was not published until a little over a hundred years ago, there is every reason to believe that it had limited circulation in manuscript form. The *Testament* was published in 1773, about twenty years after Tatishchev's death, and during a period when the nobility was becoming firmly settled in its new role. It was translated into English in 1860.[5] V.N. Tatishchev's *Conversation of Two Friends on the Use of Knowledge and Education* and his *Testament* bear witness that he absorbed the tenets that Peter the Great desired for the new service nobility. More than just listing duties and desirabilities, Tatishchev makes it very clear that these new obligations were to create a new identity for the Russian nobleman. He was to be seen as a leader in bringing Western science and culture to the newly created Petrine Russian Empire.

Works Cited

Daniels, Rudolph, V.N. *Tatishchev, Guardian of the Petrine Revolution.* Philadelphia: Franklin Publishing Company, 1973.

Iukht, A.I., *Gosudarstvennaia deiatel'nost' V.N. Tatishcheva v 20–kl–nachale 30–kh–godov* XVIII v. Moscow: Nauka, 1985.

Tatishchev, Vasilii Nikitich, *Dukhovnaia tainago sovetnika, i astrakhanskago gubernatora Vasiliia Nikiticha Tatishcheva.* St. Petersburg, 1773.

Tatishchev, Vasilii Nikitich, "Razgovor dvukh priatelei o pol'ze nauk i uchilishch." N.A. Popov ed, in *Cheteniia v imperatorskom obshchestve istorii i drevnostei rossiiskikh pri moskovskom universitete*, I. 1887.

Tatishchev, Vasilii Nikitich, *The Testament of Basil Tatishchev*, John Martinov, trans. Paris: Benjamin Duprat, 1860.

---

5. *The Testament of Basil Tatishchev*, John Martinov, trans. Paris: Benjamin Duprat, 1860.

Chapter 2

MICHAIL M. ŠČERBATOV (1773–1790) ALS KRITIKER KATHARINAS II

Erich Donnert und Eva–Maria Hartenstein

Im Geistesleben Rußlands während der Regierungszeit Katharinas II. nimmt der aus einer alten Hochadelsfamilie stammende Fürst Michail Michajlovič Ščerbatov (1733–1790) einen zentralen Platz ein. Als Militär, Politiker und vielseitiger Schriftsteller betätigte er sich gleichzeitig als Übersetzer, Historiker, Jurist, Philosoph, Pädagoge, Ökonom und Dichter.

Ščerbatovs Wirken fiel in die Periode vor der Französischen Revolution, die er zwar noch erlebte, über die er sich aber wohl nicht mehr geäußert hat. In seinen zahlreichen Schriften und Reden nahm der Fürst zu den gesellschaftlichen Problemen seiner Zeit leidenschaftlich Stellung, wobei mit Ausnahme seiner siebenbändigen "Istorija Rossijskaja", die in erster Auflage bereits 1770 bis 1791 erschien, und einigen anderen Werken des Verfassers, die sich ebenfalls mit historischen Themen, insbesondere mit der Zeit Peters des Großen[1] befaßten, die meisten anderen Schriften zu sei–

1. M. M. Ščerbatov, Istorija Rossijskaja ot drevnejšich vremën. 7 Bände, St. Petersburg 1770-1791; 2. Ausgabe: 3 Bände, St. Petersburg 1794, 1805, 1817; Neudruck: St. Petersburg 1901-1904; deutsche Teilausgabe: Russische Geschichte, 2 Bände, Danzig 1779. M. M. Ščerbatov, Kratkaja povest' o byvšich v Rossii samozvancach. St. Petersburg 1774, ²1782, ³1793; derselbe, Kratkaja povest' o načale rodov knjazej rossijskich, proischodjaščich ot Velikogo Knjaza Rjurika. Moskau 1785; derselbe, Žurnal ili podennaja zapiska...Petra Velikogo. St. Petersburg 1770-1772; derselbe, Tetradi zapisnye...Petra Velikogo 1704, 1705, 1706. St. Petersburg 1774; derselbe, Žitie i slavnye dela Petra Velikogo. St. Petersburg 1774; derselbe, Tagebuch Peters des Großen. Berlin und Leipzig 1773.

nen Lebzeiten nicht veröffentlicht wurden. Diesem Umstand verdankte er wohl auch, daß er von Verfolgungen verschont blieb.

Ščerbatovs Weltanschauung beruhte auf dem Gedanken der Vorherr–schaft und der führenden Rolle des Adels in der russischen Gesellschaft. Gleichzeitig trat der Fürst für die Beibehaltung der Leibeigenschaft ein. Ščerbatovs Kritik an den unter Katharina II. in Rußland bestehenden Verhältnissen nahm ihren Ausgangspunkt so nicht von der Leibeigenschaft, sondern wurde von einem Wortsprecher des Adels vorgetragen, der die Besorgnis hegte, daß sich die Kaiserin zu einer probürgerlichen und probäuerlichen, d.h. adelsfeindlichen Politik hinreißen liesse.

Ein wichtiges Charakteristikum der historischen Entwicklung Rußlands seit den petrinischen Reformen bestand darin, daß diese mit keiner tiefgreifenden sozialen Veränderung verbunden waren. So mußte die weitere Entwicklung des Zarenreiches unter den Bedingungen der bäuerlichen Leibeigenschaft und der Ortsbindung, Dienst- und Steuerpflichtigkeit auch der Mehrheit der Stadtbürger[2] vollzogen werden.

Für Fürst Michail Michajlovič Ščerbatov hat es niemals einen Zweifel gegeben, daß im Zarenreich der Adel der erste und führende Stand der Gesellschaft war. Um die Aufrechterhaltung und Verstärkung der Vormachtstellung seines Standes focht er ein Leben lang, und vom Adel handeln die meisten seiner Schriften. Einen weit geringeren Platz räumte Ščerbatov den anderen Ständen der russischen Gesellschaft, den Bauern, Kaufleuten und Stadtbürgern, ein, die meist nur im Zusammenhang mit dem Adel betrachtet werden. Eine Gesellschafts- und Staatslehre, die auf einem einheitlichen System beruhte und eine innere Logik besaß, hat der Fürst nie zuwege gebracht. Seine zahlreichen Einzelschriften sind völlig pragmatisch angelegt und ungeachtet des Scharfsinns des gelehrten Verfassers voller Ungereimtheiten und Widersprüche.

Obwohl Ščerbatov als Historiker eine mehrbändige Geschichte Rußlands verfaßte, die zeitlich bis zu Beginn des 17. Jahrhunderts reichte und den Fürsten als einen vorzüglichen Kenner auswies, hat er sich in seinen politischen Schriften nur sehr vage über das vorpetrinische Rußland geäußert. Ungeachtet seines Verweises auf das Wirken des Adels im Dienste des Staates und die dabei erbrachten Beispiele von Heldenmut und Tapferkeit, stellte er die russische Vergangenheit keineswegs als Vorbild für die künftige Entwicklung des Russischen Reiches hin. Die meisten historischen

---

2.   Vgl. M. Hildermeier, Bürgertum und Stadt in Rußland 1760-1870. Rechtliche Lage und Struktur. Köln, Wien 1986, S. 57ff.

Beweisstücke suchte der Fürst daher nicht in der Zeit des Moskauer Staates und davor, sondern in der Periode der Herrschaft Peters I. So besaß die petrinische Gesetzgebung für ihn geschichtlichen Rang schlechthin, und das Reformwerk des großen russischen Monarchen stellte auch für Ščerbatov zu jeder Zeit den Fixpunkt dar, an dem er sich zu orientieren suchte. Durch seine Beschäftigung mit der westlichen Soziologie und Staatsphilosophie war Ščerbatov klar geworden, daß die althergebrachte Vorherrschaft des Adels in mehreren Teilen Europas nicht mehr bestand und in anderen mit Macht dem Ende zuging. Das bedeutete, daß bereits vor der Revolution in Frankreich der Adel nicht mehr allein die Lebenswelt bestimmte, sondern sich auf dem Abstieg zu einem funktionalen Teil der Gesellschaft befand. Das Absteigen und Abgleiten des Adels von der Führungsposition in der Gesellschaft schien, so erkannte Ščerbatov, auch das historische Schicksal der russischen Feudalität zu sein. Das verbindende Merkmal für alle europäischen Adelsgesellschaften in der Zeit, in der Ščerbatov lebte, bestand somit im Übergang vom Ancien régime zur Moderne.[3]

Zu den Hauptrechten, über die der Adel verfügen mußte, gehörte nach der Meinung Ščerbatovs der Besitz von leibeigenen Bauern, der zugleich die Grundlage des Reichtums der "Wohlgeborenen" darstellte. Damit untrennbar verbunden war das Monopolrecht des Adels auf Grund und Boden. Das adlige Grundeigentum durfte auch nicht vom Staat angetastet werden. Demgemäß war Ščerbatov auch in seinen nationalökonomischen Abhandlungen bestrebt, die soziale Vormachtstellung des Adels theoretisch zu begründen.

Ausgehend von den Lehren der Physiokraten bezeichnete der Fürst die Landwirtschaft als den wichtigsten Sektor der Volkswirtschaft und verlangte ihre Intensivierung und Rationalisierung auch im Russischen Kaiserreich. So sollten Warenproduktion, Industrie und Handel ausschließlich unter dem

---

3. Vgl. A. von Reden-Dohna/R. Melville (Hrsg.), Der Adel an der Schwelle des bürgerlichen Zeitalters 1780-1860. Stuttgart 1988; K. Klusen, E. Weis, H. Roosu und G. Birsch, Der Adel vor der Revolution. Zur sozialen und politischen Funktion des Adels im vorrevolutionären Europa. Eingeleitet und herausgegeben von R. Vierhaus, Göttingen 1971; J. Blum, The End of the Old Order in Rural Europe. Princeton, N. J. 1978; B. Moore, Soziale Ursprünge von Diktatur und Demokratie. Die Rolle der Grundbesitzer und Bauern bei der Entstehung der modernen Welt. Frankfurt a. M. 1969. Für Rußland: I. Banac/P. Bushkovitch (Hrsg.), The Nobility in Russia and Eastern Europe. New Haven, Conn. 1983; K.-H. Ruffmann, "Russischer Adel als Sondertypus der europäischen Staatenwelt," in: Jahrbücher für Geschichte Osteuropas 9 (1961): 161-178.

Gesichtspunkt der Weiterentwicklung der mit Leibeigenenarbeit betriebenen Gutsbesitzerwirtschaft gefördert werden. Ščerbatov hielt es somit für möglich, die Landwirtschaft zu erneuern, ohne die Bauern zu befreien. Jeglicher Versuch, an der Leibeigenschaft zu rütteln, gefährdete nach der Ansicht des Fürsten den Bestand des Staates. Im Falle der Zuerkennung des Eigentumrechts an die Leibeigenen malte Ščerbatov das Gespenst einer grossen Bauernrevolution an die Wand. In der Beibehaltung und Verstärkung der gutsbesitzerlichen Landwirtschaft, die auf Kosten der Staats-und Kirchenländereien beträchtlich erweitert und intensiviert werden sollte, suchte er nach wie vor das Heil Rußlands. Dazu gehörte die Ausdehnung der Leibeigenschaft auch auf die noch in verschiedenen Landesteilen lebenden freien Bauern.

Eine einzigartige Stellung im Schrifttum zum Agrarproblem in Rußland unter Katharina II. nimmt Ščerbatovs "Denkschrift zur Bauernfrage"[4] vom Jahre 1768 ein. Sie läßt mit aller Deutlichkeit erkennen, in welcher Gedankenwelt die Masse des russischen Adels noch immer befangen war. Ščerbatov erklärte sich in dem Werk nur bereit, den Bauern das Nutzungsrecht auf Grund und Boden einzuräumen. Dessen Eigentümer konnten seiner Meinung nach nur die Adligen sein. Eine Bauernbefreiung würde nach Ščerbatovs Meinung den Adel ruinieren, ihn zwingen, außer Landes zu gehen und gegen sein Vaterland zu revoltieren, d.h. sich zum Aufstand zu erheben.

Bei seiner Kritik an der Sozialpolitik Katharinas II. sah sich Ščerbatov genötigt, auch ausführlicher auf den Platz einzugehen, den Handel, Industrie und Bürgertum in der Ökonomik und Politik des Russischen Kaiserreiches einnahmen. Als Physiokrat räumte er diesen nach der Landwirtschaft den zweiten Platz ein. In diesem Zusammenhang hielt es der Fürst für notwendig, daß sich auch die Adligen stärkstens in das Wirtschaftsleben des Landes einschalteten und als Kaufleute und Unternehmer betätigten. Gleichzeitig bestand eines seiner wichtigsten Anliegen darin, den Kaufleuten das Eindringen in den Adel zu verwehren. Ščerbatovs Hauptsorge im Hinblick auf die Nobilitierung reicher bürgerlicher Vertreter von Handel und Industrie drückte sich in der Befürchtung aus, daß die neuadligen Kaufleute und Unternehmer den "wohlgeborenen" Stand ökonomisch und politisch unterwanderten und von innen her aushöhlten. Für ebenso schädlich hielt er den umgekehrten Vorgang: die Verbürgerlichung von Adligen; denn in einem

---

4. Zapiska po krest' janskomu voprosu, in: M. M. Ščerbatov, Neizdannye sočinenija. Moskau 1935, S. 3-15.

solchen Falle würden sich die nunmehr Bürgerlichen ihrer Hauptaufgabe, dem Staatsdienst, entziehen.

Mit ebensolcher Schärfe wandte sich der Fürst gegen die Forderung bürgerlicher Unternehmer und Kaufleute auf Zuerkennung des Besitzrechts an Grund und Boden und leibeigenen Bauern sowie dagegen, daß adlige Mädchen nach ihrer Vermählung mit Bürgerlichen all ihre Privilegien, darunter auch das Recht auf Grund und Boden sowie auf Leibeigenenbesitz, behielten.

In seinen Spätwerken hat Ščerbatov eine Ehe zwischen Angehörigen verschiedener Stände überhaupt für unzulässig erklärt und darauf hingewiesen, daß durch Heiraten zwischen Bürgerlichen und Adligen die Adelsehre vernichtet und die Unzucht gefördert würde. Für das Verständnis der Geschichte Rußlands in der zweiten Hälfte des 18. Jahrhunderts ist es wichtig festzustellen, daß der russische Adel in seiner Masse der auswärtigen Politik und den Kriegen Katharines II. ablehnend gegenüberstand. Dieser Umstand fand in den Anschauungen Ščerbatovs einen deutlichen Ausdruck. So nahm der Fürst in mehreren seiner Schriften eine kriegsfeindliche Haltung ein. Nach seiner Auffassung waren die Kriege schädlich, und Hunger, Tod, Bauernaufstände, Steuererhöhung, Entvölkerung ganzer Dörfer und viele andere Übel mehr die Begleiterscheinungen und Folgen militärischer Auseinandersetzungen. Nicht Gebietserweiterung, sondern größere Bevölkerungsdichte und Geburtenzuwachs, verbunden mit einer wohlgeordneten Verwaltung des Reiches, bildeten nach seiner Ansicht die Grundlage für den Reichtum eines Staatswesens. Deshalb hielt es Ščerbatov für sinnlos, auf Eroberungen auszugehen, sich dünn besiedelte Territorien anzueignen und fremde Völker zu unterwerfen, die selbst in einem Zeitraum von mehreren Jahrhunderten vom russischen Volk nicht assimiliert werden könnten.

In seinen Stellungnahmen zur auswärtigen Politik und den Kriegen Katharinas II[5], seiner Denkschrift über die Militärsiedlungen[6] und anderen Werken wandte er sich gegen den Blutzoll, den das russische Volk in den verheerenden Kriegen zu entrichten hatte. Anstelle der üblichen Rekrutierungen verlangte der Fürst die Einrichtung von Militärsiedlungen, aus denen die erforderlichen Soldatenkontingente geschöpft werden sollten. Durch diese Form der Reorganisation der russischen Armee erhoffte sich Ščerbatov nicht nur eine Befreiung der Gutsbesitzerwirtschaften von den

---

5.   Vgl. A. Lentin, Prince M. M. Shcherbatov as Critic of the Catherine II's Foreign Policy, in: The Slavonic and East European Review 40 (1961/62), S. 365-381.

6.   Mnenie o poselennych vojskach, in: Ščerbatov, Neizdannye sočinenija, S. 64-83.

bedrückenden Rekrutenaushebungen, sondern auch die Erlösung von den materiellen Abgaben, die für den Unterhalt der Truppen in der Hauptsache von der leibeigenen Bevölkerung aufgebracht werden mußte. Als Schüler der westlichen Aufklärer beklagte Ščerbatov die Greuel und Massaker der Kriege und hielt nur Verteidigungskriege für gerechtfertigt. Ausgehend davon beurteilte er Katharinas auswärtige Politik und Kriege als völlig verfehlt, und er weigerte sich, der großen Kaiserin staatsmännische Fähigkeiten zuzuerkennen. Im letzten Jahrzehnt seines Lebens, in den 80er Jahren, verfaßte Ščerbatov seine reifsten Arbeiten. Beruflich wirkte er in dieser Zeit als Senator an mehreren Untersuchungen und Gerichtsverfahren mit, die 1785 in den Gouvernements Vladimir, Jaroslav' und Kostroma gegen die dortigen Würdenträger wegen deren Bestechlichkeit geführt wurden. Mit diesen Aktivitäten endete zugleich die berufliche Laufbahn des Fürsten, der noch im selben Jahr die Kaiserin aus gesundheitlichen Gründen um die Versetzung in den Ruhestand bat, was ihm auch gewährt wurde.

Aller Amtsverpflichtungen ledig, nutzte Ščerbatov nun die ihm noch vergönnten Jahre zu einer produktiven literarischen Wirksamkeit. In eben dieser Zeit entstanden jene Werke, durch die er berühmt werden sollte, so 1784 seine utopische Staatsschrift "Reise ins Land Ophir" und 1786/89 das Anklagewerk "Über die Sittenverderbnis in Rußland", die wohl schärfste Kritik am Herrschaftssystem Katharinas II. Zu den anderen grundlegenden Arbeiten des Fürsten, die in der zweiten Hälfte der 80er Jahre verfaßt wurden, gehörten auch Ščerbatovs Abhandlungen "Gedanken über den Adel"[7] und "Bemerkungen eines treuen Sohnes des Vaterlandes über die Rechte des Adels im Manifest"[8], d.h. in Katharinas II. Gnadenurkunde an den Adel vom Jahre 1785. Damit in Zusammenhang standen auch Ščerbatovs Schriften über die Bauern und Kaufleute, Landwirtschaft, Handel, Industrie, Finanzen, Staatshaushalt, Gesetzgebung und anderes mehr. Seine letzte Arbeit, die der Fürst wenige Monate vor seinem Tod, im Juli 1790, abschloß, trug den Titel: "Betrachtungen darüber, ob man Adlige zu Kaufleuten machen soll"[9].

Ungeachtet dessen, daß von Ščerbatovs Werken zu Lebzeiten des Verfassers nur wenige im Druck erschienen, war der Fürst ein lautstarker Sprecher des

---

7. Razmyšlenie o dvorjanstve, in: Ščerbatov, Sočinenija, Bd. 1, Spalten 219–268.

8. Primečanija vernogo syna otečestvo na dvorjanskie prava na Manifest, in: Ebenda, Spalten 269-300.

9. Razmotrenie o voprose-mogut li dvorjane zapisyvat'sja v kupcy?, in: Ščerbatov, Neizdannye sočinenija, S. 139-158.

Adels in der Gesetzgebenden Versammlung Katharinas II. von 1767/68; dies bewirkte offenbar, daß er ohne sein Wissen im Jahre 1772 von einer Verschwörergruppe als Kandidat für den russischen Kaiserthron aufgestellt wurde, da man von ihm eine konsequentere Adelspolitik erwarten konnte, als sie von Kaiserin Katharina II. verfolgt wurde. Jedoch nach seinem Tod 1790 fielen Ščerbatov und sein Werk rasch der Vergessenheit anheim. Dies galt auch für Ščerbatov als Historiker. Nicht er, sondern der Dichter Nikolaj Michajlovič Karamzin erlangte als russischer Geschichtsschreiber Berühmtheit, mit dem sich der Fürst, dessen voluminöse Geschichtsbände in einer außerordentlich unbeholfenen und sprachlich schwerfälligen Sprache abgefaßt waren, in keiner Weise messen konnte.

Noch um die Mitte des 19. Jahrhunderts, als in Rußland die Vorbereitungen zur Aufhebung der Leibeigenschaft durchgeführt wurden, dachte niemand daran, die Werke Ščerbatovs, dieses eingefleischten Gegners der Bauernbefreiung, zu veröffentlichen. Es kam daher einer Sensation gleich, als Alexander Herzen 1858 in seiner Londoner Druckerei Ščerbatovs Anklageschrift "Über die Sittenverderbnis in Rußland"[10] herausbrachte und damit auch den Druck von Schriften Ščerbatovs in Rußland selbst bewirkte, deren sich die Forschung rasch bemächtigte. In den jetzt ebenfalls erscheinenden Werken über Ščerbatov wurde der Fürst freilich weniger als Befürworter der Leibeigenschaft, sondern vornehmlich als Kritiker und Gegner Katharinas II. betrachtet. In den Jahren 1896 bis 1903 erschien dann die große vierbändige Ausgabe seiner Werke[11]. Ihr folgten 1901 bis 1904 eine Neuausgabe seiner siebenbändigen "Istorija Rossijskaja"[12], 1908 wichtige Materialien zu einer Biographie des Fürsten[13] und 1935 die bislang letzte Edition bis dahin nicht veröffentlichter Schriften Ščerbatovs.[14]

Mit den genannten Ausgaben der Werke Ščerbatovs ist der literarische Nachlaß des Fürsten jedoch keineswegs ediert und der Forschung zugänglich. Vielmehr befinden sich zahlreiche Ščerbatov-Handschriften und solche, als deren Verfasser der Fürst gilt, in mehreren Archiven und Museen Rußlands[15],

10. Neuausgabe: O povreždenii nravov v Rossii M. Ščerbatova i Putešestvie A. Radiščeva. Faksimil'noe izdanie. Moskau 1983.

11. M. M. Ščerbatov, Sočinenija. 4 Bände, St. Petersburg 1896-1903.

12. Anmerkung 1.

13. Knjaź D. Šachovskoj, Russkij deputat XVIII veka (Novye materialy dlja biografii kn. Ščerbatova), in: Minuvšie gody, Nov. 1908, S. 256-287.

14. Anmerkung 4.

15. Vgl. J. M. Afferica, Consideration of the Formation of the Hermitage Collection of Russian Mannuscripts, in: Forschungen zur osteuropäischen Geschichte 24 (1974), S. 237-336.

so daß auch gegenwärtig die bis 1935 veröffentlichten Arbeiten noch immer die Grundlage für die Erforschung des Wirkens M.M. Ščerbatovs darstellen.

Die besondere Aufmerksamkeit der Forschung fanden von Anfang an Ščerbatovs Anklageschrift "O povreždenii nravov v Rossii", von der auch eine deutsche und eine englische Ausgabe[16] vorliegen, sowie das umfängliche Werk "Putešestvie v zemlju Ofirskuju"[17], das bislang in keine andere Sprache übersetzt worden ist. In der ehemahigen Sowietunion sind nach 1945 nur wenige Arbeiten erschienen, die sich mit Ščerbatov und seinen Werken befassen. Zu ihnen zählen insbesondere das Buch von I.A. Fedosov sowie die Studien von P.N. Berkov, Z.P. Rustam-zade und N.Ju. Èjdel'man.[18] Zu den im Ausland veröffentlichten Arbeiten gehören die von G. Sacke, N.N. Alexeiev, M. Raeff, A. Lentin, P. Dukes, E. Donnert, J.M. Afferica, Ch. Lübke, D. Boden und W. Daniel.[19] Mit Ščerbatovs Werk "Reise ins Land Ophir" haben sich zuletzt und unabhängig voneinander E. Waegemans und

16. in: Sočinenija, Bd. 2, Spalten 133-246; M. Schtscherbatow, Über die Sittenverderbnis in Rußland. Hrsg. von K. Stählin, Berlin 1925; M. M. Shcherbatov, On the Corruption of Morals in Russia. Hrsg. und übersetzt von A. Lentin, Cambridge 1969.

17. in: Sočinenija, Bd. 1, Spalten 749-1060.

18. I. A. Fedosov, Iz istorii ruskoj obščestvennoj mysli XVIII stoletija. M. M. Ščerbatov. Moskau 1967; P. N. Berkov, "Umnyj razgovor" M. M. Ščerbatova, in: Russkaja literatura 3/1966, S. 79-81; Z. P. Rustam-zade, "Umnyj razgovor" M. M. Ščerbatova v svete ego social'no-političeskich vzgljadov, in: Ebenda, S. 76-79; N. Ja. Ejdel'man, [Einleitung und Kommentar zu]: O povreždenii nravov v Rossii (Anmerkung 10).

19. Backe, Fürst Michail Ščerbatov und seine Schriften, in: Zeitschrift für Slavische Philologie 16 (1939), S. 353-361; N. N. Alexeiev, Beiträge zur Geschichte des russischen Absolutismus im 18.Jahrhundert, in: Forschungen zur osteuropäischen Geschichte 6 (1958), S. 7-81; M. Raeff, State and Nobility in the Ideologie of M. M. Shcherbatov, in: American Slavic and East European Review 19 (1960), S. 363-379; P. Dukes, Catherine the Great and the Russian Nobility. Cambridge 1967; M. M. Shcherbatov, On the Corruption of Morals in Russia. Hrsg. von Lentin, Cambridge 1969; E. Donnert, Michail Ščerbatov als politischer Ideologe des russischen Adels in der zweiten Hälfte des 18.Jahrhunderts, in: Zeitschrift für Slawistik 18 (1973), S. 411-421; J. M. Afferica, The Political and Social Thought of Prince M. M. Shcherbatov. Diss. Harvard 1967 (und Anmerkung 15); Ch. Lübke, Novgorod in der russischen Literatur. Berlin (West) 1984; D. Boden, Sozialpolitische Züge in den russischen Erzählwerken des 18./19.Jahrhunderts. Zur Geschichte der Utopie in der russischen Literatur, in: Korrespondenzen. Festschrift für Dietrich Gerhard aus Anlaß des 65. Geburtstages. Gießen 1977, S. 36-50; W. Daniel, Conflict between Economic Vision and Economic Reality: The Case of M. M. Shcherbatov, in: Slavonic and East European Review 67 (1989), 1, S. 42-67.

E.-M. Hartenstein[20] befaßt. Angesichts dessen, daß auch Waegemans und Hartenstein sich in ihren Arbeiten ausschließlich auf die bis lang gedruckten Schriften des Fürsten stützen, dürfte das Ščerbatov-Thema nach der Erschließung weiterer Werke des Fürsten noch auf längere Sicht ein wichtiger Gegenstand der Forschung bleiben.

Was Ščerbatovs "Reise ins Land Ophir" angeht, so hat sich bereits die ältere Forschung ausführlich mit stilgeschichtlichen und kompositorischen Fragen dieses Werkes befaßt und dabei ausgiebig die westlichen Utopien zum Vergleich herangezogen. Ebenso eingehend ist die geistige Abhängigkeit Ščerbatovs von der westlichen Aufklärungsliteratur erörtert worden. Dabei wurde übereinstimmend, so von N.D. Čečulin und V.A. Mjakotin[21], auf den vergleichsweise geringen Ideengehalt von Ščerbatovs Utopie hingewiesen, insbesondere was ihre Phantastik und den sprachlich stilistischen Ausdruck betrifft. Auch A.A. Kizevetters Urteil[22] über die utopische Schrift des russischen Aristokraten ist im Hinblick auf die politische Gedankenwelt des Fürsten recht kritisch, jedoch hebt er als liberaler Historiker gleichzeitig Ščerbatovs Forderungen nach Beschränkung der Macht des Monarchen, der Einführung der Wählbarkeit bei der Besetzung von Staatsämtern und ähnliche Postulate, wie sie in der Ophirschrift erhoben werden, lobend hervor.

In der Tat als schwer zu beurteilen erweist sich der utopische Ideengehalt des Ophir Werkes und damit der Befund, ob es sich bei den von Ščerbatov vertretenen Postulaten bei einem Vergleich mit den in Rußland unter Katharina II. bestehenden Verhältnissen durchgängig um einen Schritt nach rückwärts handelt. Im Zusammenhang damit wird neuerdings, so auch von

20. E. Waegemans, Zur Geschichte des russischen politischen Denkens: M. M. Ščerbatovs "Reise nach Ophir," in: Slavica Gandensia 11/1984, S. 65-83, 12/1985, S. 259-269; derselbe (É. Vagemans), K istorii russkoj političeskoj mysli: M. M. Ščerbatov i ego "Putešestvie v zemlju Ofirskuju," in: Russkaja literatura 4/1989, S. 107-119; E.-M. Hartenstein, Michail M. Ščerbatov (1733-1790) als politischer Ideologe des russischen Adels und seine utopische Staatsschrift "Reise ins Land Ophir" (=Wissenschaftliche Beiträge der Hochschule für Industrielle Formgestaltung Halle-Burg Giebichenstein). Halle 1988.

21. N. D. Čečulin, Russkij social'nyj roman XVIII veka ("Putešestvie v zemlju Ofirskuju" g. C. švedskogo dvorjanina-sočinenie knjazja M. M. Ščerbatova), in: Žurnal Ministerstva narodnogo prosveščenija, Januar 1900, S. 115-166; V. A. Mjakotin, Dvorjanskij publicist Ekaterinskoj epochi (Knjaź M. M. Ščerbatov), in: Iz istorii russkogo obščestva, St. Petersburg 1902, S. 112-183. Vgl. auch V. Svjatlovskij, Russkij utopičeskij roman. Petrograd 1922.

22. A. A. Kizevetter, Russkaja utopija XVIII stoletija, in: Istoričeskie očerki. Moskau 1912, S. 29-56.

E. Waegemans und E.-M. Hartenstein, auch auf die positiven Elemente aufmerksam gemacht, die sich in der "Reise ins Land Ophir" finden. Zu ihnen zählen die Forderungen nach Beschränkung der monarchischen Macht zugunsten einer aristokratischen Oligarchie; Entwicklung eines Bewußtseins der Bürger des Ophirstaates im Hinblick auf ihre staatsbürgerlichen Rechte und Pflichten; Bildungsmöglichkeiten für alle Bürger von Ophir; Pflegeeinrichtungen (Waisen-, Armenhäuser u.a.m.); Öffentlichkeit des Gerichts; tugendhafte Erziehung; gerechtes Steuersystem; Ablehnung von Kriegen und Eroberungen.[23]

Diese von Ščerbatov vertretenen Postulate dürften bei einer Gesamtbewertung freilich nicht ausreichen, um "Die Reise ins Land Ophir" in die Gattung der utopischen Idealstaaten einzureihen. Obgleich Produkt der Phantasie, war dieses Werk des Fürsten keine intellektuelle Spielerei, sondern die literarische Bilanz vielfältiger politischer Erfahrungen eines hohen russischen Würdenträgers. Als Kombination von Reiseabenteuer-Erzählung und staatsphilosophischer Betrachtung handelte es sich um den ersten Versuch eines russischen Schriftstellers, den von westlichen Vorbildern übernommenen Rahmen des utopischen Romans mit Zügen der russischen Wirklichkeit auszufüllen. Den zentralen Platz in der "Reise" nehmen die gesellschaftspolitischen Erörterungen des Verfassers ein. Ščerbatovs Staat Ophir war eine Adelsrepublik, ein "wohlgeordneter" Staat, wie ihn die deutschen und österreichischen Kameralisten forderten, eine Art Mischung aus dem Reich Peters I. und Katharinas II. Er spiegelte deutlich Verhältnisse wider, wie sie im zeitgenössischen Rußland bestanden.

Wie in anderen Utopien, besaßen auch in der "Reise ins Land Ophir" die Stilmittel der Satire und Kritik eine wichtige Funktion. Jedoch vermied es der Verfasser, direkte und konkrete Kritik an den in Rußland herrschenden Zuständen zu üben. Er benutzte die Betrachtungen über die Charaktereigenschaften der Ophirianer, deren Staatseinrichtungen, Sozialfürsorge, Bildungsstätten und anderes mehr zur Skizzierung eines Bildes des künftigen Rußlands, wie es in seiner Vorstellung existierte. Als ein häufig angewandtes Mittel diente dem Autor dabei das Anagramm, d.h. die Vertauschung von Buchstaben innerhalb eines Wortes zur Zusammenfügung eines neuen Ausdrucks. So schimmerten in den Bezeichnungen von ophirischen Städten, Seen, Flüssen, Gouvernements, Völkern und Persönlichkeiten mehr oder weniger deutlich russische Namen

---

23. So systematisiert bei Waegemans, K istorii russkoj političeskoj mysli (Anmerkung 20), S. 114f.

durch (Kvamo=Moskau; Peregab=St.Petersburg; Golva=Wolga; Negija=Neva; Perega=Peter I. usw.). Auch Katharina II., Pugačёv, Friedrich II., Maria Theresia, Joseph II., Stanslaw Poniatowski und andere Persönlichkeiten des In- und Auslands wurden in fremdnamigen Bezeichnungen vorgeführt.

Das Sozial- und Staatsgefüge in Ščerbatovs Utopie stellte eine Verquickung von Absolutismus mit aristokratischem Konstitutionalismus dar. Die Beziehungen zwischen Gesellschaft und Staat wurden ganz unter dem Blickwinkel der Interessen des vom Verfasser vertretenen Adelsstandes gesehen. Die Staatsgesellschaft von Ophir besaß eine strenge Gliederung und war von ihrer Struktur her eine nahezu vollständige Kopie jenes Bildes von Rußland, das der fürstliche Autor bereits in seinen anderen Schriften entworfen hatte. Danach verfügten die erheblich voneinander getrennten Stände der ophirischen Gesellschaft über ebenso ausgeprägt unterschiedliche Rechte. Die ausgezeichnete wirtschaftliche Lage des Ophirstaates, von der Ščerbatov berichtet, beruht auf der Aufrechterhaltung der Leibeigenschaft, einem geordneten Steuer und Finanzsystem sowie auf der Organisation des Heeres in Form von Militärsiedlungen.

Der herrschende, führende und zugleich oberste Stand des Reiches von Ophir, an dessen Spitze ein Kaiser stand, stellte der Adel dar, gegliedert, wie in Rußland, in vierzehn Ränge. Ihm gehörten die den einzelnen Rängen zugeordneten hohen Würdenträger an, die die Aristokratie ausmachten; ebenso die Dienstadligen, Gutsbesitzer, Beamten, Militärs und übrigen Inhaber staatlicher Posten und Ämter. Der Adel nahm die zentralen Funktionen in der staatlichen Verwaltung wahr. Er wurde von Ščerbatov als eine auf erblichen Prinzipien beruhende, in sich geschlossene Kaste dargestellt. Er ließ aber die leibeigenen Bauern aus, über die Ščerbatov nur am Rande berichtete. Eine mittlere Position kam den Kaufleuten und Angehörigen des Bürgertums zu. Einen besonderen Platz räumte der Verfasser schließlich den Soldaten ein, die in Militärsiedlungen organisiert waren. Was in Ščerbatovs soziologischem Aufriß der ophirischen Gesellschaft fehlte, war ein eigener geistlicher Stand, deren Vertreter zu den Beamten und Ordnungshütern des Staates gezählt wurden.

Die herrschende Stellung, die der ophirische Adel insbesondere in seinen höchsten Rängen, der Aristokratie, einnahm, äußerte sich vor allem in dem ausschließlichen Recht auf Grundeigentum, leibeigene Bauern sowie Staats und Militärdienst. Die hochadligen Würdenträger übten gemeinsam mit dem Monarchen die oberste Macht im Staate aus und genossen die größten Privilegien, die es in Ophir gab. Im Unterschied hierzu nahmen sich die

Stellung und die Rechte, die Ščerbatov den Kaufleuten und Angehörigen des Bürgerstandes zubilligte, mehr als bescheiden aus. Deren Einfluß auf das ökonomische und politische Leben in Ophir war schon deshalb nicht allzu bedeutend, existierte der utopische Staat doch, wie der Fürst berichtete, auf der Grundlage der Naturalwirtschaft, was der Verfasser als einen Idealzustand hinstellte. Ungeachtet dessen gestand Ščerbatov den bürgerlichen Vertretern bestimmte Rechte im Ophirstaat zu. Dazu gehörte, daß die Kaufleute ihre Vertreter, wenn auch in beschränkter Anzahl, in die Regierungsämter entsenden durften.

Die Grundlage des Ophirreiches bildete die Arbeit von Leibeigenen, die über keinerlei politische Rechte verfügten. Jedem Bürger war genau vorgeschrieben, wie groß sein Haus sein durfte. Eben so hatte man genau festgelegt, welches Vieh gehalten, wieviel Brennholz verbrannt und welche Beleuchtung benutzt werden durfte. Nach der Zugehörigkeit zu den gesellschaftlichen Rängen wurde auch das Geschirr bestimmt, das die Bürger benutzten: die einen aßen und tranken aus tönernen, die anderen aus blechernen, die dritten aus silbernen Schüsseln, Näpfen und Krügen. Es gab Gutsbesitzer, Diener, Knechte und insgesamt ein Volk, von dem Ščerbatov behauptete, daß es in ausgezeichneten Verhältnissen lebte, wofür er freilich den Beweis schuldig blieb.

In Anbetracht der gesellschaftlichen Ungleichheit kam es auch in Ophir zu sozialen Auseinandersetzungen und Kämpfen, die im einzelnen jedoch nicht beschrieben werden. Ščerbatov versah seinen Idealstaat mit allen Attributen der Macht, die sämtliche Monarchien seiner Zeit auszeichneten. So besaßen die Ophirianer eine Armee und Flotte und unterhielten Festungen und Forts, und zwar nicht nur an den Staatsgrenzen, sondern ebenso in den Zentren des Reiches. Weiterhin gab es Gerichte, Gefängnisse und eine aktive Polizei, die über ein breites Betätigungsfeld verfügte und der staatlich organisierten und kontrollierten Gesellschaft von Ophir in maßgeblicher Weise das Gepräge verlieh.

Besonders ausführlich hat sich Ščerbatov über das Schul-, Erziehungs- und Bildungswesen Ophirs geäußert. Dabei legte er auch in aller Breite die moralischen und sittlichen Gebote sowie die gesellschaftlichen und staatlichen Pflichten der Bürger des Landes dar. Ebenso eingehend behandelte er die Stellung der Religion und der Kirche sowie der Polizei in der ophirischen Gesellschafts- und Staatsordnung. Nach seiner Auffassung übten die menschlichen Eigenschaften in Form von Tugenden und Lastern eine äußerst nachhaltige Wirkung auf die gesellschaftliche Entwicklung aus.

Den Grundpfeiler der moralischen und religiös fundierten Ophirgesellschaft
stellten Schule, Erziehung und Bildung dar.

Das sittliche Vorbild in Ščerbatovs utopischer Gesellschaft zählte zu den
wichtigsten Wegweisern der Ophirianer bei der Suche nach den richtigen
Verhaltensweisen. Zu den genannten Eigenschaften der Bewohner von Ophir
kamen deren Herzlichkeit, Großmut und Menschlichkeit hinzu. Diese
Tugenden waren dem Volk freilich nicht angeboren, sondern das Ergebnis
des wohleingerichteten Staates, vermittelt durch verschiedenartige Schulen
und Lehranstalten, Wissenschaftseinrichtungen und Akademien, Kirche,
Religion und Polizei. Nach den Angaben Ščerbatovs gab es in Ophir ein
großzügiges Erziehungs- und Bildungswesen, und die allgemeine
Schulbildung war über das gesamte Land verbreitet. So bestanden Schulen
nicht nur für adlige Zöglinge, sondern ebensolche für Kinder von Bauern,
Soldaten, Kaufleuten und anderen Angehörigen des Bürgerstandes. Von
Universitäten ist interessanter Weise keine Rede.

Religion und Kirche waren Teil der staatlichen Ordnung, und die
Ausübung des Glaubens hatte gänzlich dem irdischen Gemeinwohl zu
dienen. Auf das engste verbunden mit der Polizei, betätigten sich die vom
Volk gewählten Laienpriester, die wie die freimaurerischen Meister in den
Logen Schürzen trugen, gleichzeitig als Staatsbeamte und Polizeioffiziere.
Die ophirische Religion trug den Charakter eines abstrakten Deismus. Als
Wahrzeichen diente den Gläubigen die Sonne, die an die Stelle des Sterns
der Freimaurer[24] gesetzt war.

Im Zusammenhang mit seinen Erörterungen der Stellung, die Religion
und Kirche im Ophirstaat einnahmen, erwies sich Ščerbatov als ein scharfer
Gegner jeglicher Gewissensfreiheit. So bestand die Hauptfunktion der
Priester darin, Moral zu predigen und dafür Sorge zu tragen, daß es zu
keinerlei Störungen von Ruhe und Ordnung kam. Die in Uniformen von
Polizeioffizieren gekleideten Geistlichen hatten nicht nur das Recht, sondern
die Pflicht, sich in die Angelegenheiten der Bürger von Ophir einzumischen.
Für sie waren die Ophirianer nicht in erster Linie Gläubige, sondern staatliche
Untertanen.

Eine zentrale Rolle bei der Lenkung der ophirischen Gesellschaft kam
der Polizei zu. Diese war nicht nur für die innere Sicherheit des Landes,
sondern für vieles andere, das sich in Ščerbatovs Staat abspielte, zuständig
und verantwortlich. Hierzu gehörten die Sorgen um die gute Qualität von
zum Verkauf bestimmten Waren und die Reinhaltung der Wohnplätze ebenso

---

24. Vgl. G. V. Vernadskij, Russkoe masonstvo v carstvovanie Ekateriny II. Petrograd 1917.

wie die Garantie von funktionierenden Gesundheits- und Sozial-
fürsorgeeinrichtungen, der bewaffnete Schutz der Bürger, die
Aufrechterhaltung von Ruhe und Ordnung, die Beleuchtung von Straßen
und öffentlichen Plätzen und anderes mehr. Ein besonderes Anliegen der
Polizei bestand nicht zuletzt darin, im Zusammenwirken mit den Geistlichen
die strikte Einhaltung der vorgeschriebenen sittlichen und gesetzlichen
Normen im Leben aller Staatsbürger von Ophir zu gewährleisten.

Der Eindruck, den das Leben in Ophir insgesamt vermittelte, war der
einer bis in die sittliche Verfassung des Einzelnen hinein pedantisch
geregelten Ordnung. Dem ophirischen Gemeinwesen fehlten alle
Gleichheitsideen, die in der zeitgenössischen utopischen Literatur
Frankreichs und anderer Länder propagiert wurden und die mit der
Französischen Revolution schließlich offen hervorgebracht wurden.
Während in Westeuropa zur selben Zeit die Form der Utopie als literarisches
Vehikel radikal gesellschaftsverändernder Forderungen benutzt wurde, diente
sie Ščerbatov zum Entwurf einer oligarchischen Staatsordnung. So war die
"Reise ins Land Ophir" trotz mancher aufklärerischer Züge ein Werk, das
zur Verteidigung des Ancien régime geschrieben wurde und sich in seinem
Grundgehalt mit den Ideen der Aufklärung als unvereinbar erwies. In ihm
wurde keine Vorahnung moderner Lebensformen sichtbar und der
Gesellschaft des späten 18. Jahrhunderts keine neuen Entwicklungswege
aufgezeigt.

Chapter 3

THE ST. PETERSBURG ACADEMY OF SCIENCES AND THE DEVELOPMENT OF THE BLACK SEA REGION (1773–1795)

Robert E. Jones

From its earliest conception in the plans of Peter I, the St. Petersburg Academy of Sciences was to have many roles and functions. In addition to its purely scientific and scholarly pursuits, the Academy was also intended to serve a number of practical purposes including those of providing the government with useful information and disseminating knowledge and learning among the public.[1] From the outset the Russian government proceeded to assign tasks of a scientific or technical nature to members of the Academy to perform as a kind of state service, and inevitably the findings and reports of the Academy's scholars came to play a role in shaping and promoting the government's policies.

An important illustration of the Academy's involvement in political affairs is the role it played in advancing the expansionist policies of Catherine II in the region of the Black Sea. From the outbreak of the Russo–Turkish War in 1768 until her death in 1796 Catherine determinedly sought to advance Russia's interests in that region and to develop its economic potential. Persuaded that in the end the benefits would justify the expense of money and effort, she authorized war, immigration, fortification, and schemes of settlement and economic development that altered her government's priorities and drained its treasury. Catherine's southern policies also provoked intense and widespread opposition within governmental circles and from the noble landowners of northern and central Russia. Convinced that the prospective gains from Catherine's southern policies were not worth the costly and painful sacrifices they required, that opposition found its leaders

---

1. *Istoriia Akademii Nauk SSSR*, vol. 1 (Moscow and Leningrad, 1958), pp. 429–435.

in the Panins and then the Vorontsovs, its spokesmen in intellectuals as seemingly diverse as Fonvizin, Shcherbatov, and Radishchev, and its ultimate champion in Paul, Catherine's son and presumptive successor.[2] Within the government the opponents of Catherine's southern policies opposed and obstructed most if not all of their key elements and within educated society they disparaged Catherine's acquisitions and her efforts to protect and develop them, calling the steppe a desert and a wasteland and circulating the myth of the "Potemkin village."[3]

Although she faced widespread opposition from Russia's established statesmen and traditional elite, Catherine was not entirely alone in advocating the acquisition, defense, and development of territories adjacent to the Black Sea. Needing men who would implement her policies with the requisite zeal, she turned to favorites from outside the established elite whose personal ambition superseded any sense of class solidarity.[4] First Grigorii

2. On the opposition to Catherine's southern policies see my article "Opposition to War and Expansion in Late Eighteenth Century Russia," *Jahrbücher für Geschichte Osteuropas*, vol. 32 (1984), pp. 34–51 and A. M. Stanislavskaia, *Russko–angliskie otnosheniia i problemy sredizemnomor'e (1798–1807)*, (Moscow, 1962), pp. 56–58.

3. See for example Radishchev's *A Journey from St. Petersburg to Moscow*, translated by Leo Weiner, edited, introduced, and annotated by Roderick Page Thaler (Cambridge, Mass., 1958), p. 254 in which the author writes "If you have acquired a desert it will become a grave for your fellow citizens, in which they will disappear; in settling the new desert you will turn a fertile land into a sterile one. What shall it profit you to turn a desert into settlements, if in doing so you cause other settlements to be deserted?" This passage is on page 254 of Radishchev's own illegally published edition of 1790 and may echo the serfowners' discontent with Potemkin's policy of allowing runaway serfs to settle in Novorossiia. In my article on opposition to war and expansion, op. cit. pp. 46–49, I present the case that Radishchev's publication was much more of an attack on Potemkin and Catherine's southern policies than on serfdom and that Catherine understood it as such. On the myth of the "Potemkin Village" and its use against Catherine's policies see James A. Duran, "Catherine II, Potemkin, and Colonization Policy in Southern Russia," *The Russian Review*, vol. 28, no. 1 (Jan. 1969), pp. 23–24. In her letters to General Peter Erapkin, written during the course of her southern tour in 1787, Catherine denounced criticisms of her southern acquisitions and of Potemkin's efforts to defend and develop them as "lies" and "reckless prejudices" and called upon Erapkin to help her rebut them by disseminating the truth. Iakov Rost (ed.), *Vysochaishiia sobstvennoruchnyia pis'ma i poveleniia blazhennoi i vechnoi slavy dostoinoi pamiati gosudaryni imperatritsy Ekateriny Velikiia k pokoinomu Generalu Petru Dmitrievichu Erapkinu i vsepodanneishiia ego doneseniia v trekh otdeleniiakh* (Moscow, 1808), pp. 235, 246, 248, 258.

4. On the use of favorites by Russia's rulers to carry out policies opposed by the established elite see my article in *Cahiers du monde russe et soviétique*, forthcoming.

Orlov and then Grigorii Potemkin organized a network of allies and clients
to promote and defend an expansionist policy within the government and a
corps of clients and servitors who would implement them on the spot. In the
realm of public opinion Catherine's undertakings in the South also received
important support from the explorations and writings of the St. Petersburg
Academy of Sciences, whose members examined, catalogued, and publi-
cized the benefits to be derived from the acquisition and development of the
Black Sea coast.

The St. Petersburg Academy of Sciences became involved in the exploration and development of the Black Sea region through its well established
role in collecting and disseminating information about the geography of the
Russian Empire. Joseph Nicholas de l'Isle, brother of the famous French
cartographer Guillaume de l'Isle, came to St. Petersburg in February 1726
to direct the Academy's work on cartography and geography. In 1732 at de
l'Isle's initiative the Academy created a special department of geography to
carry out projects for exploring and mapping the Russian Empire that Peter
I had divided among several different agencies. The first major undertakings of the Geographical Department of the St. Petersburg Academy of Sciences were the Second Kamchatka Expedition dispatched to Siberia in 1733
and the Orenburg Expedition dispatched to the southern Urals in 1734. The
Academy of Sciences and its Geographical Department first became involved with the southern steppes in the 1730s and 40s through their work
on the maps and geographical information generated by the army during
Russia's military campaigns against the Turks and the Crimean Tatars.[5]

A new era of exploration by the St. Petersburg Academy of Sciences
began in the 1760s. In 1760 the Governing Senate directed the Academy to
increase its effort to collect, organize, and publish geographical information because such information "is not only useful to the entire people but is
highly necessary for all the offices of government." It also called for the
compilation of a new and more detailed atlas of the Russian Empire.[6] The

5. V. F. Gnucheva, *Geograficheskii department Akademii Nauk xviii veka* (Moscow and
    Leningrad, 1946), pp. 23–38. J. L. Black, *G. F. Müller and the Imperial Russian Acad-
    emy* (Kingston and Montreal: McGill–Queen's University Press, 1986), pp. 48–53.

6. *Polnoe sobranie zakonov rossiiskoi imperii.* First Series. (St. Petersburg, 45 vols., 1830),
    No. 10029 (Jan. 30, 1760). The only existing atlas of the empire at that time was the
    pioneering effort of I. K. Kirilov, published in 1734. Kirilov was a secretary of the Gov-
    erning Senate and a member of the Commission on Commerce. In 1734 he became a
    member of the Geographical Department of the Academy of Sciences and Director of the
    Orenburg Expedition.

Senate's concerns anticipated those of Catherine II, whose government soon initiated efforts to collect detailed information of all kinds on a vast and unprecedented scale.[7] Between 1768 and 1771 the Academy of Sciences sent thirteen scientific expeditions into the provinces and the Empire's outlying regions. Some of those expeditions were relatively limited in their goals and activities, but at least five of them were major expeditions, lasting five or six years, and were dispatched to the far reaches of the Empire. Their ostensible purpose was to observe the transit of Venus, but at the direction of the Academy all five were to explore and prepare maps of the regions through which they passed, to collect specimens, and to describe the climate, soils, crops, minerals, and anything else of use or interest. These were sent first to Academician G. F. Müller at the Academy's office in Moscow and were then forwarded by him to Academician Leonhard Euler in St. Petersburg. As its secretary, Euler presented the submissions of the various expeditions to the Conference, the governing assembly of the Academy, which decided their ultimate disposition.

When it set out from St. Petersburg in 1768, the expedition headed by Academician J. A. Güldenstädt was directed to explore the route from St. Petersburg to Tambov, Voronezh, and Astrakhan to the eastern shore of the Caspian Sea and further to the Caucasus Mountains. Güldenstädt reached the Caucasus in 1771 and spent two years travelling through the mountains and valleys as far as Tbilisi and the Black Sea coast of Georgia collecting geographical data and scientific information. In 1773 he sent the Academy its first detailed map of the Caucasus region. Then, on 21 June 1773, with Russia deeply engaged in a successful war against the Ottoman Empire, the Conference decided to send Güldenstädt's expedition into the areas occupied by Russian troops to the east and north of the Black Sea. The Academy had been receiving geographical data on occupied regions from military observers in the field just as it had during earlier Russo-Turkish conflicts, but now, with the increasing likelihood that Russia would annex some or all of that territory at the end of the present war, the Academy decided to send its own team of trained scientific observers into the region.[8]

---

7. Those efforts included the Third Revision of the poll tax rosters, the General Survey, and Legislative Commission. Robert E. Jones, *Provincial Development in Russia. Catherine II and Jacob Sievers* (New Brunswick, The Rutgers University Press, 1984), pp. 36–41.

8. *Protokoly zasedannii konferentsi Imperatorskoi Akademii Nauk s 1725 po 1803 goda*, vol. III (St. Petersburg, 1900), p. 96. Almost one year earlier, on 6 July 1772, the Conference heard a report sent to it from Ismail by a certain Major Islenev dated 25 March 1772 in which the author gave or tried to give the exact scientific locations of Bender, Akerman, Kilia Nova, and Ismail according to his own scientific observations. ibid., p. 63.

After exploring the eastern shore of the Black Sea and the Kuban,
Güldenstädt's expedition reached Cherkass na Donu in early 1774. From
there it proceeded to Azov and then through the steppe toward Kremenchug
on the Dnieper. In a report dated 22 August 1774, Güldenstädt informed the
Academy that after repairing his wagons in Kremenchug, he would proceed
to the Zaporozhian Sich and then to Perekop and finally to the Crimea.[9] He
was in Kremenchug four days later when he received the general order from
the Empress instructing all of the Academy's expeditions to return to
St.Petersburg immediately. He arrived in the capital on 24 March 1775.[10]
During his six years in the field Güldenstädt had remained in close contact with the Academy. In addition to maps, curiosities, specimens, and collections of various sorts, Güldenstädt had sent the Academy thirty–eight
reports on his activities, observations, and ideas that were read in full before the Conference of assembled academicians. For example, the minutes
of the Conference session of 27 January 1774 noted that Güldenstädt's thirty–
third report contained observations and corrections to existing knowledge
of such importance that the Conference decided to refer it to the Geographical Department without delay.[11] The minutes of the session of 22 August
1774 noted that Güldenstädt's thirty–seventh report had contained several
projects for peopling the area between the Dnieper and the Volga.[12] Neither
the specifics of these projects nor their subsequent fate is recorded in the
minutes of the Conference sessions, but Güldenstädt's reports made him
the first to regard the newly acquired territories as a favorable place for
settlement and to propose schemes for developing agriculture and towns in
those regions.

Combined with his scholarly standing as a member of the Academy,
Güldenstädt's travels in the south made him the leading authority on the
territories that Russia acquired in 1774. After his return to St. Petersburg,
Güldenstädt wrote and spoke about the benefits to be gained from the new
territories and worked to promote their development. In 1776 he published
an article entitled "On the Harbors of the Azov, Black, and Marmora Seas"
in which he sought to encourage Russian merchants to trade with Turkey
and the Levant. Güldenstädt warned that the harbors at Azov and at Temerik
on the Don had become too shallow for commercial vessels but recom-

9. *Ibid.*, p. 145.
10. *Ibid.*, p. 175.
11. *Ibid.*, p. 114.
12. *Ibid.*, p. 145.

mended Taganrog and Kinburn as ports suitable for overseas trade. He also provided a lengthy list of Russian goods that would turn a ready profit in foreign lands. Among them he included grain, a commodity that had played a very small role in Russia's foreign commerce up to that time because of a virtual prohibition on exports from St. Petersburg, but which was destined to become Russia's major export, once the steppe had been settled and Odessa had been founded. With a prescience born of broad learning and unprejudiced observation, Güldenstädt advised his readers that "The fertile Russian provinces lying between the Dnieper and the Don can provide a great quantity of that commodity if the cultivation of grain, which now, for want of markets, is neglected, be encouraged by sales of grain."[13]

On 29 December 1776 the St. Petersburg Academy of Sciences celebrated its fiftieth anniversary with a gala Jubilee session attended by the Empress, the Crown Prince, and a host of high ranking dignitaries. At a time when Catherine and Potemkin were pushing ahead rapidly with the defense, settlement, and development of the newly acquired territories in the face of intense criticism, the Academy chose Güldenstädt to deliver the featured oration at the Jubilee session. His subject, approved in advance by the Conference, was the present and future role of Russian products in international trade.[14] Güldenstädt began with a broad survey of the Russian economy for the purpose of identifying ways to increase the volume and value of Russia's exports. From that perspective he proceeded to highlight the economic potential of the new territories in the South. After identifying oxen along with their hides and tallow as Russia's principal exports, Güldenstädt explained that the greatest source of those products was the belt of provinces stretching across the steppe from the northern shore of the Caspian Sea to the Bug River. He then argued that those commodities as well as salted meat, fish, and fish products such as glue and caviar could find a new and valuable

13. Quoted in A. N. Shebunin, "Russkoe chernomor'e 70x–80x gg. xviii v. i Akademii Nauk (Trudy A. I. Gil'denshtedta i V. F. Zueva)," *Trudy instituta istorii nauki i tekhniki*, seriia 1, vypusk 8 (Moscow, 1936), p. 86. According to Shebunin, Güldenstädt's article was published in *Geograficheskii Mesiatseslov* in 1776, but I have not been able to find that title in the rare book department of the Lenin Library.

14. According to the minutes of the Conference, Güldenstädt had proposed this topic for the Jubilee oration on 24 April 1776 and, that after hearing his proposal, the director and the assembled academicians unanimously chose Güldenstädt to deliver the Jubilee oration. One week before the Jubilee session the minutes of the Conference recorded the complete agenda, noting that "M. le Professor Güldenstädt lira son memoire sur les produits de la Russie et les avantages qu'on peut retirer relativement au commerce." *Protokoly*, III: 238, 271.

market in Constantinople. He included the expansion of such trade as one,
but only one, of his several recommendations for improving Russia's balance of trade. The complete text of Güldenstädt's oration was subsequently
published in *Akademicheskie Izvestiia* in 1780.[15]
A few years later Güldenstädt was called upon to deliver a lecture of
even greater political significance. In May 1780 during a tour of the western provinces Catherine II met Joseph II in Mogilev. Travelling incognito
as Count Falkenstein, Joseph could not alter Habsburg foreign policy while
his mother, Maria Theresa, still lived, but he and Catherine began to discuss
the possibility of an alliance that would end Russia's alliance with Prussia
and provide Austrian support against the Ottomans. Significantly, Nikita
Panin, the champion of the Prussian alliance and the most influential opponent of Catherine's southern policy, was not invited to accompany Catherine
to Mogilev, while Potemkin and Bezborodko, the leading proponents of an
expansionist southern policy, accompanied her and met with Joseph.[16] Another member of Catherine's entourage was S.G. Domashnev, Director of
the Academy of Sciences since 1775.

On 5 June 1780 the Conference received a letter sent from Mogilev by
Domashnev alerting the Academy that "Count Falkenstein" would accompany the Empress to St. Petersburg where the two monarchs would attend a
solemn public session of the Academy of Sciences at which Pallas,
Laksmann, Krafft, and Güldenstädt were to lecture.[17] Since the Conference
normally decided on the agenda of its scholarly sessions, the imperious
tone of Domashnev's letter strongly suggests, as it probably suggested to

15. J. A. Güldenstädt, "Rech' o proizvedeniakh rossiiskikh sposobnykh k soderzhaniiu vsegda
vygodnago prevoskhodstva v prodazhe v chuzhie krai Rossiiskikh tovarov pred pokupkoiu
inostrannykh govorennaia Dekabria 29 dnia 1776 goda v prisutstvii ikh imperatorskikh
vysochestv v publichnom Sanktpeterburgskoi Imperatorskoi Akademii Nauk sobranni
vo vremia poluvekovago eia iubileia A. I. Gil'denshtetom Doktorom Meditsiny
Professorom Istorii Natural'noi i Chlenom Imperatorskoi Akademii Nauk, Volnogo v
Sanktpetersburge Ekonomicheskago Obshchestva i proch." *Akademicheskie Izvestiia*,
1780, chast' iv, pp. 354-379 and chast' v, pp. 19-52 and 141-165.

16. John T. Alexander, *Catherine the Great. Life and Legend* (Oxford: Oxford University
Press, 1989), pp. 241-244. Maria Theresa died some six months later, and the alliance
was concluded by May 1781.

17. *Protokoly*, III: 471. A supplement to the minutes notes that Count Falkenstein objected to
attending a special session of the Academy and preferred to attend one of its regular
sessions. It also turned out that Joseph did not accompany Catherine on her return to St.
Petersburg. Instead he went first to Moscow with Potemkin and then travelled from Moscow to St. Petersburg in late June.

the academicians, that the list of speakers had been decided at a higher level
and that Domashnev was merely transmitting it rather than prescribing it on
his own authority. The academicians may also have concluded that the four
speakers had been chosen because they could lecture in German. Güldenstädt
in particular seems to have missed the point of his selection, for in
Domashnev's absence he proposed, and the Conference placed on the agenda,
a lecture "on a people in the Caucasus related to the Hungarians."[18]
The error was soon corrected. A supplement to the minutes of the Conference session of 12 June at which the agenda had been approved noted
that since Domashnev had allowed Güldenstädt to substitute "a matter more
important and of more direct utility" for the "subject of pure curiosity" that
he had prepared to entertain Count Falkenstein, the latter had decided to
present a proposal to establish trade between Russia and Germany by way
of the Black Sea and the Danube.[19] The oration that Güldenstädt finally
presented in German before Joseph II was entitled "Gedanken über eine
zwischen Russland und Deutschland auf der Donau und dem Schwartzen
Meer zu eröfnende Handlung."[20]

As a presentation of the St. Petersburg Academy of Sciences to the Holy
Roman Emperor and heir to the Habsburg dominions, Güldenstädt's topic
appears even more significant in light of a document written some five years
earlier. In April 1775, as Russia prepared to open commerce on the Black
Sea, the Austrian government had sent a note to the Russian plenipotentiary
in Constantinople stating that Austria did not envy Russia's possession of
ports on the Black Sea; that Austria was interested in the growth of trade in
the Black Sea region, and in ties between Russia's Black Sea trade and
Austria's trade along the Danube; and that to that purpose Austria wanted to
open commercial offices in Russia's Black Sea ports.[21] Without committing

---

18. The Conference approved the agenda on 12 June 1780. For some unstated reason Krafft
   was to be replaced by Leksell. *Ibid.*, pp. 473–474.

19. *Ibid.*, The supplement, dated 1 July 1780, the date of Joseph's attendance at the Academy, was signed by Jean Albert Euler. The original reads as follows: "Son Excellence M.
   de Domashneff ayant permis à Monsieur le Professeur Güldenstädt de substituer au
   sujet de pure curiosité qu'il avoit indiqué dans cette séance du 12 Juin pour entretenir le
   Comte de Falkenstein, une matière plus importante et d'une utilité plus directe, celui–ci
   choisit et proposa de donner un projet de commerce à établir sur le Danube et la Mer
   Noire entre la Russie et l'Allemagne. Ce qui fut approuvé et effectué comme on le voit par
   le protocol extraordinaire du 1 Juillet 1780."

20. *Ibid.*, p. 477.

21. A. N. Shebunin, *op. cit.*, pp. 75–109.

Catherine, Güldenstädt's oration took up the Austrian proposal and suggested an encouraging response.

As the resident expert on the Black Sea region, Güldenstädt assumed responsibility for the Academy's explorations and research on that subject. In 1776 Güldenstädt presented the Conference with a program for future study of the newly annexed territories. In it he expressed his doubts that future expeditions would find anything completely new and then proceeded to list several subjects that merited further investigation: the mouth of the Dnieper, the products of the Black Sea, the mountains of the Crimea, and the native peoples of that peninsula.[22] Güldenstädt's list had a practical and political as well as a scientific purpose. The government was beginning to switch its attention from the eastern to the western side of the Crimea and to envision the Dnieper rather than the Don as the main artery of Russian exports. Catherine had recently given the order for the construction of a port at Kherson, and it and Kinburn had become the focus of Russia's commercial ambitions. Research into the commerce of the Black Sea had obvious commercial import. Güldenstädt's suggestions regarding the Crimea seemed to assume that the Crimea was part of the Russian Empire, which it was not, but Catherine and Potemkin were already pursuing a policy of Russian domination of the Crimea that would eventually lead to its annexation.

Meanwhile, Güldenstädt continued to collect and compile information about the Black Sea region and put it into usable form. Thus the minutes of the Conference on the compilation of the geographical calendar for the following year note that Güldenstädt had promised that his contribution would be "geographical, historical, and statistical information about the new borderline of the Russian Empire between the Terek River and the Sea of Azov."[23] The minutes for 5 July 1779 record that Güldenstädt had agreed to provide an historical and geographical description of the new guberniias of Azov and Novorossiia as soon as he received the necessary information from their governors.[24]

Güldenstädt died in March 1781, but his death did not by any means mark the end of the Academy's involvement in the Black Sea region, as Güldenstädt's work was soon taken over by others. On 13 August 1781 the

---

22. V. F. Gnucheva, *Materialy dlia istorii ekspeditsii Akademii Nauk v xviii vekakh* (Moscow and Leningrad, 1940), pp. 135–136.

23. *Protokoly*, III: 388.

24. *Ibid.*, p. 417.

minutes recorded that adjunct member Johann Gotlieb Georgi had on that day submitted a work entitled "On the rivers of the Russian Empire that flow into the Black Sea" that was to be inserted into the almanacs of the following year.[25] More significantly, on 3 May 1781 Director Domashnev announced that a new expedition would be sent out to explore Russia's new southern territories as far as the mouth of the Dnieper. The expedition would be led by Vasilii Zuev, a young adjunct member of the Academy, and would follow a program of instructions to be drafted by Academicians Pallas and Lepekhin.[26] In its original form the program drafted by the two academicians contained twenty–six points that were mainly concerned with topography, natural history, and agriculture, but the Geographical Department then added fourteen points of a practical geographic and economic nature, especially with regard to the rivers flowing into the Dnieper and the Black Sea.[27]

Zuev's expedition set out on 20 May 1781 and returned to St. Petersburg on 30 September 1782. Officially, the Academy had instructed Zuev to travel as far as the mouth of the Dnieper at Kherson, and Zuev's own account of his travels, published in 1787, also ends with his arrival in Kherson.[28] However, both parties understood that Zuev was also to explore the Black Sea and the Crimea. From Kherson Zuev travelled to Constantinople by frigate and then returned to Kherson by way of the Danubian principalities. On his second departure from Kherson he entered the Crimea, but his stay in that peninsula was cut short by a rebellion against Khan Sihan Giray and his Russian supporters. Zuev fled the Crimea and returned to St. Petersburg. He found himself in disfavor and began a period of acrimonious relations

25. *Ibid.*, p. 582.

26. *Ibid.*, p. 529. Zuev's biographer, B. E. Raikov, claims that the decision announced by Domashnev was "doubtlessly dictated from above." *Akademik Vasilii Zuev. Ego zhizn i trudy* (Moscow and Leningrad, 1955), p. 91. Gnucheva, *Materialy*, p. 119, had previously argued that the initiative for Zuev's expedition came from "governmental circles eager to improve trade on the Black Sea after the opening of Kherson in 1779." Neither author presents evidence in support of the argument that the decision was imposed on the Academy, but the absence of previous discussion by the Conference suggests that the decision to launch a new expedition came from outside the Conference, and the context noted by Gnucheva gives plausibility to her argument.

27. Raikov, *op. cit.*, pp. 93–99. Shebunin, *op. cit.*, 90–92. The program of the Zuev expedition was not recorded in the minutes of the Conference.

28. Vasilii Zuev, *Puteshestvennye zapiski Vasil'ia Zueva ot S. Peterburga do Khersona v 1781– 1782 godu* (St. Petersburg, 1787).

with the Academy and several of his colleagues that resulted in his dismissal from the Academy in 1784.[29]
In the course of his struggles within the Academy Zuev wrote to Princess E. R. Dashkova in October at a time when her appointment to replace Domashnev as Director of the Academy of Sciences was anticipated, but not yet official. Zuev complained that the Academy had neglected him and his work in spite of what he regarded as the important findings of his expedition to the south. He explained that in addition to his regular reports he had sent the Academy a map of the western shore of the Black Sea from Ismail to Constantinople, a map of the entire liman of the Dnieper with soundings from the mouth of the river to the open sea, a packet of seeds collected in the steppe, a map of the southern border of the empire from Gur'ev to the mouth of the Dnieper, a map of the Black Sea with soundings acquired in Constantinople, and a packet of seeds he himself had collected in that city.[30] Obviously several of Zuev's submissions had military and commercial as well as scientific value.

Zuev also took up Güldenstädt's efforts to acquaint the reading public with the benefits Russia would derive from the territories bordering the Black Sea and to encourage their development. In 1784, the year in which it dismissed him, the Academy published Zuev's article on the Black Sea trade. Written while Zuev was struggling to regain favor and retain his post, the article followed Güldenstädt's example in proclaiming the economic potential and commercial opportunities of the South, but it diverged from Güldenstädt's dry economic analysis in its effort to carry favor with the proponents of an active southern policy and in its willingness to bend the truth in order to make its case. On the first page of his article Zuev openly and explicitly defended Catherine's southern policies, declaring

> Catherine the Great crowned the happy position of Russia, in relation
> to seafaring with the addition of the Black Sea to its boundaries, by
> which, one might say, a path was opened for Russian merchants to
> carry their goods to three parts of the earth—Europe via the Danube,
> Asia via the Black Sea, and Africa via the Mediterranean. The great
> empress did not have the expansion of the empire as a motive for this

---

29. According to Raikov, Zuev was the grandson of a peasant and son of a common soldier in the Semenovskii Guards Regiment who had been educated at the Academy's gymnasium. On the circumstances of his dismissal see Raikov, *op. cit.*, pp. 187–202.

30. M. I. Sukhomlinov, "Akademik Zuev i ego puteshestvie po Rossii," *Drevniaia i novaia Rossiia (1879)*, no. 1, pp. 96–110.

annexation, but rather the provision of a way for her subjects to enrich themselves and the creation of a happy condition for even later generations of the Russian nation.[31] Zuev then proceeded to explain how Russia could take advantage of its new opportunities in the South. He estimated that fully half of the export goods that were now transported to St. Petersburg could more profitably be diverted to ports on the Black Sea via the Dnieper and the Don, but in doing so he made light of two serious obstacles that had so far hindered Russia's efforts to develop commerce on the Black Sea: the Dnieper Rapids and the lack of a deep water port accessible from the rivers. He argued that the Dnieper Rapids were not all that dangerous and added that in any event "They will soon be destroyed by the efforts of Faleev, who has sacrificed part of his estate for the cleaning of those rapids and the creation of a safe passage through them." As for a suitable port for the Dnieper trade, Zuev wrote that "The city of Kherson so close to the mouth will be the collection point for boats and the loading dock for sending goods carried there to far away places."[32] He closed his article with a long list of price comparisons between Russian and Turkish goods in the manner of Güldenstädt and with a description of Ottoman ports and cities.[33]

During his journey down the Dnieper, Zuev had observed the ongoing efforts to eliminate the Dnieper Rapids as an obstacle to navigation. Potemkin had entrusted those efforts to M. L. Faleev, a former merchant recruited by Potemkin to help carry out his developmental projects in the new territories. In the account of his journey, published in 1787 and based on his reports to the Conference from the field, Zuev took a more objective and skeptical view of Faleev's work than he did in the article published in 1784. Of Faleev's efforts to blast a channel through the rapids Zuev noted that Faleev "has had some success and may be will finish completely if a firm determination be applied." Of the canals that Faleev was creating around the most serious ridge blocking the channel Zuev opined "If he succeeds in creating the upper and lower canals, fine, but it is an extraordinary ambition."[34] As for the port of Kherson, Zuev had sent the Academy a map with

---

31. Vasilii Zuev, "O rossiiskoi torgovle po chernomu moriu," *Sobranie sochinenii vybrannykh iz Mesiatsoslovov na raznye gody*, chast' 5 (St. Petersburg, 1790), p. 377. This publication notes that Zuev's article was originally published in *Mesiatsoslov* in 1784.

32. *Ibid.*, p. 379.

33. *Ibid.*, pp. 380–401.

34. Zuev, *Puteshestvennyia Zapiski*, p. 256. On Faleev, including Shcherbatov's denunciation of Faleev as an example of what was wrong with Catherine's regime, see Shebunin, op. cit., pp. 99–101. On the Dnieper Rapids as a hindrance to commerce see my article, "The Dnieper Trade Route in the Late Nineteenth and Early Twentieth Centuries," *The International History Review*, vol. xi, no. 2 (May 1989), pp. 303–312.

soundings of the liman of the Dnieper and therefore knew or at least sus-
pected what the Russian government did not want to admit even to itself—
that Kherson was not a suitable harbor for the overseas export of grain and
other heavy commodities.

Zuev's article of 1784, extolling the potential for profitable commerce
on the Black Sea and ignoring the serious obstacles to the realization of that
potential, reflected the author's desperate attempt to save his career at the
Academy by writing what those in authority over him wanted him to write.
His assessment of the situation and the fact that the Academy published the
article strongly suggest that at that juncture the authorities wanted a man of
learning and high repute to praise the commercial potential of Catherine's
southern acquisitions and gloss over the problems that still had to be overcome because the southern policy of Catherine and Potemkin was under
attack from their opponents.[35]

The publication of Zuev's observations in book form in 1787, simulta-
neous with Catherine's own voyage to the Crimea, marked the end of the
Academy's political engagement with what might be called "the southern
question." After the annexation of the Crimea in 1783 Potemkin arranged
for the Academy to send K. I. Gablits into that peninsula at the head of a
new expedition charged with describing the new territory "according to all
three realms of nature." Academician P. S. Pallas also travelled through the
Crimea in 1793-1795 and then settled there in semi-retirement. Although
Gablits and Pallas limited their activities and their subsequent publications
to observations of geology, natural history, and related topics within the
Crimean Peninsula, they continued to supply the government with maps
and information of practical value. Unlike Güldenstädt and Zuev, however,
they showed little interest in the larger and more controversial questions
surrounding Catherine's foreign and domestic policies in the Black Sea region.

From 1773 to the end of Catherine's reign the St. Petersburg Academy of
Sciences played a significant role in the exploration and development of the
new territories bordering the Black Sea. Its members provided the Russian

---

35. Another, more important attempt to respond to criticism of Catherine's southern policy
can be seen in the introduction to the Charter to the Nobility, promulgated on 21 April
1785, in which Catherine praised Potemkin and his rival Rumiantsev by name and then
explicitly presented their victories over Turkey and the subsequent annexations in the
South as the immediate source of a charter guaranteeing the personal and corporate privileges of the Russian nobility. See Robert E. Jones, "The Charter to the Nobility of 1785:
A Legislative Landmark?" *Canadian–American Slavic Studies* vol. 23 (1989), pp. 13–
15.

government with maps, soundings, economic observations, and other information that it used in implementing its policies in that region. More remarkably, in the 1770s and 80s, the publications of the Academy openly sought to persuade Russians of the economic advantages and opportunities that the new territories had brought to the empire and its subjects. In doing so the Academy and its members entered directly into the bitter controversy over the southern policies of Catherine and Potemkin.

Chapter 4

STOLYPIN'S LAND REFORM OF 1906-1914

George Yaney

1. Institutionalized conflict

It is basically a very good thing that Soviet spokesmen now dwell on the problems of their government rather than singing hymns to its glory. It is even better that there are now several centers of government and that each one subjects the proposals and "achievements" of its neighbors to criticism. Best of all, the leaders within each government are vulnerable to domestic opposition. Statements cannot come before the public simply as flat assertions demanding only a simple choice between applause or disapproval. They come, rather, as contrary positions that must continually be hammered out in serious debates. Every plan is tested by ridicule; every achievement is doubted. It is difficult now for a citizen who pretends to be politically conscious to hide from thought. There are many who see harm, danger, and even disintegration in this state of affairs, but surely if there is any validity in the concept of homo sapiens, the emergence of institutionalized political conflict in the Soviet Union is a wholesome and promising phenomenon.

However, the habit of seeing all the actions of government as mistakes, failures, and crimes makes it difficult to recognize achievement. If every leader is labelled a scoundrel, every policy a failure to act, and every development a sign of disintegration, real achievements may pass without notice. This problem presents itself in any country, but it becomes a serious threat in the society of Russian intellectuals, creatures notoriously prone to assume that achievement and efficacy must be judged solely and rigidly by abstract standards taken from traditional European ideologies.

The uncritical acceptance of European models by Russian intellectuals goes back hundreds of years. During his last years, Peter the Great enacted European forms of administration directly into Russian law and hired European administrators to enforce them, at salaries well above what native Russians of equivalent rank received. Thereafter, Peter's way of thinking gained an ever widening following in the capital cities of Russia, and, two hundred years after his time when the tsarist regime's strenuous efforts to Europeanize brought it down, a chorus of intellectual voices accused it of not Europeanizing rapidly enough.

2. The So-called Stolypin Land Reform

One of the tsarist government's best known Europeanizers was Petr Stolypin, prime minister and minister of internal affairs from 1906 until his assassination in 1911. It may be instructive to today's would-be Europeanizers to draw some comparisons between his experience and that of the current administration. It would be a gross error to assume that present-day administrators should necessarily pursue the same aims as the tsarist government did, but even if one deem tsarist reformers foolish or malicious, their ordeal has relevance. Their manner of interacting with a distrustful population during and after the violent upheavals of 1905-06 should certainly interest the cruelly deflated officials who are now trying to blunder out of the mess left by decades of rigidly centralized, would-be communistic government.[1]

A land reform was enacted during 1905-06, and it fell to Stolypin to take charge of carrying it out. The enactors, including Stolypin, believed that individual peasants should be liberated from villages and families so that they could function effectively in the "free market." Accordingly, Stolypin granted the peasants individual civil rights. Acting through the peasant bank, he offered individual heads of families the financial means to claim shares of village land as their own property. He believed that "capitalistic" holders of property could enrich themselves by their own economic enterprise and that villages working collectively could not. During the years of implementation, however, the original goal was set aside. Stolypin's ministry of internal affairs gave up its original intention to play a leading role in carrying out the reform, and its officials were supplanted by surveyors and agronomists working under the auspices of the ministry of agriculture. These new cohorts de-emphasized the measures for separating peasants from their vil-

---

1. I have discussed the so-called Stolypin land reform in greater detail in my *The Urge to Mobilize* (Urbana, Illinois, 1982), esp. chapters 8 and 9.

lages—by 1914, individual separations had been virtually abandoned — and devoted their energies to helping villages to act collectively to modernize their agriculture. Many of the resultant measures imposed greater restraints on individual property rights than had the pre-Stolypin villages. This, apparently, was the way the peasantry wanted it.

The government's sharp change in direction during 1907-11 is ordinarily depicted as an indication of weakness and/or error, but one can also say that the tsar's officials *interacted* with the peasantry. Instead of swallowing the European preconception that it is the task of government administrators to operate as parts of a mechanical instrument,[2] they forged new purposes out of their experience. Most peasants defended their institutions, and in so doing they found new ways to act collectively. Instead of carrying out their orders, therefore, the officials responded. Instead of loaning money to individuals, the peasant bank put most of its funds at the disposal of villages. Instead of lecturing the peasants on official doctrine, many officials actively assisted them to articulate their impulses in language understandable to bureaucrats. Not all the statesmen in St. Petersburg perceived the change of direction, and not all of those who perceived it reacted positively. One man who did both was the minister of agriculture, Appolon V. Krivoshein. Krivoshein understood what was happening, and he was able to prevent his more doctrinaire associates from interfering with it. Thus, the so-called Stolypin land reform (more accurately, Krivoshein's reform) succeeded. The belief that it failed arose from the inability of most intellectuals, including Stolypin himself, to recognize achievements that did not conform to European preconceptions.

Failure and success are treacherous words. In recent years, a few historians have begun to notice that the peasants of Russia were not growing poorer during the decades prior to 1905. Many peasant farmers were improving their agricultural methods and enriching themselves. Agricultural production and productivity were both on the rise.[3] Peasants who went to work in the towns significantly increased their incomes. They sent money to their families in the villages, and the villages provided them with an escape from the kind of suffering endured by many British laborers during the industrial

---

2. The most famous articulation of this preconception is Max Weber's. See his *Wirtschaft und Gesellschaft* (3 vols. Tübingen, 1922), III, p. 650-78, 753-54.

3. See Peter Gattrell, *The Tsarist Economy: 1850-1917* (London, 1986), p. 207; Heinz-Dietrich Löwe, *Die Lage der Bauern in Russland: 1880-1905* (St. Katherinen, 1987), p. 371-72; Paul Gregory, *Russian National Income, 1885-1913* (Cambridge, 1982), p. 193.

revolution in that highly civilized country. It is not entirely clear, then, that the peasants of Russia were in great need of dramatic reforms in 1906. It may be that from their point of view Stolypin's attempted attack on their institutions is not properly described by the word "success."

If we consider the whole of Russian society, however, the picture becomes a little brighter. Capital city intellectuals were profoundly out of touch with the realities of their own society, and it was surely helpful for all concerned that substantial numbers of them could at last penetrate the villages and find channels for meaningful communication with the peasants. If the Reform set off conflicts in villages and capital cities alike, it also furnished new ways to articulate these conflicts. Krivoshein's reform did not bring unity of purpose to Russian society, but it began at last to draw members of the rural population into the cities' ideological conflicts, thereby introducing authentic meanings into hitherto empty slogans. Russia was growing together—albeit painfully—until the strains of the first world war destroyed the fragile networks of long range trade and transport on which her people were learning to depend.[4]

What do we learn from Krivoshein's reform? That a program of social reform conceived by bureaucrats in a centralized government does not succeed because its initiators know the correct thing to do, nor does it fail because they do not. Measures of centrally directed social reform originate in desperation, not in sure knowledge, and their consequences are inherently unpredictable. The writing of edicts does not suddenly make the future clear. A reform imposed by a centralized administration "succeeds" only when and if people in the locales find themselves compelled to cope with the government's agents, thereby discovering new ways to cope with each other, new issues to fight over, and new meanings in their mutual interaction.

Unfortunately, our perception of these elements in Krivoshein's reform is clouded. In Stolypin's time, the weight of European scholarship in history and the social sciences saw the world of human affairs in the context of

---

4. Leopold Haimson takes a different view ("The Problem of Social Stability in Urban Russia, 1905-1917," *Slavic Review*, XXIII, December 1964, 619-42; XXIV, March 1965, 1-22). He indicates that social conflict grew steadily sharper during the period 1905-14, and he concludes that society and government were disintegrating. He is correct about the conflict, but his conclusion does not follow. Even if a revolution had taken place in 1914-15, it would not necessarily have signified disintegration or even reform, though, if successful, it would certainly have interrupted the tsarist government's progress toward decentralization and rapid economic development.

one-dimensional, rationalizing progress, and no enlightened man could conceive of a meaningful reform that did not calculably proceed from and lead to this progress.[5] A few Russian observers were beginning to step aside from this frenetic positivism to look directly at the realities of village life in the Russian Empire. The remarkable studies of Peter P. Semenov (Tien-Shanskii) and A.I. Engelgardt date from the 1870s,[6] and after about 1900 Aleksandr Chaianov and his associates stirred up the waters with new insights into economic relations within the villages.[7] On the whole, however, Russian scholars clung to the European perspective. Modern capitalist man was presumed to be individualistic; unmodern peasants were not individuals, and the purpose of reform was to make them so. The Russian peasantry were assumed to be stifled by their village institutions, passive victims suffering helplessly from poverty, oppression, backwardness, and/or illiteracy. The only meaningful collective action of which they were capable was rebellion. Peasants who responded actively to a changing environment within the context of their own culture were hidden from view behind the conventional metaphor, "dark masses," and it was easy to believe that they were desperately in need of reforms hatched in the capital cities.[8]

5. Philosophers of science began to abandon this worldview only in the 1960s. See esp. the pioneering efforts of the contributors to Frederick Suppe (ed.), *The Structure of Scientific Theories* (Urbana, Illinois, 1974).

6. See Semenov's "Muraevenskaia volost," in F.L. Barykov et. al. (eds.), *Sbornik materialov dlia izucheniia selskoi pozemelnoi obshchiny* (St. Peterburg, 1880); and A.I. Engelgardt, *Iz derevni* (Soviet edition, Moscow, 1937)

7. Some of Chaianov's works have been republished (in Russian) in A.V. Chaianov, *Oeuvres choisies de A.V. Cajanov* (8 vols., The Hague, 1967). From Stolypin's time until the end of the 1920s, Soviet investigators turned out the most original and probing studies of peasant life in the world—e.g., M.Ia. Fenomenov, *Sovremennaia derevnia* (2 vols., Moscow, 1925).

8. Lenin himself resorted to "dark masses" more than once during the years when he was attempting to govern. Some recent works in which active, self-reliant peasants put in an appearance are David Ransel, *Mothers of Misery* (Princeton, 1988); V.A. Aleksandrov, *Selskaia obshchina v Rossii* (Moscow, 1976); Daniel Field, *Rebels in the Name of the Tsar* (Boston, 1976); Reginald E. Zelnik, "The Peasant and the Factory," in Wayne Vucinich (ed.) *The Peasant in Nineteenth-Century Russia* (Stanford, 1971); R.H. Rowland, "Urban In-Migration in Late Nineteenth-Century Russia," in Michael Hamm (ed.), *The City in Russian History* (Lexington, Kentucky, 1976); A.A. Trifonov, "Formirovanie naseleniia Moskvy v dorevoliutsionnym period," *Russkii gorod* (vyp. 7, 1984); Boris G. Litvak, "O nekotorykh chertakh psikhologii russkikh krepostnykh pervoi poloviny XIX v.," in B.F. Porshnev (ed.) *Istoriia i psikhologiia* (Moscow, 1971). These works have made no discernible dent in the prejudices associated with progress and modernization.

And today, the progress that goes on within non-European societies still remains largely concealed from the perception of modern scholars. Our imaginations respond to a very limited number of images: Ben Franklin devoting himself to self-enrichment and deeming himself independent, Vladimir Lenin leading crowds of simpletons into utopia and deeming himself ideologically correct, Frederick Taylor building men and machines into perfect systems and deeming himself efficient. Speaking generally, these are the only forms of social evolution that are intelligible to modern men, and this is why it has been difficult for historians to see the villagers of Stolypin's time experiencing progress as a crushing demand upon them to act collectively and to surrender much of what they considered to be their individuality. Scholars are as yet very far from grasping the proposition that a people are more likely to improve their common lot by inserting modern concepts into established institutions than by following instructions from outsiders. This general refusal to observe explains why a progressive like Ghandi insisted that he was opposed to progress. It also explains why modern Japan remains a mystery to Europeans, Americans, and the Japanese themselves.

What is "success" in socioeconomic reform? Little can be said at the present stage in scholarly development, but it may be suggested that serious reform is underway when a people are seen to redefine their institutions in the course of struggles to organize themselves to defend these institutions. The best way to administer "reforms," if reforms there must be, is not to direct people but to involve them in broader conflicts. Krivoshein's reform "succeeded" because the government's agents and the peasants became enmeshed in each others' disagreements.

3. The Relevance of Krivoshein's Reform

Administrators in the formerly Soviet republics now labor under much the same kind of misunderstanding as Stolypin's once did. Today as yesterday, many Soviet intellectuals (and a host of "experts" in Europe and America) strive chiefly to lead Russia toward democracy and the free market. Like Peter I and Josef Stalin, they begin their "thinking" by selecting certain Western concepts and erecting them into a high platform of holy truth, whence plans can be formulated and decrees issued.

Mikhail Gorbachev's most remarkable achievement was to avoid this syndrome. The spirit that moved him was the same as that which Krivoshein expressed in a note that he wrote to Tsar Nicholas II in early 1906, urging

—in effect—that the government leave off its incessant investigations and planning conferences and set up local agencies to commence reforms.[9] Krivoshein believed that plan formulation served only rhetorical purposes. Serious reform could only arise from interaction between administrators and peasants, and the function of the central authorities was to respond to this interaction. The essential aim in any serious social reform is to make it impossible for people to escape an awareness of their interdependence. But what should the new governments do? How can administrators play a leading role while dismantling the machinery through which leading roles have customarily been played? Above all, how can tasks be identified and achievement recognized? How is something as vague and uncontrollable as an awareness of interdependence stimulated and harnessed? The experience of Krivoshein's administrators offers no specific answers to these questions, but it tells us something about perspective.

Awareness of interdependence is bound to be unpleasant. If a peddler has visited a village regularly for many years and the villagers are satisfied with him, they are not likely to give much thought to their dependence on him. They will awaken only when their satisfaction is interrupted: when he ceases to come, or raises his prices, or insists on immediate payment for his goods. The peddler has never ceased to feel his dependence on the villagers, but even his awareness rises to a new sharpness when the villagers threaten to buy from a new competitor. In times of socioeconomic change— when farmers learn to grow cash crops, new railroads and canals suddenly render people and goods mobile, factories render artisans obsolescent, etc— everyone becomes in some sense a peddler. The sensing of new dependence becomes an everyday experience. Ideally, at least some people learn to form new networks of communication, but no one will be happy with the new relationships. Suspicion and hostility will flourish. Trust will be long in growing.

When an individual senses his dependence on others, he finds himself in Gulliver's plight, bound down to the ground by people whose existence had been unknown to him the night before. One thinks of Doctor Zhivago returning from the war to find people occupying most of his house. In the novel, Zhivago accepts this new closeness to the working class, but the usual feeling in such circumstances is a primal fear, which can easily slide into resentment. The first thought that comes is likely to be a desire to get

---

9. Krivoshein's note is printed in B.B. Veselovskii (ed.), *Agrarnyi vopros v Sovete Ministrov, 1906 g.* (Moscow, 1924), p. 105-10

free from the interlopers. Punish offenders, exclude aliens, preserve one's rights, find a protector, assemble citizens. Such enterprises sometimes bring superficial successes, and the ensuing relief may be labelled independence, but even victory brings a new dependence. New ties make themselves felt, and in most cases they go deeper and cause more agony than the preceding ones. This is especially true in modern times, when cultures smash into each other with unprecedented force and penetrate each other deeply, establishing hidden strongholds within each other that sustain a perpetual confusion of identity.

As people begin acting collectively to cope with newly recognized dependence, the role of the go-between becomes crucial. People urgently need new ways to communicate, and someone must discover these ways. This basic fact poses a dangerous contradiction. A would-be go-between can only open channels between hitherto separate groups by inspiring trust; yet his activities are likely to appear dishonest and corrupt. If he is an administrator, he bends and breaks the regulations that he is supposedly obliged to enforce, and he routinely deceives both superiors and subordinates. An elected representative finds ways to deceive his constituents. Both types will need more financial support than they legitimately receive, especially if they find ways to work effectively, and their ways of getting funds may well be illegal. It follows that the go-betweens—i.e., the only people who can actually make a reform happen—are likely to bring down upon themselves all the fear and frustration to which the growing awareness of dependence invariably gives rise. It is necessary for them to protect themselves against this eventuality, and the measures they take are not likely to be morally or esthetically pleasing. Even those who are ethically inspired may become extortioners, or profiteers, or tyrants. In short, the go-between's role is complex. His work is difficult to observe; his contributions are virtually impossible to understand.

How then shall we recognize achievement in modern Russia? By looking for signs that the citizenry are feeling the force of the ties that bind them to each other; by looking for signs that people are strengthening their new ties by wrestling against them; by trying to identify the go-betweens who are giving expression to the new interaction, and to perceive what people are doing to cope with these go-betweens.

Krivoshein's experience tells us something about leadership. In particular, he shows us that a leader who changes direction is not necessarily acting from weakness. It has been fashionable in modern European culture to focus attention on the historical impact of "successful" leaders like Otto von Bismarck, whom we credit with an ability to envision the future and to impose their visions on others. Rarely do we honor a leader who "merely" does what he must and "fails" to adhere to principles or reach goals. In fact, however, it may require more fortitude to abandon plans, programs, and ideologies in the face of a refractory reality than to persist in them. A leader who sacrifices one deeply held conviction when his experience brings it into contradiction with another is not vacillating or manifesting dishonesty. His determination to implement policies while changing their substance testifies to his seriousness. Krivoshein's career is meaningful because it illustrates this principle. So, for that matter, was Lenin's. So was Gorbachev's. One hopes that Yeltsin will live up to his predecessors even as he condemns them.

4. Reminder

As I said at the outset, I am not suggesting that present-day Russian leaders have lessons to learn from Krivoshein. I bring up the latter's reform only to suggest that the Soviet people are in need of new perspectives if they are to recognize their achievements and cope with their difficulties. It is significant that some of their forefathers exhibited a remarkable ability to adopt new perspectives, but the perceiving of examples should not be twisted into uncritical imitation.

Gorbachev certainly needed no such reminder. He and his administration demonstrated an ability to respond to experience that was far superior to anything that Stolypin's government could manage. Unlike any other statesman in history, he conducted his reforms in a spirit of contrition. In the past, reformers and revolutionaries have proceeded by blaming others; Gorbachev not only renounced his government's past sins but also admitted his own share in them. What is more, he made his unprecedented confessions to the whole world, abandoning all manner of claims and trusting deeply in the good will of his enemies. Lessons drawn from the European past have little meaning for the regimes that emerged under his bewildered yet forceful direction. The Americans want Russia to follow the precepts of Thomas Jefferson, a slaveholder who ruthlessly invaded Indian lands while preaching about natural rights. The British would have Russia learn about "freedom" from their long history of bloody conquest and racist arrogance. The Germans offer lessons in law and administration taken from a scholarly tradition that led them into two world wars and the horrors of Nazism. None of these "models" are of much help. Russia and the other successor states are moving along paths that have never been tried.

Chapter 5

MONEY TALKS? A NOTE ON POLITICAL STABILITY IN LATE IMPERIAL RUSSIA

James Cracraft

The paper money of late Imperial Russia is among the copious graphic or indeed visual sources that historians have ignored in our traditional, nearly exclusive preference for purely verbal documents. Why such a preference (or resistance) should persist, in our age of textual criticism and of imagery *par excellence*, is a fascinating question, but not one that can be pursued here. Rather will this short essay argue, on the basis of intensive study of certain aspects of the graphic material just mentioned, that on the eve of World War I the Imperial system was as "stable" as it had ever been and that its core ideology remained both coherent and consistent, *pace* the familiar views to the contrary of assorted Marxist and other historians. The essay thus hopes to contribute, however modestly, to the "collective rethinking of the Imperial field—its categories, methods and fundamental concepts"— that was initiated in 1991 by the Social Science Research Council.[1]

---

1. See Jane Burbank, "Revisioning Imperial Russia," *Slavic Review* 52, no. 3 (Fall 1993), [555]–67: Professor Burbank reports on a workshop sponsored by the SSRC and held at the University of Iowa on November 1–3, 1991; a second workshop on the same general theme, also sponsored by the SSRC, was held at the Kennan Institute of the Wilson Center, Smithsonian Institution, on September 9–12, 1993. Earlier versions of this essay were presented in the second of these workshops and in the Russian and East European Studies Program of the University of Wisconsin, Madison (December 9, 1993), where it benefitted from numerous helpful comments. The essay has also benefitted from extended discussion with my junior colleague at the University of Illinois at Chicago, Jonathan Daly. I am especially pleased to publish it in this collection honoring my long-time senior colleague, Edward C. Thaden, whose very productive career has been devoted to the history of Imperial Russia.

More precisely, my case involves the "state credit notes" (*gosudarstvennyi kreditnye bilety*) issued by the Imperial State Bank in St. Petersburg between 1898 and 1912 in denominations of one, three, five, ten, twenty–five, fifty, one hundred, and five hundred rubles.[2] These I will treat as an obviously important "image–set" created by the Imperial system (its incumbent regime) for dissemination among its subjects, ostensibly for economic reasons alone, and submit them to historical analysis. My aim will be to discover in these images any underlying message or "ideology," meaning the structure of values and interests—not only economic—that informs *any* representation of reality (*pace* again, the Marxists).[3] I will also briefly consider the contemporary *reception* of these images, or the evident responses of the system's subjects to the messages they project.[4] I will then ask what all of this might tell us of broader historical significance, as previewed above.

But first let me clarify certain basic points of reference. By "the Imperial system" is meant that distinctive political *system* which was destroyed as such by the Bolshevik revolution after dominating Russia and contiguous territories for about two hundred years. The term refers, in other words, to that *hegemonic* order which was brought into being under Peter the Great and was comprised until 1917 of the "autocrat" and his/her family and court together with the Imperial elite (nobility plus bureaucracy) in all of their groupings, departments, appurtenances, cultural forms or expressions, and multifarious operations. The term Imperial *regime* then refers to the system's policy– and decision–makers at any given point in the Imperial period, the top executive officers as a body (compare U. S. usage, "the Administration"). Both system and regime existed to be sure within a huge, multiform, widely dispersed *society*, the ensemble known formally as the Russian Empire; and society was of course ruled and exploited by the Imperial system under its incumbent regime through a complex, mutually reinforcing

---

2. I have had access to a private collection of late Imperial paper money. For minimal technical details, see Albert Pick's *Standard Catalog of World Paper Money*, 3rd ed. (Munich, 1980), 880. New interest in Imperial paper money among Russian scholars and collectors is evident in A. I. Malyshev, V. I. Tarankov, and I. I. Smirennyi, *Bumazhnye denezhnye znaki Rossii i SSSR* (Moscow, 1991), the first comprehensive catalogue of Russian paper money ever published; for details of the notes in question, see 53–76 and 345–46 (nos. 1.11.53–1.11.66) with (poor) photo–reproductions of the whole series on 409–15.

3. Cf. W. J. T. Mitchell, *Iconology: Image, Text, Ideology* (Chicago, 1986): I am deeply indebted, in clarifying both terms and purposes, to this remarkable work.

4. Cf. David Freedburg, *The Power of Images: Studies in the History and Theory of Response* (Chicago, 1989): another seminal work.

process of coercion and consensus. Yet however we characterize their functions and interrelationships, it is important that we keep these terms and their referents straight. Imperial regimes—of rulers and their various relatives, appointees, and favorites——came and went whereas the *system* endured, essentially unchanged, for at least two centuries.[5] Exactly how and why the Russian Imperial system eventually seized up and collapsed thus constitutes a major historical problem and one that remains, I would argue, largely unsolved.

The State Bank was created (1866), it will be remembered, in tandem with the so–called Great Reforms of the 1860s and 1870s, which sought to modernize (further Europeanize, or Westernize) the Imperial system in various ways because of its poor showing in the Crimean War of 1854–1855; but it became a bank of issue only in 1897, in connection with the monetary reform engineered by the famous minister of finances, S. Iu. Witte. The leading photographer in Russia of the time, Karl Bulla (he enjoyed court patronage), has left us a picture of the Bank (still standing) as it appeared ca. 1900: a colossal, typically Imperial building dating to the reign of Catherine II (architect Quarenghi) and located on the Catherine canal in the heart of official St. Petersburg, its imposing facade of classical columns and pilasters and rusticated stone adorned in ascending order with huge metallic replicas of the cipher of Nicholas II with the Imperial crown, the Romanov double–headed eagle also with crown, and the traditional Orthodox cross. Another huge eagle stood guard over the elegantly forbidding front fence and portico, also arrayed in classical style. Thus the Bank's own "image" was clear enough. It was imposing, even awesome; official, formal, monumental; also elegant, even glamorous: this building houses, its exterior ob-

---

5. On the Imperial system in Russia, see the detailed work of John P. LeDonne, *Ruling Russia: Politics and Administration in the Age of Absolutism, 1762–1796* (Princeton, 1984) and *Absolutism and Ruling Class: The Formation of the Russian Political Order, 1700–1825* (New York, 1991). On political systems and the question of "hegemony" more generally, I have found the following especially helpful: Harry Eckstein, *Regarding Politics: Essays on Political Theory, Stability, and Change* (Berkeley and Los Angeles, 1992); T. J. Jackson Lears, "The Concept of Cultural Hegemony: Problems and Possibilities," *American Historical Review* 90, no. 3 (June 1985): 567–93; and the introductory portions of Philip Corrigan and Derek Sayer, *The Great Arch: English State Formation as Cultural Revolution* (Oxford, 1985).

viously said, an important institution, indeed a major agency, of the almighty Russian state.[6]

I select for more detailed description the acme of this Imperial image–set, the 500–ruble note issued by the State Bank in 1912. The relatively spare obverse of this note states centrally, in fine print, that the Bank exchanges credit notes for gold coin "without limit" at the rate of one ruble equals one–fifteenth of an Imperial consisting of 17.424 measures (*dolei* = 0.7774234 grams) of pure gold.[7] Also, the obverse prominently displays two classical scrolled escutcheons, one (left) showing the Romanov eagle with crown and crests and the other (right), the cipher of Nicholas II with crown, both trimmed with laurel leaves, fruit and other symbols of fertility (or natural wealth). The right escutcheon bears the figure 500 and the date, 1912; the left, the finely printed message: "1. The Exchange of State Credit Notes for gold coin is guaranteed by the entire wealth of the State. 2. State Credit Notes have currency throughout the Empire equally with gold coin. 3. For Counterfeiting Credit Notes the guilty will be subject to deprivation of all rights and banishment to hard labor." The note is finely engraved and printed in several inks: green, the predominant color, blue, and lavender. It is very much in the contemporary European monetary style except that it is, if anything, more finely executed. The contemporary Swiss National Bank considered the 100–ruble note (1910 issue) in this series a "technical masterpiece" and took it as a model for improving the aesthetic and anti– counterfeit qualities of its own currency.[8] The remaining notes in the series carry

6. Bulla's photograph of the State Bank is reproduced in Mikhail P. Iroshnikov, *Before the Revolution: St. Petersburg in Photographs, 1890–1914* (New York, 1991), 138. See also the contemporary guidebook by V. Kurbatov, *Petersburg, khudozhestvenno–istoricheskii ocherk* (St. Petersburg, 1913), especially 210–212, with photograph and verbal description concluding: "...one of the most successful and best thought–out projects of civil architecture [in the city]"; Kurbatov also considered the Bank's fence "one of the most elegant in the history of art" (212). Another photograph of the Bank, this time as decorated for the Romanov Tercentenary celebrations in 1913, is printed in Mikhail Iroshnikov et al., *Nikolai II: poslednii rossiiskii imperator* (St. Petersburg, 1992), 406. For the building in Soviet time, see A. N. Petrov et al., *Pamiatniki arkhitektury Leningrada*, 3rd ed. (Leningrad, 1971), 255 and photograph ([254], no. 1); and for its original plans as well as recent photos, Giacomo Quarenghi, *Architetto a Pietroburgo: Lettere e altri scritti*, ed. Vanni Zanella (Venice, 1988), nos. 46–53.

7. The Imperial was a gold coin equal to ten gold rubles and used mainly in international transactions; its gold content had been established by decree in December 1885.

8. Michel de Rivaz, *Ferdinand Hodler, Eugene Burnand und die schweizerischen Banknoten* (Bern, 1991), 339–40. For further examples of contemporary European bank notes see Deutsche Bundesbank, *Das Papiergeld im Deutschen Reich 1871–1948* (Frankfurt/Main, 1966), especially 48–57; Carmelo Storico, *La Carta Moneta Italiana 1746–1960* (Palermo, 1967), especially 141–67; etc.

Figure. Reverse of 500-ruble State Credit Note, issued 1912. Private Collection. Actual size: 275x127mm.

identical wording and comparably fine designs, the main overall difference being one of size: the larger the denomination, the larger the note.

The reverse of our 500–ruble note features prominently, against a background of similarly classicist architecture and decoration reflecting the currently fashionable *style moderne*,[9] an equally stylish female personification of Imperial Russia holding in her outstretched hand a scepter surmounted by the Romanov eagle (see Figure). The scepter obviously is linked to the Imperial crown and orb pictured above and below a portrait of Peter the Great, which is easily, and no doubt intentionally, the most striking feature of the entire note. The portrait is highly specific. It reproduces in fine steel engraving the famous image of Peter first painted from life in oil by Karl Moor (Carel de Moor) at The Hague in 1717, during Peter's triumphal second embassy to Europe. Moor's painting (later whereabouts uncertain) was reputedly Peter's own favorite among the dozens of likenesses taken during his life, and at his order it was copied almost immediately by the well–known Dutch engraver Jacobus Houbraken. The Houbraken engraving was repeatedly reproduced thereafter, in Russia as well as abroad, in books and single sheets, until it became the single best known image of Peter the Great

9. E. A. Borisova and G. Iu. Stepnin, *Russkii modern* (Moscow, 1990)—authoritative text, beautifully illustrated.

in the fullness of his power.[10]

The bank notes under review have been authoritatively judged "master-pieces" on aesthetic as well as technical grounds.[11] Yet it surely also is note-worthy that four of the eight denominations in the series carry ruler por-traits, and that these are of Alexander III (25 rubles, 1909 issue), Nicholas I (50 rubles, 1899 issue), and Catherine II (100 rubles, 1898 and 1910 issues) in addition to Peter (500 rubles, 1898 and 1912): the lesser denomination notes—1, 3, 5, 10—bear only the Imperial eagle or allegorical figures of Russia.[12] *Not* thus represented in the series are the other monarchs of the eighteenth century (Catherine I, Peter II, Anna, Elizabeth, Ivan VI, Peter III, and Paul), Alexanders I and II, and the reigning ruler, Nicholas II (who *is* represented, following custom, on contemporary coinage). Why not? What do these other rulers (excepting Nicholas II) have in common but their rela-tively brief time in office (five of the nine), death by assassination (four of the nine), lackluster if not perverse character and achievements (most of the nine), and the ambiguity if not forgetability of their reigns (this from the perspective of the Imperial regimes of 1898–1912, for whom the reign of Alexander II, to take the most obvious omission, was far from beneficent)? And what, in their ascending denominational order, do Alexander III, Nicho-las I, Catherine II, and Peter the Great have in common—except for their relative longevity on the throne and more or less unscathed reputations as successful, if not positively enlightened, autocrats? Then, more or less ar-guably, was Russia great and strong!

The selection of rulers for portrayal on this series of notes, and in the order portrayed, from the 25–ruble Alexander III to the 500–ruble Peter I, cannot have been accidental; and further research may establish definitively the rationale and process of decision–making here, at the highest levels of the Imperial system in what proved to be its last years. Meanwhile, we can readily see in this series of Russian bank notes of 1898–1912 (eight de-nominations, 14 individual notes, 36 separate issues[13]) beautifully defined

---

10. Details in my forthcoming volume, *The Petrine Revolution in Russian Art*. The first 500–ruble note of this series (issued in 1898) presents a different—less imposing as well as historically dubious (romanticized)—portrait of Peter: see Malyshev et al., *Bumazhnye znaki*, 414 (no. 1.11.65).

11. Thus Malyshev et al., *Bumazhnye znaki*, 70–72; and see again Michel de Rivaz, *Schweizerischen Banknoten*, 339–40.

12. Malyshev et al., *Bumazhnye znaki*, 409–15 (nos. 1.11.53–1.11.66).

13. The 1898 one–ruble note was issued again in 1903, 1910, and 1912; the 1898 three–ruble note, in 1903; etc. See again Malyshev et al., *Bumazhnye znaki*, 345–36 (nos. 649–84) for a complete list.

images of Imperial authority, dignity, strength, and bounty—images that were conveyed by what was presumably a widely distributed, highly valued, and most desirable medium, one that commanded acceptance. And from available contemporary sources we can establish much of the immediate context in which this series of notes was issued.

Indeed, in them is figured, with impressive clarity and brevity, Witte's monetary reform of 1897 (1895–1898): Witte was then, of course, head of the Imperial Ministry of Finances, which controlled the State Bank. Historians divide in their assessment of the ultimate consequences of this reform, which introduced the international gold standard and gave the State Bank the authority to issue as many as 600 million rubles' worth of these "credit notes" with 50 percent gold backing above which amount it could only issue notes with 100 percent backing.[14] Yet there is no doubt that it was Witte's reform and that it stabilized the Empire's hitherto grossly fluctuating currency, making it freely convertible in foreign markets. The reform thus greatly facilitated not only the state's ability to float foreign loans (saving it from bankruptcy, according to Witte, in the crisis of 1904–1905), but also foreign investment in Russia—which Witte considered essential to Russia's economic modernization (which he considered essential to maintaining the Empire as a great power, his ultimate objective).[15] Moreover, rarely after 1897 did the State Bank exercise its authority to issue paper rubles—"credit notes"—with less than 100 percent gold backing. Often (1898–1905, 1909–1911), relying on the enormous gold reserves that were built up prior to the 1897 reform as

14. Cf. V. E. Vlasenko, *Denezhnaia reforma v Rossii 1895–1898 gg.* (Kiev, 1949); Theodore H. Von Laue, *Sergei Witte and the Industrialization of Russia* (New York, 1969), especially 138–46; Olga Crisp, "Russian Financial Policy and the Gold Standard at the End of the Nineteenth Century," in Crisp, *Studies in the Russian Economy before 1914* (London, 1976), 96–110; Arcadius Kahan, "The Russian Economy, 1860–1913," in Kahan, *Russian Economic History: The Nineteenth Century,* ed. Roger Weiss (Chicago, 1989), 1–90, especially 50–52; and Peter Gatrell, *The Tsarist Economy 1850–1917* (New York, 1986), especially 224–26. Documents in A. I. Bukovetskii, ed., *Materialy po denezhnoi reforme 1895–1897 gg.* (Petrograd, 1922). Witte's importance has at last been fully recognized among historians in Russia: see B. V. Anan'ich and R. Sh. Ganelin, "Sergei Iul'evich Vitte," *Voprosy istorii* 1990 no. 8 (August): 32–53—"one of the greatest reformers in the history of Russia" (32), etc.

15. See *The Memoirs of Count Witte,* ed. and trans. Sidney Harcave (Armonk, NY, 1990), especially 189–91 and 246–49. The official history/rationale of the reform is fully laid out in A. Gur'ev, *Denezhnoe obrashchenie v Rossii v XIX stoletii: istoricheskii ocherk* (St. Petersburg, 1903). For detailed background information, see M. Kashkarov, *Denezhnoe obrashchenie v Rossii,* 2 vols. (St. Petersburg, 1898); and I. F. Gindin, *Gosudarstvennyi bank i ekonomicheskaia politika tsarskogo pravitel'stva 1861–1892 gg.* (Moscow, 1960).

well as after it, the State Bank held gold considerably in excess (from 1 percent to over 40 percent) of the total ruble value of its notes in circulation. In 1914 its approximately 1.7 billion rubles' worth of credit notes in circulation (of a total of about 2.3 billion rubles circulating in notes and gold and silver coin) were secured by gold in a proportion somewhere between 92 and 100 percent (expert estimates vary)[16]—making it, in this sense, one of the strongest currencies in the world.[17] In short, the Witte series of paper rubles (1898–1912) was, in all of Russian monetary history to that point (or since!), uniquely strong and stable.

To be sure, the policies of the Witte regime heavily favored capital investment over wage increases, industry over agriculture, production over consumption, and domestic products over imports, thus making life more difficult, at least in the short run, for the great majority of the Empire's subjects. Knowing this, Witte favored retaining as long as possible the autocratic core of the Imperial system—or, as he would have preferred it, enlightened bureaucratic absolutism—as the *sine qua non* in Russian circumstances of the necessary economic modernization. Put bluntly, Witte needed absolute power, based on the monarch's confidence and exercised through his highly trained corps of administrators and technical experts, in order to pursue his lofty goal as quickly as possible and with maximum efficiency; for his policies to this end were extremely unpopular. This much is fairly well known. But Witte's bank notes remind us that he acted here solidly within the hallowed Imperial tradition of enlightened bureaucratic absolutism in the service of economic modernization and political aggrandizement——the tradition founded by Peter the Great and thereafter best

---

16. Cf. Prof. Z. S. Katsenelenbaum, *Denezhnoe obrashchenie Rossii 1914–1924* (Moscow/Leningrad, 1924), 8–12 (English edn. = S. S. Katzenellenbaum, *Russian Currency and Banking 1914–1924* [London, 1925], 4–8); Kahan, "Russian Economy," Table 1.22A [45]; and Vlasenko, *Denezhnaia reforma*, tables on 182, 185. See also the memoirs of V. N. Kokovtsov, Witte's assistant (1896–1902) and successor (1904–1914) as minister of finances, *Out of My Past* (Stanford, 1935), 463. Kokovtsov declares here (443) that "as his [Witte's] subordinate I carried out his financial and political policies to the best of my ability, and as his successor I continued the former in a large measure, especially as regards currency and the liquor monopoly."

17. William Wiseley, *A Tool of Power: The Political History of Money* (New York, 1977), 66. In 1913, Wiseley shows (363, Table 1), Russia had the largest gold reserves in the world. A recent study of the Bolshevik regime's initial trade with the West indicates that this gold, as the indispensible means for securing vital goods and credits, was critical to the new system's survival: Christine A. White, *British and American Commercial Relations with Soviet Russia, 1918–1924* (Chapel Hill, NC, 1992).

represented among his successors precisely by Catherine II, Nicholas I, and, most recently, Alexander III, a ruler for whom Witte himself secretly professed an admiration verging on adulation.[18] It was also a tradition, as brilliantly exemplified in Witte's bank notes, that strove to explain and justify itself by the most advanced aesthetic and technical means at hand.[19]

Viewed in this context, we see why the choice of rulers for portrayal on the larger denominations of the Witte series of paper rubles—popularly known, accordingly, as the "Romanov notes" (*romanovskie bilety*)[20]—was certainly not accidental. Nor was the choice of means for portraying them— the best available—any less so. In fact, the basic "ideology" of the Imperial system in its last decades is more clearly and succinctly revealed in this image–set, taken as a whole, than in the relevant verbal sources that survive from the period—scattered and fragmentary in form, as well as inconsistent or incoherent in content, as they are.[21] As broadcasted in and by this highly estimable medium, that ideology plainly projected a triple message: (1) these fine notes are as good as gold; (2) the State Bank that issued them is really solid (as solid as it looks); and (3) the system thus represented, the Russian Imperial system, is therefore good—durable, beneficial, enlightened—as

---

18. See *Witte Memoirs*, 170–78 and *passim* (Witte died in February 1915; his memoirs, secretly written after his fall from power in 1906 and deposited abroad, were published posthumously: see *ibid.*, editor's introduction, xiii ff.). The official rationale of Witte's monetary reform made it clear that the reigns of these four rulers marked the major advances in the monetary history of Russia to that time: see Gur'ev, *Denezhnoe obrashchenie*, 15–20 (Peter the Great), 26–48 (Catherine II), 77–157 (Nicholas I), 187–218 (Alexander III). We also note here, in the chapter devoted to monetary matters in the reign of Nicholas II to date, the statement that "the Minister of Finances" (Witte) had deemed it "most opportune" to proceed (1895) with the reform "because, thanks to the peaceful policy of Alexander III, our political situation and that of the European powers was tranquil, accounts were not in deficit, the economic resources of the population were somewhat developed, the international [trade] balance was steadily tilting in our favor, the state's credit had achieved unprecedented heights, a huge gold reserve had been built up, and finally, and especially important, the ruble's exchange rate had attained significant stability" (220–21). In other words, Nicholas II had contributed nothing to the reform except insofar as he had followed his father's, Alexander III's, policies. Witte's contempt for Nicholas II is clear from his *Memoirs, passim*.

19. Catherine II's patronage and promotion of printing and the visual or graphic and plastic arts (the visual media), like that of Peter the Great, are well known. Less well known perhaps are the similar roles played by Nicholas I and Alexander III—and, in his way, Nicholas II.

20. Malyshev et al., *Bumazhnye znaki*, p. 72.

well as elegant and imposing. This was incontestably a powerful message for the incumbent regime to send to both subjects and creditors, especially when parts (1) and (2) of it were demonstrably true. And the message could only have redounded to the system's prestige, reinforcing its hegemony.

Indeed, the value of these graphic sources as evidence of the nature and the persistence of the Imperial system's core ideology is only enhanced when we turn to the question of their reception. It should be stressed that this is always a difficult matter for historians to investigate: how finally to measure or assess the responses of millions of people to *any* official image or, for that matter, verbal text? In this case, however, we can state with assurance that money in a reasonably modern (monetized) economy was and is in many respects a uniquely effective medium not only of exchange, but of communication; and we can fairly surmise that virtually none of these state credit notes was deliberately refused or destroyed by potential recipients nor its basic message ignored. Then too, on the issuance beginning in 1898 of the Witte series all previously issued notes were recalled to the Treasury and destroyed, this fact "accounting," in the words of Pick's *Standard Catalog*, "for their uniform scarcity today."[22] We should also remember that one purpose of Witte's reform was to *decrease* the number of lower–

---

21. Cf. Andrew Verner, *The Crisis of Russian Autocracy: Nicholas II and the 1905 Revolution* (Princeton, 1990), who complains (70) that in this period "The ideology of autocracy was neither unchanging nor rationally coherent...." Constantine Pobedonostsev, the longtime (1880–1905) administrator of the Russian Orthodox Church who is often cited as the leading ideologist of the Imperial system in its last decades, is the best case in point: the principal statement of his views, the collection of occasional essays entitled *Moskovskii sbornik (Moscow Miscellany*, published in five editions 1896–1905), is little more than a fragmentary and often plagiarized polemic against various opponents, real or imagined, of the system. See Robert F. Byrnes, *Pobedonostsev: His Life and Thought* (Bloomington, IN, 1968), 290, 304, 371, and *passim*; "a part–time philosopher" concerned as such mainly with church or religious matters, as Byrnes says (267), or again, "more a pedant turned propagandist than a thinker": Edward C. Thaden, *Conservative Nationalism in Nineteenth–Century Russia* (Seattle, 1964), 201. Thaden finds only one "first–rate Russian thinker" of conservative bent active in the last decades of Imperial Russia, L. A. Tikhomirov (1852–1923), a marginal figure who never held office and who had the "dubious distinction of being hailed in the early 1930s as the father of Russian fascism" (205). Nor is there any indication that Tikhomirov's book of historical, legal, and religious ruminations on "the principle of monarchical statehood" (*Monarkhicheskaia gosudarstvennost'* [Moscow, 1905; reprinted St. Petersburg, 1992]) had any influence in its time.

22. Pick, *Standard Catalog*, 879. Cf. the high "rarity" ratings (*stepen' redkosti*) for pre–1898 paper money issues listed in Malyshev et al., *Bumazhnye znaki*, 9, 318 ff.

denomination notes (1, 3, 5, 10 rubles) in circulation and to *increase* that of the "romanovs" (25, 50, 100, 500; also, 50– and 500–ruble notes had never been issued before); so that by 1903 the lower accounted for only 7.2 percent (face value) of the paper money in circulation (by 1914, after 25 successive new issues—11 of lower–denomination notes, 14 of romanovs—and the general expansion of the economy, including both price and wage inflation, that percentage had risen to 48.2).[23]

Thus between 1898 and 1914 the *only* paper money in circulation in Russia were the Witte notes, with those of larger denomination predominating numerically, quite possibly, as well as in face value. But in what volume did this paper money circulate, especially by comparison with the new gold and silver coins that also formed part of Witte's reform? Of *all* money in circulation in Russia in 1898, 23.7 percent was in coin and 76.3 percent in notes; in 1904, the percentages were 61.3 and 38.7 respectively (the highest year for coins—the bulk of them, by a factor of more than three to one, *gold* coins); and by 1914, the percentages had reverted to 28.8 coin and 71.2 paper. Never between 1898 and 1914 did paper money as a percentage of all money in circulation in Russia fall below 38.7, and most often it ranged between 60 and 70 (just as the percentage of gold coins in circulation always heavily outweighed that of silver). Lastly, official records show that at any one point between 1898 and 1914 notes to the value of between one billion and two billion rubles were in circulation—this total constituting the bulk of all money in circulation, as just mentioned, while the bulk of this paper, also as just mentioned, was usually in the notes of larger denomination, the good old "romanovs."[24]

These figures indicate clearly that the Witte state credit notes—exceptionally fine in appearance, as solid as gold in fact, uniquely strong and stable—circulated widely in Russia in what proved to be the Imperial system's last years. Furthermore, it can be readily inferred from these figures that the "romanovs" circulated widely (as well as almost exclusively) among groups whose support was critical to the system's continued success: industrialists, merchants, and traders including the many foreign investors and operatives; higher–salaried officials including those of the armed forces and the church; managers and other professionals of higher income; the extended Imperial family itself: any and all wealthy or better–off people in Russian society at

---

23. Vlasenko, *Denezhnaia reforma*, 163 (table).

24. Vlasenko, *Denezhnaia reforma*, 185 (table).

the time.[25] In 1913 or 1914, in other words, the elite of Imperial Russia (or, by now, the several elites) obviously had a deep financial interest in the maintenance of the system (though not necessarily the current regime), an interest that would have been shared, if not perhaps as deeply, by the rapidly expanding classes of wage–earners and ordinary consumers.

And we can thus see why the precipitous devaluation of Imperial Russia's paper money in the ensuing years of World War I, caused mainly by the regime's precipitous increase in the issuance of such money to pay for the war, provides a particularly telling marker of the system's precipitous collapse.[26] Even so, it is clear that as late as August 1917 millions of ordinary people in Russia still clung to their state bank notes, evidently in the hope-

25. While industrial workers earned an average 284 rubles per year in 1913 (with great regional and sector variations), business directors and managers received annual salaries ranging from 7,000 to 12,000 rubles and senior officials, from 4,000 to 8,000 rubles (15,000 to 26,000 rubles per year for ministers and their deputies). But price/wage inflation in the Empire's last decades makes it difficult to generalize; so do such facts as that up to 50 percent of the topmost Imperial elite still derived income from landholdings as well as official salaries, and that most officials also received travel, food, and housing allowances. For these and other figures see Diane Koenker, *Moscow Workers and the 1917 Revolution* (Princeton, 1981), 84–88; Victoria E. Bonnell, ed., *The Russian Worker: Life and Labor under the Tsarist Regime* (Berkeley and Los Angeles, 1983), 126 (n. 15), 144 (n. 31), 167, 202–203; Gatrell, *Tsarist Economy*,94–95; Don Karl Rowney, "Higher Civil Servants in the Russian Ministry of Internal Affairs: Some Demographic and Career Characteristics, 1905–1916," *Slavic Review* 31, no. 1 (March 1972): 109; Dominic C. B. Lieven, "The Russian Civil Service under Nicholas II," *Jahrbücher für Geschichte Osteuropas* 29, no. 3 (1981): 366–403 and especially 401, 402 (tables 13, 16); and Paul R. Gregory, *Russian National Income, 1885–1913* (New York, 1982), [254–55] (table). Gregory also estimates (146–47), on the basis of contemporary Ministry of Finances data, that in 1909–1910 some 1.5 percent of *families* in Imperial Russia had annual incomes of 1,000 rubles or more (up from 1 percent in 1905), a figure that translates into several million people.

26. Recent research in both official (especially police) and Bolshevik party archives as well as in the contemporary press confirms earlier published indications that by early 1917 the enormous fall of the ruble (to about one–quarter of its 1914 pre–war value) and the resulting runaway inflation—prices by an average of 300 percent, leading to severe deprivation and shortages of vital necessities—constituted the chief cause of discontent with the regime among both ordinary and better–off people: see I. P. Leiberov and S. D. Rudachenko, *Revoliutsiia i khleb* (Moscow, 1990); Jonathan W. Daly, "The Watchful State: Police and Politics in Late Imperial Russia, 1896–1917" (PhD dissertation, Harvard University, 1992), 383–87; and Iu. I. Kir'ianov, "Massovye vystupleniia na pochve dorogovizny v Rossii (1914–1917)," *Otechestvennaia istoriia* 1993 no. 3 (May–June), 3–18. It might be noted that in early 1917 there were over nine billion rubles' worth of state credit notes in circulation—up from 1.7 billion in early 1914 (Malyshev et al., *Bumazhnye znaki*, 74).

ful conviction that their value would be maintained or indeed restored.[27] Runaway inflation, it might be argued, as much as anything else, would also destroy the Provisional Government, rushing as it was to print still more money—and in oddly new, quite ephemeral guises.[28]

At the same time, these findings regarding the status and appearance of the Witte notes tend to oppugn the well–known thesis, drawn from quite different evidence (mainly of social unrest), that in 1914 the Imperial system stood on the brink of collapse: that its collapse was only *postponed*, not precipitated, by Russia's entry into World War I.[29] A kind of populist bias—"history from below"— and/or preoccupation with the phenomena of revolution—the "te-

---

27. Thus the minister of finances' report to the Provisional Government of August 1917, which states in part: "The demand for bank notes is so great that [there is] no time to print them in the needed quantity, and the situation may become critical, inasmuch as the [gold] reserves of the treasury are extremely limited. Bank notes accumulate for the most part in the hands of peasants and workers. And to extricate the bank notes from their owners is very difficult. As a result, millions of bank notes are at present concentrated in the hands of the popular masses" (Robert Paul Browder and Alexander F. Kerensky, eds., *The Russian Provisional Government, 1917: Documents*, vol. 2 [Stanford, 1961], 516–17).

28. Between March and September 1917 the Provisional Government more than doubled the amount of paper money in circulation (Malyshev et al., *Bumazhnye znaki*, 84, 74).

29. Articles by Leopold Haimson are usually considered the *locus classicus* (non–Soviet) of this thesis: "The Problem of Social Stability in Urban Russia, 1905–1917," *Slavic Review* 23, no. 4 (December 1964): 619–42; *Slavic Review* 24, no. 1 (March 1965): 1–22, 47–56. Soviet historiography meanwhile posited an "undeviating sequence" of events from 1905 to 1917, as Professor Wildman has noted: "Lenin's ideological precepts, the assimilation thereof by the party, organizational preparations, the masses' response to the party's influence and the maturing of the 'crisis,' by which time the party and the masses are primed for revolutionary action"; and *voilà*, "the overthrow [of]...the Russian monarchy" (Allan K. Wildman, *The End of the Russian Imperial Army: The Old Army and the Soldiers' Revolt (March–April 1917)* [Princeton, 1980], 121). Wildman's own work strongly supports the thesis that it was the war's "intolerable strains" that brought down the Imperial system; but in explaining how and why this was so he minimizes the "purely economic causes" of popular "alienation" from the system and of the "massive groundswell of popular feeling that shattered [February 1917] the autocratic framework" (*ibid.*, 374–75, 122, and *passim*). Similarly, more recent studies of the role of the urban masses in 1917, although well aware of underlying economic factors, tend to slight them in favor of the surface drama of social and political unrest: cf. Koenker, *Moscow Workers and 1917*, especially 78–100; or David Mandel, *The Petrograd Workers and the Fall of the Old Regime* (New York, 1983), 1– 110. On the other hand, Robert B. McKean, *St. Petersburg between the Revolutions* (New Haven, 1990), indicates that only a minority of St. Petersburg workers were militant in 1914, and that it was the effects of the war that radicalized the worker masses.

leology of 1917"—have perhaps distorted our picture of the system's viability in 1914.[30] We should not replace one *idée fixe* with another, to be sure, whether the replacement is economic or narrowly monetarist (or something else) in nature. But *on the basis of these findings alone* we may infer that as 1914 began, the Imperial system was as "stable" as it had ever been, if not more so. Its hegemony, however much weakened or contested since the glory days of Alexander III or Nicholas I, was still intact.[31]

The monetary index of system stability (as we might call it), with its universalist postulate of a positive correlation between monetary and system stability, has never been systematically applied to Imperial Russia. Nor have Imperial Russian historians, in common with most modern historians, paid much attention to the visual remains of their period. It is hoped that in both respects this brief but intensive look at the Witte notes in their historical context will encourage further work, work which could well contribute to a "rethinking" of the field.

30. Not to mention the shortsighted view, as expressed classically by Bernard Pares, that "The dynasty fell by its own insufficiency, and the immediate occasion of its fall was the rule [from later 1915] of the Empress and Rasputin" (Pares, *A History of Russia* [London, 1965; first published 1926], 531).

31. The economic case for the Imperial system's viability in 1914 has been put most succinctly perhaps by the late Alexander Gerschenkron, notably in his "Problems and Patterns of Russian Economic Development," in Cyril E. Black, ed., *The Transformation of Russian Society: Aspects of Social Change since 1861* (Cambridge, MA, 1960), 42–72 (especially part III, 52–61): thus, on the basis of its industrial development to 1914 "one might surmise that in the absence of the war Russia would have continued on the road of progressive westernization" (58). Professor Haimson, in the work just cited (n. 29), explicitly contests this view (622). But see also the generally positive (and generally ignored) conclusions regarding Russian economic development by 1913–1914 variously offered in works cited above (nn. 14, 25) by Crisp, Kahan, Gatrell, and Gregory.
   Of course, "stability" is a relative concept, and in applying it to the *political* situation in Russia on the eve of World War I historians might distinguish system stability from both regime stability and social stability: a political *system* (following Eckstein, *Regarding Politics*, n. 5 above) "that has demonstrated considerable staying power, a capacity to endure without great or frequent changes in authority pattern," is capable of "effective decision making," and is "authentic," will remain stable in the face of almost any amount of social instability (whether caused by exogenous or endogenous factors, or by both) so long as the incumbent regime is also stable. When severe regime instability coincides (perhaps causally) for any length of time with severe social instability, the system collapses (as happened in Russia after 1914 and in the Time of Troubles of 1598–1613, but did *not* happen through all the palace coups of the eighteenth century nor in the 1812 invasion nor with the Decembrist 1825 Uprising nor with the 1881 assassination of Alexander II nor—though it apparently came close—in the 1905 Revolution).

Part Two:
Eastern Europe

FROM THE RENAISSANCE TO THE COUNTER–REFORMATION: THE DUBROVNIK OF ĐIVO GUNDULIĆ (1589–1638)

Zdenko Zlatar

"EVERY AGE, we might say, has its own style, or perhaps we might say more modestly but more broadly, its own climate—and that is a truth which applies not merely to art and literature."[1] According to Lucien Febvre, it applies to history as well. Here I would like to apply Febvre's approach to Dubrovnik during the lifetime of its greatest poet, Đivo Franov Gundulić [Joannes Francisci Gondola].[2]

One of the richest sources for the social and cultural history of Dubrovnik is the extremely fine and completely preserved series *Testamenta*, which includes wills made between 1282 and 1815. I have gone through hundreds of wills made up by patricians between 1578 and 1608 in order to see how they reflect social, religious, and cultural changes that took place in Dubrovnik in general and within the patriciate in particular during the pe-

---

1. Lucien Febvre, "Amiens: From the Renaissance to the Counter–Reformation" in Peter Burke, ed., *A New Kind of History: From the Writings of Lucien Febvre* (New York, 1973), 193-207, first published in *Annales d'Histoire sociale III* (1941) and reprinted in Lucien Febvre, *Au coeur religieux du XVI siècle* (Paris, 1957).

2. I have written the first study of Gundulić in English. His unfinished and (until the early 19th century) unpublished epic *Osman*, singing of the defeat at Hoczym (1621) and deposition and murder of Sultan II (1622), and glorifying the role of the Poles as fellow Slavs and of the Polish heir to the throne, Wladyslaw [future Wladyslaw IV (1632-1648)], as the impending liberator of the Balkan Slavs from the Ottoman yoke, was modelled on Tasso's *Jerusalem Delivered*. It represents the crowning achievement of Old Croation literature. *See* Zdenko Zlatar, *Gundulić's Osman: The Slavic Epic* [forthcoming].

riod of transition from the Renaissance to the Counter- Reformation. In this I had followed the fine example of Lucien Febvre. What should be pointed out about the wills is their unprevaricating nature: a man or a woman about to die, or expecting the possibility of an untimely death (e.g., when leaving on a risky mission) is not about to deceive him/herself and others. And while quite a few of them reveal human quirks, stubborness and pride sometimes bordering on vanity, they are not sly or coy.

The first thing that strikes one about these wills is the class nature of Ragusan society. Of course, one should expect to find traces of this in the wills of those who belonged to the ruling class of Dubrovnik. Yet, their class tenor is not only unmistakable, it is very assertive, even haughty. Yet, paradoxical as it may sound, this relishing of their supreme position in Dubrovnik did not prevent many, if not most of them, from expressing solicitous, sometimes tender, and occasionally very compassionate feelings about those who served them. Certainly, Christian charity figured prominently at such a solemn occasion as when drafting a last will. On the other hand, many managed to assuage their guilty consciences by leaving appropriately small amounts of money to those whose misfortune it had been to serve them. But many went much beyond these social and religious conventions: and these instances reveal to us a much more complex, human and sophisticated society than we were expected to believe.

A whole book could be written on the relationships between the privileged and unprivileged classes in Dubrovnik, but this is not the place. What I can do is highlight certain moments indicative of the social fabric of Early Modern Dubrovnik. A more detailed discussion of the patriciate as a ruling class is given in my book, *Our Kingdom Come.*[3] Here I shall not deal with the evolution and structure of the patriciate as a ruling class, but only with its relationship to non-privileged classes.

Ragusan society was not a class system, but one based on estates, as in the rest of Western and Central Europe. Yet, its upper estates evinced certain characteristics more appropriate to castes, rather than estates. Thus, all three prominent and well-off upper estates, the ruling patriciate, the two confraternities of St. Anthony and St. Lazarus, did not marry outside of their own ranks. The patriciate was closest to a caste, and indeed between 1462 and 1666 it was a complete caste, for it refused to mix with any other

---

3. *See* Zdenko Zlatar, *Our Kingdom Come: The Counter–Reformation, the Republic of Dubrovnik, and the Liberation of the Balkan Slavs* (East European Monographs, Distributed by Columbia University Press, Boulder, 1992).

estates, and was genetically sealed. Though the two privileged confraternities accepted new members and thus new blood into their ranks, the members of the two did not mutually intermarry. Thus, the entire upper and middle
strata of Ragusan society lived in a strictly segregated social order, refusing
to cross these social boundaries in principle. As it has been pointed out, this
division of the mercantile and financial elites of Dubrovnik into mutually
exclusive and often intensely jealous groups, facilitated the rule of the patriciate in Dubrovnik, for it did not have to face the challenge of a united
middle class, grown rich on trade and finance. Instead the two privileged
(but rigidly excluded from all power) groups of citizens belonging to the
confraternities of St. Anthony (the *antunini*) and of St. Lazarus (the *lazarini*)
aped the patriciate both in its ostentation and in its exclusiveness.

That is why any Marxist interpretation of Ragusan society is fraught
with difficulties: as largest landowners and exclusive participants in a government which still carried many quasi-feudal noble attributes (their insistence on the noble status, its title of *ser* etc.), the patricians could be seen as
feudal lords as opposed to the rest of the Ragusan population; but as active
and biggest participants in Ragusan trade and finance, the patricians had all
the bearings of Early Modern capitalists, and thus could be seen as belonging to the middle class, together with the members of the two privileged
orders of the *antunini* and the *lazarini*. The same is true, of course, of the
Venetian patriciate, and I think that this special class role of these patrici-
ates accounts for the absence of a bitter class conflict in Early Modern Venice
and Dubrovnik. This is not to say that there was no conflict involving the
patriciate: but the conflict, as I demonstrated, was *within*, not *between* the
patriciate and other groups.[4]

The testaments are full of references to patricians' generosity: thus
Mattheus Christophori Bona leaves to his maid Maria Antonova 200 scudi
so that she could get properly married; in her last will Nicha, the widow of
Bernardus Pozza left all her bedding, "i.e. mattresses...and all such goods
found adorning my Chamber, and I leave her these on account of her faithful service she rendered me during my illness;" Lutianus Francisci Caboga,
in his will, ordered his heirs to keep his old servant, Vizza from Lopud
[Isola di Mezzo], by paying her eight scudi as long as she lived, while two
other maids, Zvieta and Catarina, living in his own house, were to be paid
three ducats for each one of their eight years of service plus ten scudi each

---

4. *See* Zdenko Zlatar, "The 'Crisis' of the Patriciate in Early Seventeenth–Century
    Dubrovnik: A Reappraisal" in *Balcanica* VI (1975), 111–131.

to enable them to marry, not counting the value of clothes and other goods already given them, "because they served me faithfully;" Savino Aloysii Gozze gave his servant, Nicolo di Pietro Bandiero, "who served me without pay" [gratis] 150 scudi and a half of one of his estates in Konavle [Canali].[5] Reasons other than gratitude for faithful service often were stated almost bluntly: this was especially the case where feeling of obligation and sometimes even of love were the result of illicit sexual relationships. It was quite acceptable for patrician men to have love affairs with their maid servants, and often these resulted in illegitimate children. Ragusan patricians did not deny their illegitimate offspring in their last wills, and often expressed their tender feelings toward their bastard sons and daughters in uncompromising terms. Thus Jacobus Laurentiii Sorgo stated openly that he felt conscience-bound to one Madusa or Mandaliena, wife of Francesco di Marco Vitcovich, who had served him and his wife faithfully for twelve years, and left her all linen found in his house, "especially in my bedchamber," and the rest to his patrician sister Maria, widow of Luca Pauli Sorgo, with this proviso that if her sister objected "or even tried to object to this final will of mine" she would be dispossessed and everything would go "to the said Madussa...I say all my goods...;" Marinus Secundi Zamagno acknowledged one Francesco as his "natural son" [figliulo naturale, a euphemism for an illegitimate son] and left him parts of his estates during his life as a priest, so that he could use the usufruct, such as wine, from them with an admonition to his parents to treat him as they would treat the dying man, and another one to his legitimate heirs to feed and clothe Francesco until the age of thirty while he is studying "living in the fear of God;" a very poignant case is that of Joseph Prodanelli, the last of his patrician house, who left to his 'natural son' all his estate in Breno, while the rest of his possessions went to his only surviving sister "nun in [the monastery of] St. Clara;" and Martolizza Draghoe Cerva ordered his heirs to treat his 'natural daughter' [figlia naturale] by the name of Annizza, married to Paolo di Pietro Lalich "with no less love than I have"—a rather tall order.[6]

Not surprisingly, in view of what was said about the segregated nature of Ragusan society, relations between patricians and privileged citizens were exclusively business–oriented. Thus Andreas Marini Restis, having been actively engaged in Ragusan trade in the Balkans, mentioned the late Biagio

---

5. Historijski arhiv, Dubrovnik [HAD], *Testamenta de Notaria* [TN], *51*, 44'–45'; *52*, 1–3; *52*, 5–6; *52*, 43–44'.

6. TN *52*, 90'–91; *51*, 82–84'; *53*, 206–206'; *53*, 212'–213'.

Bisia, "who died in Filippopoli" [Plovdiv in Bulgaria] and the latter's goods, namely "a silver dagger and a curved Turkish sword called a scimitar" so that Bisia's heir "or anybody else" could use them; he went on to declare himself a debtor to Girolamo Darsa, a rich merchant of common background for 900 tubes of special cloth called "montanine, partly in Ancona and partly on their way from Sofia."[7]

Often patricians tried to repair the damage done to nonpatricians through the stubborness of some of their own members to acknowledge their debt: thus Stephanus Joannis Gondola, the uncle of our poet, who died in Venice in 1602, but who wrote his testament as early as 1585, mentioned a bale from Antwerp [d'Anversa] which had not been paid and in case his partner, Raffael Gozze refused to do so; and in his long testament Nicolaus Lutiani Bona left 200 ducats to be given to Paulo Barbiero, Giovanni Barbiero and Bernardo Barbiero, all three merchants in Belgrade (mercante di Belgradi), but he swore "by that formidable and final step that my soul will make from this fragile body" that he owed "nothing to anybody, nor do I feel obligated to anyone; for I am sure that as a member of a company among us I lost more than 10,000 ducats."[8]

Expressions of pity, rather than of business propriety or obligation, governed the relationship between patricians and the outcasts of Ragusan society: the poor, the slaves, and the lepers. A great majority of wills contains provisions leaving some alms for the poor: thus Franciscus Michaelis Caboga ordered all his mobile goods to be sold, and "one third given as help toward marrying poor girls, a third as help and subsidy for poor noble women, and a third as help for liberating Ragusan slaves." Franciscus Marini Goze stated that he owned a slave named Marco in Messina to whom he was giving freedom and leaving it up to him whether he wanted to serve his heir in Dubrovnik or not freely—in each case Marco was to be given a small sum of money. Nicha, the widow of Bernardus Pozza, left 1 grossus to every beggar found in the city at the day of her death, "up to the sum of 3 ducats." And when Joannes Marini Restis died in office as the Rector [president] of the Ragusan Republic, the first thing he mentioned in his will was alms for the lepers "who live outside of the City," i.e. outside the city walls.[9]

The poor, the slaves and the lepers were the outcasts of Ragusan society whether they lived inside or outside the city walls; as such they could and

---

7. TN *51*, 130–131'.

8. TN *51*, 193–195; *52*, 212–214.

9. TN *51*, 85–87; *51*, 177'–178; *52*, 1–3; *52*, 142–143'.

did provoke pity. Better–off commoners who rubbed shoulders with patricians in real life were mentioned in business-like fashion in patrician wills. All these were looked down upon by the patricians, even when the latter expressed feelings of compassion, gratitude or even filial love. The wills, of course, tell us quite a lot too about the relationships within the patriciate as such. They reveal a similar gradation of responses, and a basic inequality at the very core of the patriciate.

What strikes one immediately is the inequality of female versus male members of the patriciate, of single versus married patricians, of those belonging to the Church orders as opposed to those serving the government, of young (under the age of 25 or even 30) versus the old. Ragusan society was quite typical of the European scene as a whole, and there is no need to belabor the point. What one has to stress is the constraining and oppressive atmosphere dominating patrician social life, unbroken even by sincere feelings of love and friendship. As a very tight group within a rather provincial city from a cultural point of view, the Ragusan patriciate exhibited the features so typical of many later colonial societies: distrust of foreigners unless they quickly ceased being so; disdain for everybody outside one's own charmed circle; contempt for lower classes; scorn for the poor and unfortunate; hatred of all deviants; uncritical praise for every native trait, good or bad. Above all, the patricians considered themselves second to none.

Since only the male members of the patriciate could participate in government, and since only they perpetuated the name of the house [*casata*], the patricians preferred having male to female children. Thus in his last will Natalis Christophoris Goze left everything to his daughter Aniza, wife of Paulus Sorgo and their sons with the proviso that his property could not be used to provide dowries for their daughters, but "that it is passed from a male to a male heir in perpetuity." Only in case they did not have any sons were daughters to inherit anything. Sometimes patrician provisions were even more stringent: Bernardus Gabrielis Cerva made his sons, Iunius, Stephanus and Gabriel his heirs with the proviso that they could not sell any of his estates, "but that they pass them on to their male heirs." In case some of them did not have boys their portion was to be passed on to the boys of their brothers. Under no circumstances was any portion of his estates to be left to girls.[10]

Daughters of Ragusan patricians had only two choices in life: they could either marry or enter a nunnery. In fact during the lifetime of our poet (1589–

---

10. TN *51*, 67–67'; *51*, 70–71'.

1638) many were left without a real choice: if they happened to be younger daughters and the family was not wealthy enough to provide suitable dowries for all of them, their oldest sister was usually singled out for marriage (unless for some reason a younger one married earlier, or was passed over), and the rest had to accept a monastic life willy nilly. Frequently the patrician fathers waited until their daughters came of legal age (circa 25) before allowing their marriage which put many eligible girls at risk. Thus Vicentius Junii Pozza specified in his will that "if my daughter Maria gets married before the age of twenty-five, in that case she will get nothing but the said 1,000 ducats for her dowry; for it is my will that a husband be found for her when she has reached the age of 25 and then can have my bequest of 2,600 ducats...and whether my daughter should or should not get married I leave this entirely to the will of my wife, Domina Nica."[11]

Though very many patrician girls were condemned to spend the rest of their lives in nunneries against their will, the patrician wills consistently discriminated against them as though they chose to enter religious life out of preference. The same Vincentius Junii Pozza left his younger daughter Jella 1,000 ducats for her dowry, "according to the provisions of the City," but in case "she wants to become a nun" [si volesse monacare] she was to get only 500 ducats to dispose of as she pleased, and the remainder was to be put into Italian savings associations called Monti and she was only to get the interest, "for I want these 500 ducats to pass on to my heir after her death."[12]

Not only were patrician daughters forced to give up a part or all of their inheritance in favor of their married sisters and brothers if they 'chose' [rather were forced to] to enter religious life, but often they were also obliged to stand aside for male but illegitimate ('natural') sons of their fathers: thus the same Vincentius Junii Pozza made his son Junius his "universal heir" with the proviso that if the latter died before reaching the age of thirty and without any sons, "legitimate or natural," only in that case was his inheritance to go to his sisters, Vincentius' daughters, divided up in equal parts.

The only way Ragusan patrician women could inherit real power was when they became widows: if their husband chose to, Ragusan patrician women [vladike] were given all the rights that their late husbands enjoyed, but only during their lives, for after their deaths, most of the inheritance was passed on to their sons. In certain cases their dead husbands gave them

11. TN 53, 62'–64'.
12. TN 53, 62'–64'.

rights over their minor sons only while the latter were under legal age. Thus the same Vincentius Junii Pozza (who had written one of the longest as well as most revealing testaments mirroring Ragusan social life) enjoined his 'universal heir,' his only son, Junius, to obey his mother, Domina Nicca; "and if it happens, which I do not believe, that my son and heir becomes disobedient to my wife and his mother, it is my will that the said Domina Nicca, without having to justify her action to anyone, can throw my son out of her house; and in that case of [my son's] disobedience can Domina Nicca give or transfer the right of possession of [my estate in] Konavle to whomever she sees fit, but only during her life; so that the right of enjoying my estate will be given only during her life, and not longer."[13] In other words, after his mother's death, her 'disobedient' son would inherit the estate nonetheless.

One of the greatest sixteenth–century Ragusan poets of the late Renaissance, Dominicus Ragnina [Dinko Ragnina], who died in 1607, in his second addition to his last will, designated his nephew, Johannes Blasii Ragnina, with the proviso that the latter "honors, serves and obeys Domina Frana, my dearest daughter and his mother, for if he does otherwise, I leave it up to Domina Frana to reserve judgment on his inheritance during her life; but I hope, since he has a good nature and knows the obligations to one's parents, he will not fail to obey my wishes."[14]

Even when they were designated 'universal heirs' male patricians under age were expected to obey their mothers and, in case they were left without parents, their guardians [epitropi], nominated by the government. Stephanus Christophori Zamagno made his "beloved and only son" Christophorus his "universal heir of all my goods, mobile and real estate, actual and potential, present and future" with the proviso that "he cannot dispose of anything before reaching the age of twenty-four." His relative, Marinus Secundi Zamagno in his will ordered all his goods to be sold and the proceeds to be invested in the savings account in the Italian Monti, so that the invested capital "could not be removed from the Monti until the younger of my sons and heirs reached the age of thirty; ...and I order that until the younger of my sons reaches the aforementioned age, my sons cannot divide up any of my goods..." And in his will Lutianus Francisci Caboga went so far as to place his younger son, Bernardus, not only under the wardship of the four

---

13. TN 53, 64'.

14. TN 53, 122'.

15. TN 51, 19–21; 51, 82'–84'; 52, 5–6.

epitropi [all patricians], but under the authority of his older son, Scipio, "on account of Bernardus being so little and young."[15] There were very good reasons why the elder patricians took such stern precautions to keep their young sons obedient and in check after their death: Ragusan young patricians were notorious for their riotous and often criminal behavior. These instances of their misbehavior cannot naturally be gleaned from the last wills. We have to turn to the criminal records of the Ragusan courts kept in the Chancery papers for such information. Of course, the amount of information found there is immense.[16] I shall therefore restrict myself to a single but well–known case: that of young Stephanus Marini Georgi [Stijepo Đurđević][17] (1579–1632) who was to become related by marriage to our poet, Đivo Gundulić, in his old age. I chose Stephanus Georgi not only because he was a near contemporary of our poet, but because he was a minor poet himself, and was involved in the gravest crisis affecting the Ragusan Republic, namely the so–called Great Conspiracy. I could have chosen, however, dozens of almost similar cases: the pattern is always the same. A young patrician, in his teens or early twenties, invariably before he gets married, commits violent acts, for which he is rather leniently punished by his elders (many of whom are his relatives sitting in judgment on him on the ruling councils), then settles down and presides in judgment over a younger generation of patrician misbehaving young men. In Dubrovnik there is still a saying, harking back to the relative license accorded to patrician youth in olden times: *Starost, skladnost*—which can be freely translated as "Old age makes one behave (properly)." This was certainly true of Stephanus Georgi and the period of our poet's life.

Educated in the same Renaissance high school attended somewhat later by our poet, Stephanus entered the Grand Council at the required age of twenty on November 8, 1598. But even before he was considered legally of age to join the Grand Council, the legislative assembly of all male patricians, Stephanus was already in trouble with the law. As a teenager Stephanus was fined 100 perperi for an unspecified (probably minor) offense which he committed in the company of his friends, a group of similar patrician youth representing some of the best families in Dubrovnik: Paschal Simonis

---

16. HAD, *Lamenta de Criminale* (247 vols.); *Lamenta de Intus et de Foris* (74 vols.).

17. D. Pavlović, "Stijepo Đorđić (Đurđević) —dubrovaćki pesnik XVII veka" in *Glas SKA [Drugi razred]* 84 (Belgrade, 1935), 209–275; *id.*, "Prilozi biografiji Stijepa Đurđevćia" in *Zbornik filozofskog fakulteta* (Belgrade, 1955), 329–338; *id.*, *Iz književne i kulturne istorije Dubrovnika (Studije i članci)* (Sarajevo, 1955), 46–79.

Benessa, Stephanus Marini Gozze, Michael Petri Luccari, Johannes Orsatti Gondola (a relative of our poet), Vito Nicolai Gozze and Hieronymus Vladislavi Menze. It seems that they were 'raging' all over the town, especially at night, frequenting taverns and brothels. This was in 1594.[18]

Two years later, in 1596, during the carnival season, Stephanus in company with six other young patricians and a woman "of a dubious reputation" broke into a dwelling occupied by an artisan, beat him and his wife up, and left after wounding both with swords. Before the court Stephanus and his mates refused to say who stabbed the pair. The court, as in similar instances, was rather lenient considering that all culprits were under age and of patrician background, and made them pay 50 perperi of damages each.[19] In the same year when he was admitted to the Grand Council, in 1598, Stephanus attacked a gardener, Ivo Tarantino, who had not been paid for arranging Stephanus' garden, and when the latter protested, chased him and cut off three of his fingers.[20]

In 1600 Stephanus was again involved in violence when he attacked and wounded a leather maker for a supposed insult; before the court young Stephanus denied everything: "I do not know anything about it, I did not do anything." The whole trial dragged on for a while, until the people who treated the wounded man testified that Stephanus with his brother Jacobus visited a leather maker the day after the incident and tried to persuade him to drop the charges in return for 5 scudi if his wound healed or 100 scudi if he lost his arm. The court found Stephanus guilty, ordered him to pay 50 perperi for damages, and to spend thirty days chained in prison.[21]

While waiting for the verdict Stephanus was involved in another misdemeanor: together with his brother Jacobus and his friend, Jacobus Eliae Bona, Stephanus attacked and seriously wounded another young patrician, Mattheus Simoni Benessa. Again the incident happened at night, in the Ragusan quarter of Prijeko, notorious for its fast life. The three young patricians were accompanied by two 'fast women' and became embroiled in a quarrel with Mattheus Benessa who at first dared them to attack him ("I do not fear you, though there were a hundred of you!"), but was then stabbed by Stephanus. The wounds were serious and life–threatening for a while,

18. HAD, *Consilium Minus 63*, 49.

19. HAD, *Lamenta de intus et de foris 7*, 46.

20. *See* D. Pavlović, "Valo Valović [Valentin Sorkočević], dubrovački pesnik XVI veka" in *Godišnjica Nikole Čupića 46* (1937), 191–192.

21. HAD, *Lamenta de Criminale* (1600), 198.

but Mattheus recovered, and being involved in the quarrel himself, with-drew the charges. The court still imprisoned the attackers for several months while the trial was going on, and fined each 50 perpers in addition to spend-ing a month in prison, in a chained condition.[22]

Barely out of prison Stephanus Georgi became involved in another inci-dent during the Carnival of 1601 when he and his two brothers, Jacobus and Marinus, disguised as Moors [alla morescha] jumped a tailor in his work-shop, beat him with sticks and bats, broke his head and both of his arms.[23] Two years later, in 1603, Stephanus attacked another tailor, wounded his left arm, and beat and abused him for a long time.[24] It is quite clear from the above incidents that Stephanus, like most of his young patrician contempo-raries, had an exaggerated view of his own patrician status, and found satis-faction and pleasure in mistreating the members of the lower orders. But it would be a mistake to assume that he vented his excess energy only on the less privileged Ragusans, as the above attack on young Benessa, a fellow patrician, proves.

In 1604 Stephanus continued his violent life by wounding a cleric, Vincenzo di Marco, who had together with other fellow clerics arrested and imprisoned a woman called Maria and nicknamed "Pede" for living an im-moral life. "Pede" used to receive male visitors, including young Stephanus, at her place. Enraged by the arrest of "Pede" Stephanus broke into Vincenzo's place and wounded him five times.[25]

It should be pointed out that his violent temper was held against him when his candidacy for minor governmental offices came up: regularly he was defeated on votes.[26] While other young patricians calmed down and settled to enjoy the fruits of a respectable career in government before they turned thirty, Stephanus Georgi chose to get involved in a series of intrigues designed to turn the Ragusan Republic into an anti–Turkish state to be used by Western princes as a springboard for the liberation of the Balkan Slavs. These events that make up the so–called Great Conspiracy are presented in. detail in *Our Kingdom Come*. The reason why his brother Jacobus became one of the leaders of this Great Conspiracy had much to do with his and Stephanus' riotous behavior.

22. *Lamenta de Criminale* (1600), 306–309.

23. HAD, *Lamenta de intus et de foris 11* (1601), 81–82.

24. *Lamenta de intus et de foris 13* (1603–1604), 284.

25. *Lamenta de intus et de foris 14* (1604–1605), 306–314.

26. HAD, *Consilium Maius 30* (1599–1604), *31* (1605–1610).

At the beginning of 1609 Stephanus' brother Jacobus, together with Jacobus Resti, Marinus Resti and Sebestanus Menze attacked Domenicus Facenda, one of the richest commoners. The reason was the latter's denuncation of Jacobus Georgi and Jacobus Resti to the Senate. The charge was that the two young patricians were meeting secretly with his beautiful wife, Paula. She was the greatest beauty in early 17th–century Dubrovnik: when after her death Đivo Bunić Vučić [Johannes Seraphini Bona (1591–1658)] wrote four poems dedicated to "The Death of Lady Paula" [*U smrt gospode Paule Dunka Facende*] in the first of them he sang: "The undying beauty was found in thee" ["Neumrla ljepota u tebi bila je"].[27] Domenicus Facenda's denunciation of Jacobus Resti and Jacobus Georgi provoked the attack of the two in company with others. Facenda was seriously wounded and for a while it seemed that he would not survive. The Senate took this latest crime very seriously: the first proposal was for the decapitation of the attackers, but was lost on votes (1 for, 6 against). Instead the majority verdict insisted on their banishment from the city for twenty years.[28] Jacobus Resti and Jacobus Georgi went to the court of the Duke of Savoy where they became involved in the Great Conspiracy.

The violent behavior of brothers Georgi and other young patricians was a typical case of the patriciate's inordinate power—what the Italians call *prepotenza*. It existed both earlier and later than the lifetime of our poet (1589–1638), but it was particularly prevalent and acute during his youth, i.e. circa 1589–1620. Such a sorry state of Ragusan patrician youth was another aspect of the immoral and violent behavior of the Ragusan ruling class that the Counter-Reformation Church in Dubrovnik tried to stem if not wipe out. The Counter-Reformation attempts to impose strict moral behavior on the patriciate in general and the aristocratic youth in particular provoked a split in the patrician ranks. The origins of this split are analyzed in *Our Kingdom Come*. Two factions emerged within the patriciate: one for and another against the imposition of the Counter–Reformation reforms in Church and State. The leader of the pro-reform party was Franciscus Gondola [Gundulić] (1539–1589), a relative of our poet. He was stabbed to death inside a church by a hot–headed young follower of the anti-reform party, Marinus Andreae Bobali. In that same year of 1589 our poet was born.

The violent tenor of life in late 16th- and early 17th-century Dubrovnik

---

27. M. Ratković, ed., *Djela Điva Bunića Vučića*, Vol. 35 of *Stari pisci hrvatski* (Zagreb, 1971), 158.

28. HAD, *Acta Consilii Rogatorum 82* (1601–1611), 41.

was symptomatic of a deeper psychological crisis which the Ragusan Republic in general and its patriciate in particular were experiencing: what I have called a 'crisis of confidence.' A crude Marxist interpretation sees this crisis of the patriciate in strictly and exclusively economic terms, i.e. as the decline of the patrician involvement in Ragusan trade, especially in the Balkans, which led to their impoverishment and challenge by non–patrician, middle classes, i.e. the *antunini* and the *lazarini*.[29] Yet such a monocausal explanation is crude and falsifies a much more complex phenomenon; its economic factors were important, but neither paramount nor unilateral. In my opinion, the roots of this 'crisis of confidence' were neither primarily economic nor social, but religious and cultural.[30]

What I am suggesting is that Dubrovnik went through that transitional period between the Renaissance and the Counter–Reformation which everywhere, according to Febvre, was characterized by painful religious doubts. By religious I mean the pangs of guilty conscience (and, as we saw, the patriciate had plenty of reason to feel guilty) which resulted in a morbid sensitivity that was often tinged with sublimated eroticism, all characteristic hallmarks of Counter–Reformation *mentalité*.[31] Febvre suggested the use of personal papers, such as inventories, and I shall resort again to the last wills to ascertain this shift in feeling.

Testaments written during the first three quarters of the sixteenth century, while outwardly pious, do not contain any exaggerated expressions of religious feelings, any hyperbolic descriptions of a person's inescapable fate of death and judgment, or any lachrymose protestations of one's unworthiness in order to be saved. They are noted for their quiet decorum, business–like tone full of important, often trivial details, and stern admonitions and commands to one's heirs. They are, in short, typical of the Renaissance view of humans who, even as sinful beings, were a measure of all things, capable of rationally facing the inevitable with dignity and calm. Expressions of "not knowing either the day nor the hour of one's death" are

29. D. Pavlović, "O krizi vlasteoskog staleža u Dubrovniku XVII veka" in *Zbornik radova Instituta za proučavanje književnosti* II (Belgrade, 1952), 27–38, with a brief summary in French.

30. Z. Zlatar, "The Crisis...;" also *see* chs. 1 & 3 of my *Our Kingdom Come*. The book is dedicated to Professor Edward C. Thaden.

31. L. Febvre, *op. cit.*, 245–246: "But after 1560 everything evidences...a clear invitation to sensibility—a sensibility which was not without a certain eloquence."

32. Ibid.,: "Among the effects inventoried before 1560 there can be found things which aided people to pray to God in spirit...directly and silently, without any ostentation."

simple acknowledgment of the ultimate human destiny. They exude calm resignation to one's death.[32]

The period between roughly 1590 and 1620 is a transitional one, and there are still sentiments expressed in this vein: one can still hear humanist voices valuing stoical virtues, as in Savinus Petri Sorgo's will where he leaves all his books to his "real friend, Nicolaus Natalis Tudisi," to be read "in memory and love of me."[33] Or the traditional statement that the "human condition that cannot be assured of a single hour of [one's] life, in conformity with the Evangelic admonition to stay vigilant" in the last will of Stephanus Christophori Zamagno. But the latter is already unsure of his eternal fate and cannot face the prospect peacefully without appealing "to my merciful Creator and Savior to deign to receive my soul by His Grace among the Saints in Heaven, through the intercession of the Holy Virgin Mary, my benevolent protectress."[34]

One would expect women to switch to the new sentimentality earlier than men, but no such clear-cut case emerges in late 16th-century Dubrovnik. In the testament of Maria, widow of Laurentius Michaelis Bobali, there is a calm and restrained repetition of the traditional formula: "considering the fragility of human life and subject to innumerable perils, and nothing being more certain for man than his death, and nothing less certain than the hour of his death, and wishing to conform to that [admonition of the] Gospel which says: 'Be prepared, for you know not either the day or the hour'...;" whereas somebody like Jacobus Francisci Sorgo already evinces that infatuation with masses at several altars simultaneously for the duration of the whole year, which is a sure sign of excessive religiosity and morbid uncertainty of the Counter–Reformation sensibility.[35]

In the same year of 1600, however, some patricians still stick to simple, heart-felt but restrained formulas, such as that in the will of Natalis Christophoris Gozze: "and thus I render my first account to God of my sins by confessing...;" while others are slowly and partially adopting the elements of the new florid style, as did Savinus Aloysii Gozze when he wrote three years later his own will: "Finding myself in the decrepit state of my life, accompanied with many infirmities and fearing a sudden coming of

---

33. HAD, TN 51, 2'–5 [what a pity he did not list the books!].

34. TN 51, 19–21.

35. TN 51, 40–42; 51, 63'–65.

36. TN 51, 67–67'; 52, 43–44'.

death...I pray to the Divine Majesty for a favor to *find conceits, shape my words and move my pen...*"[36] After 1600 such 'conceits' are to be found in more wills, though they are by no means universal: thus Petrus Simonis Menze waxes and wanes in the opening of his will dated in 1603[37]: "Considering the infinite conditions to which every mortal is subject, and also the means of repentance...as well as conforming to the admonition of my Creator..." Even so such expressions appear timid when compared to the beginning of the will of Nicolaus Lutiani Bona, dated 1606: "Having invoked the name and help first of the omnipotent and ever merciful God, Father, Son and the Holy Ghost, and of the Glorious Virgin Mary, his mother, and of all the triumphant celestial Host to whom I recommend most devoutly my soul in the hour of my death and for ever, and to the Mother Earth my fallen body." And when he adds some rather convoluted expressions about the gradual failing of the body while the mind is forced to go beyond physical pain to his duties toward his posterity, we can suspect that he is posturing somewhat.[38]

We should have no suspicion of one thing: a greater attention to the outward observances, especially to funeral masses, bequests to religious bodies, alms to the poor etc. Thus Maria, widow of Laurentius Michaelis Bobali left the huge amount of 240 ducats for alms to the eight monasteries of Dubrovnik so that they can pray continually "for the soul of mine and my departed ones." And in 1600 Marinus Secundi Zamagno had a small chapel built on his estate so that every year funeral masses could be offered for the salvation of his soul. Domina Aniza, the widow of Jupanus Zamagno, left 200 ducats to be invested in the Monti, and whose interest was to provide for annual masses "for ever" on the altar of the Ragusan Cathedral for the benefit of her soul. And Domina Nicha, the wife of Aloisius Pozza, left the interest of 100 scudi to be used "for ever" for clothing the poor and "celebrating the masses".[39]

This obsessive and almost selfish preoccupation with one's salvation is in marked contrast to the practical emphasis found in earlier wills, like the one of Stephanus Joannis Gondola, an uncle of our poet, who died in Venice in 1602, but whose testament was registered in 1585. In it this successful merchant and respected patrician left 200 ducats for the erection of a Jesuit [*Giesuini*] college in Dubrovnik, or, that of the Capuchins if the former

---

37. TN *52*, 58'–60.

38. TN *52*, 212–214.

39. TN *51*, 40–42; *51*, 82'–84; *51*, 170–171; *51*, 183'–184.

were not admitted. It is curious that he called the orders "religions" [*Religione*], thus indicating that they stood for a tighter religious discipline of post-Tridentine Catholicism.[40] How different such a bequest is from Domina Nicha's, widow of Bernardus Pozza, who left 200 scudi to the Dominicans so that they could "celebrate every week three masses ... one for my soul, the second for my departed husband, and the third for my [departed] parents. Moreover, they are to offer two chanted, funeral masses each one for ten years, one on the anniversary of my death and the other on the All Saints Day."[41]

More and more outward observances figure in the wills after 1600: thus Johannes Mariae Nicolai Gozze ordained that on the altar in the Franciscan Church a mass be held every day and "a candle be burning on the altar for ever." He ordered the same be done "eternally" [*in perpetuo*] in a village church where he had an estate. For this he left the sum of 500 ducats. A similar bequest was left by Aniza, the widow of Johannes Dominici Ragnina, in 1606 to the Dominicans to celebrate 80 "low masses" (i.e. not chanted) "every year in perpetuity for my soul and those of my consort, mother and father, and my two late sons, Domenicus and Michael." And Vincentius Junii Pozza requested that a chanted mass be officiated on the "privileged altar of the Crucifixion" in the Cathedral every year "for ever" [*perpetuis temporibus*], another at the altar of Crucifixion in the Church of St. Blasius, Dubrovnik's patron saint, and a third on the altar of Crucifixion in the Dominican Church.[42]

As the seventeenth century wore on, and especially after 1620, one's preoccupation with salvation assumed such sensitivity tinged with elements of morbidity, that one can unmistakably sense being in another age. It is sufficient to offer two telling examples: the last will of our poet's mother, Giva, the widow of Franciscus Ioannis Gondola, written in 1627; and that of the most famous Ragusan poet of the 17th century after Gundulić, Joannes Seraphini Bona [Đivo Bunić Vucić] (1591/2–1658). The testament of Gundulić's mother is especially interesting because it is written in Croatian, not in Italian or Latin, and is a particularly fine example of the common speech of 17th-century Ragusans.[43]

40. TN *51*, 193–195.

41. TN *52*, 1–3.

42. TN *52*, 120–120'; *52*, 228'–229'; *53*, 62'–64'.

43. It was published by Alfred Jensen in his *Gundulić und sein Osman: Eine südslavische Literaturstudie* (Göteborg, 1900), 87–89.

The entire first half of Giva's will is taken up with the bequests to churches, monasteries and nunneries so that they would say innumerable masses for the salvation of her soul: thus she left money to three main churches in Dubrovnik in order to enable them to say masses every day for her for a full year, and if possible to be said by her own confessor. Then she provided for chanted masses on the anniversaries of her death, her late husband's death (our poet's father), and of her and her husband parents' deaths. Giva specified at which altar these masses were to be said, and who was to say them.

A quarter of a century later, in 1651, Đivo Bunić Vučić wrote his elegant testament in Italian; in it his preoccupation with death and his own salvation were suitably expressed in fine, ornate sentences. Thus he starts out by saying that he knows that he is mortal, and born to die, and only then does he quote the standard admonition about not knowing the moment of one's death. This is followed by his supplication to God, the Virgin Mary, and the saints to allow his soul to enter paradise among the elect, and to forgive his sins.[44]

It is when we turn to his bequests that the staggering amount (relatively speaking) left to various churches and monasteries hits us: after his death in 1658 in a separate addition these various religious bodies acknowledged receipt of these sums in grateful terms. Bunić Vučić justified leaving such sums on the grounds that they will help to "take [his] soul out of the Purgatory." The crowning detail on this obsession was his order for 600 (!) masses to be given straight after his death "at the privileged altars, where the soul is being taken out of the Purgatory."[45] Judging by his early poetry dominated by what we would call nowadays youthful 'rages' Bunić Vučić might have felt a particular need for forgiveness: this would also explain his switch later in life to suitably Counter-Reformation kind of poetry, of which his fine long poem entitled *Mary Magdalen, the Penitent*, in three cantoes, is the best example. There is no question, however, that his style both in this poem and in his last will is very typical of an age excessively concerned with the uncertainties of life and obsessed with one's own salvation in quite sensitive (not to say sensual) terms. Perhaps Bunić Vučić felt that he and his beloved city were somehow living on borrowed time. The sense of impending doom was certainly prophetic: for in 1667 a big earthquake destroyed most of Dubrovnik from which it has never fully recovered. Instead of an almost arrogant note of confidence pervading in 16th–century Dubrovnik, there is a tone of sensitive vulnerability permeating the 17th century.

Into this volatile, violent and vulnerable city our poet was born.

---

44. M. Ratković, ed., *Djela Dživa Bunića Vučića*, 69–72.

45. *Ibid.*, 70.

Chapter 7

POLISH PARLIAMENTARISM DURING THE PERIOD OF THE PARTITIONS

Lech Trzeciakowski

Poland's loss of independence at the end of the 18th century interrupted for a certain period of time the history of the Polish parliament—an institution able to boast of a tradition extending back several hundred years. The Polish lands themselves had come under the rule of three absolutist states in which the binding principles of government ran contrary to the existence of a national representation responsible for jointly ruling the country. However, the stormy events witnessed by Europe during the course of the 19th century brought about the partial rebirth of Polish parliamentarianism. The institution's history during the years 1795–1918 can be clearly divided into two periods. Two factors—the forms adopted by parliament and the functions it performed—lie at the basis of this periodization.

At the onset of the first period, which began in 1807 and lasted until 1846, Napoleon's victorious wars shook the existing European order and led to the creation of a small Polish state known as the Duchy of Warsaw. Despite the defeat of the French emperor, the short-lived existence of this Polish state made it impossible for the great powers to ignore the Polish question. At the Congress of Vienna they were forced to create two autonomous entities: The Kingdom of Poland, which was a part of the Russian partition, and the Free City of Cracow. As had been the case with the Duchy of Warsaw, both the Kingdom of Poland and the Free City of Cracow possessed their own representative organs. Napoleon's fall, followed by the Polish defeats in the November uprising of 1830/31 and the Cracow uprising of 1846, led to the liquidation of these two political entities as well as their representative bodies.

The second stage in the development of Polish parliamentarianism during the partitions extended from 1848 to 1918. The characteristic trait of these years was the lack of independent Polish legislative bodies and the activity of Polish representatives in the parliaments of the partitioning powers that evolved in the wake of the revolutionary events of 1848 in Prussia and Austria, and of 1905 in Russia.

The fall of the Polish state as a result of the partitions was a tragedy for the politically conscious part of the Polish nation, a tragedy made all the more painful by the fact that independent Poland's parliamentary monarchy had ensured precisely this segment of the nation a fundamental influence in political decision–making. Shortly after the last partition in 1795, however, a new Polish state, the Duchy of Warsaw, arose thanks to Napoleon's victories over Prussia and Russia in 1806 and 1807 as well as the Poles' constant drive to regain their freedom. This state consisted of only a part of the lands belonging to the former Prussian partition, to which in 1809 after Napoleon's victory over Austria a portion of the lands previously seized by the Habsburg monarchy were added. On 22 July 1807 Napoleon turned the Duchy of Warsaw into a French satellite state with a constitution based on the French model. The legislative body, referred to in the constitution as the sejm główny, the main diet, did not possess legislative initiative which rested in the hands of the ruler. The role of the sejm which consisted of two chambers, the senate and the house of representatives, was limited to decisions concerning taxation, changes in civil and criminal law, and the monetary system. The extent of discussion in the sejm's forum was seriously limited. Members of the state council, the body responsible for preparing legislative projects, as well as members of the individual sejm commissions responsible for considering the proposals presented to them, had the right to participate in parliamentary discussion. Thus, in comparison to the pre-partition sejm's role in state affairs the influence of the Duchy of Warsaw's legislative body on the state's fate was very limited.[1]

This, however, was merely one side of the coin. On the other was society's new role in electing the parliamentary body. Article 4 of the constitution stated: slavery is repealed; all citizens are equal in the eyes of the law; personal rights are under the protection of the courts.[2]

1. Andrzej Ajnenkiel "Polskie konstytucje," Wiedza Powszechna, Warszawa 1982, pp. 101–108.

2. Ustawa konstytucyjna Księstwa Warszawskiego z 22 VII 1807, in: Wybór tekstów źródłowych z historii Polski w latach 1795–1864," opracowali Stefan Kieniewicz, Tadeusz Mencel, Władysław Rostocki, Państwowe Wydawnictwo Naukowe, Warszawa 1956, p. 127.

Yet this did not mean that all of the citizens of the Duchy received the right to vote. In the case of the szlachta, the Polish gentry, this right was based on an estate-property census, and in the case of the townspeople and peasantry on a property census. The enfranchisement of peasants was an event without precedent in Poland. This privilege applied exclusively to rent-paying peasants; it did not affect peasants who, though now personally free, were still forced to perform labor services. All in all, approximately 110,000 citizens, i.e., 2.7 % of the Duchy's population—36,000 members of the szlachta, 40,000 townspeople and about 35,000 peasants—possessed the franchise in 1811. The representation of the specific estates in the parliament was not proportional to the number of voters. The szlachta was guaranteed 2/3 of the seats in the representative chamber. The passive voting right, awarded to citizens who were above the age of 24, was reserved for those who were able to read and write Polish and who resided in the electoral district. The low level of political consciousness of the majority of voters as well as the lack of allowances for representatives seriously limited the deputies' social base. As a result, there were few members of the middle class and intelligentsia in the chamber of representatives; they represented merely 19–25% of the deputies. Despite the fact that the number of deputies from non-aristocratic spheres was very small, the enfranchisement of almost 80,000 townspeople and peasants was an event which had enormous influence on the development of political consciousness among these two social groups. In this respect, the Duchy of Warsaw compared favorably with the neighboring states.[3]

According to the constitution, the sejm's rights were limited, yet its members were not all that willing to accept this situation. The tradition of the sejms of old Poland remained alive. Despite the procedural limitations, the representatives manifested significant activity. Deprived of the right to participate in parliamentary discussions, they stated their views during informal meetings, after which open letters were published in order to inform public opinion of the deputies' positions. Occasionally, laws were rejected. Internally, the sejm was not homogeneous. Some of the representatives supported progressive changes such as those introduced by the new legislation, particularly the Code Napoleon. The conservative groups strongly opposed

3. Tadeusz Mencel "Prawa wyborcze w Księstwie Warszawskim i Królestwie Polskim / 1807–1830/ na tle porównawczym, in: Pamiętnik X Powszechnego Zjazdu Historyków Polskich w Lublinie 9–13 września 1969 r. Referaty i dyskusja IV Sekcje X–X, Polskie Towarzystwo Historyczne, Warszawa 1971, pp. 35–42.

84 ESSAYS IN RUSSIAN AND EAST EUROPEAN HISTORY

these changes. Conflicts also arose between representatives of the szlachta and the townspeople over proposed taxes. The activity of parliament's members allowed it to play a significantly more important role in the Duchy of Warsaw's political life than the Napoleonic system had foreseen.[4] The constitution of the autonomous Kingdom of Poland, bestowed by Tsar Alexander I on 23 November 1815, was the most liberal basic law in contemporary Europe. It instituted a legislative body consisting of a senate whose members were named by the ruler and a representative chamber numbering 128 elected members. Electoral participation was determined on the basis of property and education. About 100,000 citizens, i.e., 2.8% of the population, had the franchise. In relative terms, this was a very high percentage, particularly if we remember that in France at the same time about 80,000 individuals, i.e., 0.3% of the population, possessed the right to vote. In comparison to the Duchy of Warsaw's constitution, the powers of the legislature itself were broader. The sejm, though deprived of parliamentary initiative, possessed broad rights concerning discussion of and voting on de facto almost all issues related to the state's functioning. A characteristic phenomenon was the even clearer domination of the sejm by the szlachta than during the period of the Duchy of Warsaw. Its representatives comprised 82.3% of the sejm's membership in 1818, 88.3% in 1825 and 84.4% in 1830. This strong position of the gentry in the legislature was a general European phenomenon. In France, for example, landowners occupied 58% of the seats in the house of deputies in 1820.[5]

A few years after the establishment of the Polish kingdom the Poles' dreams of a benevolent Alexander I began to dissipate. Gradually a reactionary course gained in strength. Limitations imposed on civil rights, followed by measures which undermined the very concept of autonomy for the Polish Kingdom, exemplified this drift towards reaction. Censorship was introduced. Efforts were undertaken to liquidate public court hearings. The powers of the public prosecutor were increased. These steps led to sharp protests of the liberal deputies.

Legislative projects presented by the government to the parliament were rejected. The tsar's reaction to this opposition was decisive. Leaders of the opposition were persecuted. Two leaders of the opposition party, the broth-

4. Andrzej Ajnenkiel "Historia sejmu polskiego." Vol. II, Part I, W dobie rozbiorów. Państwowe Wydawnictwo Naukowe, Warszawa 1989, pp. 23–28; Barbara Grochulska "Księstwo Warszawskie," Wiedza Powszechna, Warszawa 1966, pp. 110–120; 133–136.

5. Andrzej Ajnenkiel "Historia sejmu...," pp. 30–39; Tadeusz Mencel, op. cit., pp. 46–49.

ers Bonewentura and Wincenty Niemojowski, had their elections annulled. Later, Wincenty Niemojowski and Teodor Morawski were arrested. For five years Alexander I did not call the sejm into session and in 1825 forced a series of reactionary laws through the legislature.[6]

Alexander I's successor, the gendarme of Europe Nicholas I, despite the fact that he also refused to convene the sejm for several years, faced the stiff opposition of its members. In 1828 a specially established parliamentary court under the chairmanship of Piotr Bielinski investigated a plot by members of the Patriotic Society who had come to the attention of the tsarist officials after the suppression of the Decembrist revolt in Russia. The Polish conspirators had maintained contact with the Decembrists; hence it is not difficult to imagine how much Nicholas I counted on an exemplary punishment of the Polish patriots. The parliamentary court, however, did not bend to pressure and refused to recognize the accused as being guilty of high treason. As a result relatively mild sentences were meted out, while three of the accused were even acquitted.[7]

Faced with a war with Turkey, Nicholas I agreed to certain concessions. He confirmed the parliamentary court's verdict, though not without great resistance, and decided to convene the sejm in 1830. Once again the legislature became a scene of conflict between the liberal camp and the conservative party allied with the Kingdom's government. It proved possible to defend the provisions of the Code Napoleon in matters relating to divorce, but the criticism of the extremely reactionary ministers of education and internal affairs, both of whom stood in the service of the partitioning power, passed without echo.[8]

The outbreak of the November uprising in 1830 transformed the sejm into the main governing body of the Polish kingdom. Within the sphere of its powers fell the authority to appoint the government, to ratify international treaties, and to nominate as well as dismiss the supreme commander. Thus the sejm took over the constitutional powers of the king. The position achieved by the parliamentary body was supported by a decisive majority of public opinion which was enchanted by the sejm's leading role. Undoubtedly, this would have been very advantageous under conditions of peace; however, such a fusion of legislative and executive authority could not prove

6. Andrzej Ajnenkiel "Historia sejmu...," pp. 39–43.
7. Hanna Dyląagowa "Towarzystwo Patriotyczne i sąd sejmowy," Państwowa Wydawnictwo Naukowe, Warszawa 1970, pp. 276–324.
8. Andrzej Ajnenkiel, "Historia sejmu...," pp. 49–50.

successful in the face of a war conducted by the independent Polish state against Russia. The sejm's omnipotence often went to absurd lengths as, for example, when war plans and even the tactics of the general staff became objects of debate. Such an important issue as the solution of the peasant problem—in the form of a general conversion of servitude into rent or an act granting the peasants land—drowned in a sea of chatter among the deputies, amidst whom there was no shortage of strong opponents of social reform. However, the sejm proved itself capable of undertaking measures which were judged by contemporaries and continue to be judged by historians today as being worthy of the highest recognition. These measures served to elevate the authority of the legislative body. Among them were such grave resolutions as the official declaration of the uprising as a national uprising on 18 December 1830, and Nicholas' I dethronement as Polish king on 25 January 1831. The latter was an act of enormous consequences. From this moment on there existed an independent Polish state which found itself in a state of war with tsarist Russia. The dethronement of Nicholas I was a challenge thrown in the face of the gendarme of Europe, the mainstay of the Holy Alliance. These significant events in the history of Polish parliamentarianism, all of which entered forever its great tradition, cannot however alter the fact that during the time of active struggle for Poland's independence the Poles did not need even the best representative body, but rather an outstanding individual capable of accepting the burden of decision-making.[9] Yet there was no such person of great talent available who was prepared to guide the nation, and this is not the place to consider the possibility of ultimate success had power been in the hands of a genius.

The existence of a parliamentary body was so deeply embedded in the Poles' consciousness that even after the November uprising's defeat, attempts were made in Paris to renew the activity of the legislature of which the majority of members were in exile. But basic political differences made the renewal of the sejm's sessions impossible.

The Free City of Cracow, which came into existence as the result of a compromise between Russia and Austria during the Congress of Vienna, was a republic that did not possess full political sovereignty. The three partitioning powers exercised supervision over the city through their residents.

9.   Władysław Zajewski "Rola sejmu w Powstaniu Listopadowym," in: Powstanie Listopadowe 1830–1831. Dzieje wewnętrzne. Militaria. Europa wobec powstania. Władysław Zajewski /Ed./. Państwowe Wydawnictwo Naukowe, Warszawa 1980, pp. 98–114.

Executive power rested in the hands of a thirteen–member senate. The assembly of representatives appointed nine members of the senate together with the body's president. The university and the cathedral chapter nominated the remaining senators. The assembly of representatives numbered 41 members, the majority of whom were elected, the rest appointed by the university and the cathedral chapter. The right to vote was based on a property tax and education. It was important that not only did peasant landowners receive the franchise, but also that nonlandowning peasants could choose one delegate for every 10 households. This represented an improvement in comparison to the conditions existing previously in the Duchy of Warsaw as well to those in the Kingdom of Poland. But also in the Free City of Cracow sharp conflicts between the conservative and liberal camps arose. The mainstay of the former was the senate, whereas the latter had its center in the assembly of representatives which was dominated by the middle class. The conservatives strove to limit society's influence on the exercise of power and acted in close understanding with the guardian powers. The main promoter of unfavorable changes was Count Stanisław Wodzicki who came from an aristocratic background. Sharp confrontations erupted over several issues: the question of autonomous powers for the university, the principle of judicial independence, and the departure from the custom of periodically convening the assembly of representatives. In this fight the middle–class/ liberal camp experienced a short–lived victory. The majority of the assembly of representatives rejected Wodzicki's candidacy for the presidency of the senate in 1827 and elected Józef Nikorowicz,the president of the court of appeals, instead. This success did not last long. The partitioning powers did not confirm the election and named the compliant Count Wodzicki president. Now the reaction was triumphant. The next years witnessed the slow demise of the superficially independent Free City of Cracow until its liquidation and annexation by Austria in 1846.[10]

This period in the history of Polish parliamentarianism ended with dramatic events; the defeat of the November uprising in 1831 was followed by the defeat of the Cracow revolution in 1846. At the source of Polish parliamentarianism's fate were events that remained outside the sphere of influence of a nation deprived of its freedom. These were the partitioning powers' efforts to restore at least a portion of the conditions which had existed under the ancient regime. Within this context there was absolutely no room for liberal political principles and the legislative bodies connected

10. Andrzej Ajnenkiel "Historia sejmu...," pp. 67–74.

with them. The Polish conservative groups hostile to liberalism did not by themselves bring about the institution's demise, but facilitated and accelerated the final decisions made in Petersburg, Vienna, and Berlin. The Poles' inability to influence their fate already at this point in time became their curse. The defeat of a legal parliamentary opposition strengthened the conviction in Polish political thought of the need to search for solutions in armed struggle; this belief led to a series of unsuccessful conspiracies and uprisings that resulted in a sea of blood and tears.

Yet the years during which a relatively free parliamentary life had existed remained significant; they promoted the existence of a modern political culture that strove to solve growing problems by way of discussion between the authorities and the society's representatives; a more general suffrage, furthermore, encouraged a growth in political consciousness among ever broader groups of society.

The revolutions of 1848 and 1905, which shook the foundations of partitioning states, brought about the creation of legislative bodies in Prussia, Austria and Russia. All three of these parliaments were deprived of law–making initiative. In 1848, as the Landtag in Berlin, the German National Assembly in Frankfurt on the Rhine, and the Constituent Assembly in Vienna convened for the first time, Polish politicians faced serious dilemmas:

1. Should the Poles participate in the elections and send representatives to the partitioning powers' legislatures? Would this not signify an acceptance of the status quo in the Polish lands? 2. Should the Poles, in the event of their participation in the elections and acquisition of seats, join existing political factions in accordance with their political views, or should they create national political groups without regard to political differences?

On a certain scale Poles already had some experience operating in a situation in which the representative body was divided on the basis of nationality. In the second decade of the nineteenth century in Prussia, provincial parliaments (Provinzial–Landtage) with only advisory power had been created. The right to vote was based on the class structure of the provinces which had mixed national populations. In provinces inhabited by Poles the opportunity thus arose to send Polish representatives to the local parliaments. The Poles were strongest in the provincial parliament of the Great Duchy of Poznań, where they even possessed a slight majority. This political entity had been created at the Congress of Vienna as a part of Prussia, with the difference that the Polish population was granted the right to use its mother tongue in the schools, the governmental administration, and the courts. Contrary to original intentions, the Polish delegates used the parliamentary forum to defend their national rights which were progressively violated by the Prussian administration, e.g., through the germanization of the school system. It was characteristic that during a session of the Poznanian parliament the deputy Konstanty Kossecki appealed to the Poles to use consistently legal opposition, presenting the Irish leader Daniel O'Connel as a model worthy of imitation.[11]

Despite the resistance of the advocates of armed struggle for independence, ultimately the opinion won that favored participation in elections as a legal form of struggle for separate national identity. The Poles decided to participate in elections to the Prussian Landtag and the constituent assembly in Vienna which were based on universal, but two–stage elections. However they also opted to boycott the elections to the German national assembly in the recognition that this would be an indirect form of support for the incorporation of the Prussian partition into a unified German state, an act contrary to the provisions of the Congress of Vienna. It is important to note that reference to the 1815 commitments made by the great powers in the Polish question for many years represented the foundation upon which the Poles based their defense against the partitioning powers' policies of denationalization.

After the victory of the counterrevolution in Austria the legislative body was not convened for a number of years, while in Prussia the year 1849 witnessed the introduction of a new, antidemocratic electoral law. The elections remained and retained their two stages with, however, one fundamental modification. All citizens in possession of the franchise were divided into three classes. Each class then chose the same number of electors who in turn voted for candidates to the parliament. As a result, a few of the wealthiest taxpayers often chose the same number of electors as several hundred of the less well-to-do.

Within the Prussian partition elections took place under specific conditions. Due to migration encouraged by the authorities, the German population attained a slight preponderance, not only numerically but also in terms

---

11. Witold Jakóbczyk "Studia nad dziejami Wielkopolski w XIX w. /Dzieje pracy organicznej/ Vol. I 1815–1850," Poznańskie Towarzystwo Przyjaciół Nauk, Poznań 1951, pp. 21–22; Herbert Obenaus "Polen und Deutsche auf dem Posener Provinziallandtag von 1827 bis 1847. Politische Restauration und nationale Bewegung im Grossherzogtum Posen," in: Ideologie, poglądy, mity w dziejach Polski i Europy XIX i XX wieku. Studia Historyczne. Księga Pamiatkowa ofiarowana prof. drowi Lechowi Trzeciakowskiemu w 60 rocznicę urodzin. Jerzy Topolski, Witold Molik, Krzysztof Makowski/Ed./ Uniwersytet im. Adama Mickiewicza, Poznań 1991, pp. 77–89.

of wealth. This situation was of fundamental significance in the context of the electoral law of 1849. The leading segments of Polish society—the gentry, the secular intelligentsia, and the clergy—conducted electoral campaigns under the slogan of "national solidarity" while treating social status and political orientation as secondary issues in the face of the German threat.[12]

The Poles began to create electoral organizations which initially remained loosely structured. In the Austrian partition this function was performed by the national committee convened by the Poles beginning in 1843. The Poles in the Prussian partition had at their disposal a system of well-functioning committees for elections to the Landtag as well as to the North-German Confederation of 1867, and from 1871 onwards to the Reichstag. The elections to the general German representative body were based on a democratic electoral law. The franchise was universal, direct, secret, and equal .

In 1860, following a 12-year pause, the Austrian emperor transformed the state council, which had previously been limited to an advisory function, into a two-chamber parliament. At the beginning, the representative chamber consisted of members of the provincial parliaments. Beginning in 1873 the representatives were chosen in direct elections based on a complicated estate-property census, from 1907 onwards on a universal franchise. In Galicia, where the political situation was different and regional autonomy was introduced in 1867, Polish political life developed freely. Here rivalries existed among various political groups and electoral propaganda was organized not by a separate committee, but by individual parties seeking votes. In the eastern portion of Galicia political rivalry arose based on national divisions between Poles and Ukrainians.

In Russia a parliamentary body came later into existence than in the other two partitioning states. During the years 1905–1907 the tsarist authorities had altered the electoral law three times; it remained based on class differences, two stages, and the absence of universality. At one point workers employed in small factories were discriminated against, then the unemployed, poor peasants, and national minorities faced discrimination. Due to the sharp political conflict between the conservative groups and the workers' parties in the Russian partition, political parties conducted electoral campaigns on their own.

---

12. Lech Trzeciakowski "Die Herausbildung der Wahlklientele im preussischen Teilungsgebiet 1848–1914," in: Patronage und Klientele. Ergebnisse einer polnisch–deutschen Konferenz. Hens–Henrich Nolte /Ed./, Bohlau Verlag Köln Wien 1989, p. 114.

The creation of legislative bodies had an enormous influence on the awakening of interest in political affairs among broad groups of society. At the onset of the 20th century the rate of participation hovered around 80 percent and in certain districts even reached 95 percent. There were, of course, periods when this trend slowed down and even suffered setbacks. Especially the drop in significance of the parliamentary body caused fluctuation in electoral participation. Such a regression occurred for example in Prussia during the period of the counterrevolution, the so-called Manteuffel era (1850–1858), when the Landtag was reduced to the role of a submissive executor of the executive power's orders. Hence, in the elections of 1855 merely 16.1 percent of those entitled to vote actually made use of their right, but this was a merely temporary phenomenon.

Not only the increasing percentage of people participating in elections, but also the growing number of individuals involved in electoral campaigns provide evidence of the rise in political consciousness. In 1848 the gentry, members of the clergy, intellectuals, and occasionally peasants were involved in preparations for elections in the Prussian and Austrian partitions. By the beginning of the twentieth century, however, not only the traditional leaders of society conducted electoral propaganda, but also masses of peasants and workers as well as members of the lower middle-class and bourgeoisie. It is significant that organizers of electoral campaigns counted a great deal on the participation of women, even though they were deprived of the right to vote. Thus electoral proclamations from the Poznanian province stated in 1914:

> Above all, let mothers and wives participate in these meetings. Those mothers and wives who will provide good cheer during the difficult electoral struggle awaiting you.
> Let your wives, daughters and mothers come, because they are raising the future generation.[13]

The number of Polish parliamentarians ranged from thirteen to twenty, that is from 3.3 to 5.1 percent of the delegates in the Prussian Landtag. In the Viennese state council they made up 15.7 percent (81) of the membership in 1907 after the reform of the electoral law, and in the Petersburg Duma they comprised from 3.3 to 9.5 percent (14–46) of the deputies.[14] Did the Poles join groups according to their political views or did they

---

13. Biblioteka Raczyńskich w Poznaniu. Akta Centralnego Komitetu Wyborczego na Wielkie Księstwo Poznańskie. Odezwy i Komunikaty., Rkp. 919, fol. 171.

14. Andrzej Ajnenkiel "Historia sejmu...," pp. 290–292, 294–296, 300–301.

form Polish factions? In 1848, amidst the lofty slogans of brotherhood among nations, Polish delegates to the Landtag and the constituent assembly in Vienna voluntarily joined German political groups. Shortly thereafter any desire to cooperate within German political parties vanished. It became evident that the majority of the German democratic and liberal representatives in the Prussian Landtag and the Frankfurt parliament was unwilling to support the Polish cause in the parliamentary forum; the Polish delegates to the Landtag, therefore, formed their own parliamentary faction in 1849. The Polish representatives in the Viennese state council and the Petersburg Duma followed the example of the Poles in the Prussian partition. The majority of Polish deputies belonged to Polish factions. In exceptional instances, social–democratic and peasant politicians remained for short periods of time outside of these Polish groups.

The numerical participation of Polish representatives in the legislative bodies of the partitioning powers never exceeded 16 percent, and generally remained at the level of a few percent, and thus provided only slight chances of influencing the state's policies. But what motivated the Poles to march to the ballot boxes in such numbers and vote for their candidates? The motives differed from partition to partition. The most rational motive existed in the Austrian partition. In 1860 a process began which brought the Poles increasingly wider rights and ended with the bestowal of autonomy seven years later. Furthermore, given the monarchy's complicated nationality situation, the emperor sought support from Polish conservatives who in turn responded with complete loyalty. Poles occupied many of the highest posts in Vienna. They reached the rank of premier, minister, and even foreign minister of Austria-Hungary. The Polish faction held almost 16 percent of the seats in parliament which made it the third largest group. Often the Poles were able to cast the deciding vote concerning parliamentary projects. Under these circumstances mass participation in elections had practical significance; the more Polish delegates were in Vienna, the greater was the Polish influence in the state.

During the Duma's first period, it also appeared as if the acquisition of the largest possible number of seats in the tsarist legislature would have practical significance. Initially, the Polish deputies, who in political and social terms represented conservative landed as well as nationalist middle–class elements, believed that the tsar would look favorably upon their efforts to obtain national autonomy. These hopes quickly dissipated. There remained the defense of national rights through parliamentary means, a policy which proved equally unsuccessful in the face of the russification policies reactivated after the revolution's defeat.

In the case of the Prussian partition, the hopes of attaining anything disintegrated already in 1848. In the Prussian Landtag, which greatly influenced the government's anti–Polish policies, parties hostile towards the Poles dominated throughout. In the Reichstag the situation developed somewhat more favorably, however, yet the authorities were able to gain a majority for their anti–Polish policies. Thus the struggle for seats seemed to have minimal significance. The small number of Polish delegates could not effectively resist the growing insistence on germanization. Yet the number of people voting for Polish candidates did not decrease, but grew even in areas such as Upper Silesia which were considered germanized. Within the collective consciousness of Polish society the conviction was firmly rooted that electoral participation was a patriotic obligation and the best show of Polish strength and unity under Prussian rule. The acquisition of every single seat and even of new votes in districts in which it proved impossible to defeat the German opponent was proclaimed a great victory. Consistent defense of national rights and of the Polish question under Hohenzollern rule was demanded of every parliamentarian. The title of poseł—representative—was recognized as one of the highest in the social hierarchy. Next to the excellently organized system of various Polish cultural and economic organizations, electoral campaigns represented the most effective weapon in the struggle for a separate national existence.

The more than one–hundred year history of Polish parliamentarianism during the tragic period of the partitions' existence be it in the form of purely Polish parliamentary bodies or of numerically modest Polish representations in the partitioning states' parliaments, played an enormous role in the development of the Poles' political and national consciousness. Parliamentary activity was one of the important factors that prepared Poles to act in the hour of freedom that was yet to come.

Chapter 8

THE DUALIST CHARACTER OF THE UNION ACT IN PORVOO 29TH OF MARCH, 1809

Osmo Jussila

The opening ceremonies of the first Diet of Finland took place in the small coastal town of Porvoo on March 28, 1809. There the Finnish nation, represented by four estates, and their new monarch, Alexander I, met each other. The union of the Finnish nation and her monarch was confirmed and sealed by a solemn ceremony the next day: the representatives swore first their oath of loyalty, and the Emperor and Grand Duke confirmed their religion, fundamental laws, rights and privileges.

A dominant view in Finland has been, and to some extent still is, what might be called the theory of State–agreement; it claims that the Russian Emperor and the Finnish people through their representatives at the Diet made a two–sided agreement in Porvoo: the Finns accepted the Emperor as their ruler, accepted him not as an autocrat but as a constitutional monarch whose power was limited by Finnish fundamental laws; the Emperor, in turn, took the Finnish people with all their rights as his subjects. By and through this agreement Finland was raised from the status of a province to the rank of a state, in real–union with the Russian state.

This theory was developed by a well–known Finnish–Swedish physician and professor Israel Hwasser as early as 1838–39. According to the formulation of Hwasser the Finnish people at the Porvoo Diet emancipated themselves from Swedish rule, constituted themselves into a nation, and made a separate peace treaty with the Russian Emperor. In this way a state was formed which contained its own Diet and representative constitution. According to the theory the Diet of Finland had the same role, power, and status as the Swedish Diet before 1809.

The majority of Russian historians and jurists in the 19th and at the beginning of the 20th century did not accept this Finnish theory of state–agreement, nor did a group of Finnish historians of my generation. My basic view has been so far that there was no state–agreement and no special agreement at all, but only a one–sided confirmation of laws and privileges on the one hand, and the oath of loyalty from the Finnish side on the other. In the footsteps of my Russian idol, professor B.E. Nolde, I have emphasized the fact that Russians followed in Finland an old and long tradition of their occupations and annexations, the nearest antecedent to Finland being that of the Baltic provinces in 1710–12. In the Baltic provinces as well as in Finland an essential part of the accomodation was the right to have "landtage." I have also to stress that the Finnish estates or corporations did not capitulate in the same way as the Baltic corporations; in Finland they could not make demands or put forth any terms of capitulation because the Finnish army had already surrendered unconditionally before. Thus the position of Finnish estates at the Porvoo Diet was considerably weaker than that of the Baltic corporations and towns at the time of capitulation. At the beginning of 1809, Finland was already totally occupied by Russian troups; the Emperor had commanded his new subjects to send representatives to the Diet, and they obeyed without reservations. Therefore I observed in one paper: "In fact, the Emperor did not conclude an agreement or peace treaty with the Finns but gave one–sided assurance just as before 1809 many other Russian czars had given assurances to various countries which they had occupied."

But nothing is permanent. After I read again some histories of the Romanov dynasty, books and articles concerning various Russian annexations, especially of the Baltic provinces, and last but not least Laczlo Peter's paper on Hungary and the Habsburgs, I had to revise my basic view. Some specialists on Baltic history, among them R. Wittram, have suggested that the capitulations of 1710 were in fact "Verträge staatsrechtlichen Charakters im Sinne des früheren ständisch–mittelalterlichen Staatsrechts." This theory could be elaborated further: perhaps the capitulations were an example of those dualist "Herrschaftsverträge" described by W. Näf in his famous study *Herrschaftsverträge und Lehre vom Herrschaftsvertrag* (1949). The land was transferred by agreement or treaty from the sovereignty of one ruler to that of another.

But the annexation of Livland and Estland happened a hundred years earlier than that of Finland. Can it then be compared at all with Finland, one may ask? If not, one may take an example of a much later date, the annexation of the Duchy of Courland in 1795 which took place in connection with the third division of Poland. There one cannot find an act of capitulation similar to that of Livland and Estland. What one does find, however, are signs of feudal thinking and even elements of a *Herrschaftsvertrag*. There the act of union was, at least formally, quite voluntary: the Seim of Courland, *Landtag*, asked the Russian Emperor to take their Duchy under her rule (pod Derzhavu). After the Seim's members had sworn the oath of loyalty, the Empress confirmed by her *gramota* the religion and rights of her new subjects, the Duke of Courland relinquished his ducal rights and the title "Duke of Courland" was added in the titulature of the Russian monarch. The act of union was supported by the argument that the indirect "feudal relation" of the ducal government to Poland, the *polnische Ober–Lehns–Herrschaft* had been detrimental for Courland. Besides the Duke also the Nobility and the *Landtag* issued a manifesto, declaring that they were leaving Poland, and signed an *Unterwerfungsakt* to the Imperial Majesty of Russia. One argument for renouncing the feudal relationship with Poland claimed that it had violated the rights promised to Courland. Another argument for union with Russia implied that Courland was too small to be an independent country and needed the protection of mighty Russia.

The fact that the capitulations of Livland and Estland had the character of an agreement derives partly from the international politics of the time. Other European powers desired the Baltic provinces, and it was therefore vital for Russia to couch its occupation of those provinces in the form of a capitulation.

How were these feudal agreements or *Herrschaftsverträge* suited to the system of autocratic Russia? I suppose they were similar to other innovations and models taken over by Peter the Great from Western Europe. They were only forms, a West–European façade, which did not touch or change the basic structure of autocracy. I would suggest that the capitulations of 1710 were some kind of Russian pseudo–*Herrschaftsverträge*.

It seems to me now quite evident that at least some of the main elements of such *Herrschaftsverträge* were present when Finland was united with Russia in 1809. Although neither Sweden nor Finland had known vassalage or serfdom, their social system can be called, and was called at the time, feudal or at least *ständisch*. M. M. Speranski, the main Russian architect of the union, labelled the Swedish constitution as feudal. In his memorandum of 1811 he compared the Finnish and Russian social and political systems and explained:

> The constitution of Finland is a very old monument of feudalism and communal principle.... A similar constitution had also been in Russia and is still partly existing.

He referred to the peasant communes, the *krestjanskie miry*. The main point—at least here—in Speranski's feudalism was communal principal (corporative society). Also Finnish society, estate corporations and the monarch (Grande Duke), had a dualist character in the eyes of Speranski. Furthermore, also in Finland international concerns were a factor. The war was still going on in 1809, not only in Finland, but also in Europe at large. Sweden had not yet abandoned hope of getting Finland back, and even Napoleon had his eyes on Finland. Therefore it was important for Russia to give the union the semblance of a voluntary union. Israel Hwasser's claim of 1838, however, that the Finnish nation emancipated itself from Swedish rule and made a state–agreement with the Russian monarchy is highly exaggerated. This applies all the more to Courland in 1795. The central act of the Porvoo Diet was called *hyllningsakten (Huldigung)*, on the 29th of March. The estates' corporations swore an oath of loyalty and the Emperor gave his confirmation gramota'. He promised to respect the religion, the fundamental laws and privileges of every Estate in particular and of all the inhabitants in general. The act was also called unionact, *föreningsakten* in Swedish, between the Emperor and his new Finnish subjects.

The formal setting in Porvoo was dualist like in a genuine *ständisch* system: the monarch and the land met each other. Emperor Alexander I addressed his words especially to the estates. There was not yet any Finnish state–organization or a Finnish prince to meet the Russian Emperor as there was in Courland with its Duke.

In my view Professor Nolde was right when he observed in his book of 1911 on Russian constitutional law that "the act of 15/29 of March 1809 is a very typical 'zhalovannaya gramota' which were given to many autonomous provinces of Russia. There are differences only in details." He observed that, for instance, the Finnish gramota did not contain the typical remark of the eighteenth century gramotas that the Emperor had given the confirmation on behalf not only of himself but of all his successors and forever, nor does it have the usual expression that the rights and privileges will be preserved by "imperial word." The gramota of Porvoo, therefore, was more an expression of the individual imperial will and did not contain

the usual contractual and obligatory elements. But I must disagree somewhat with Professor Nolde as to one point: at least in appearance the con-
tract of Porvoo did contain strong contractual elements. According to Nolde
there was some modernization of terminology in the Porvoo *gramota*. He
refers especially to the term *korennye zakony* which proves in his view that
the political terminology at the beginning of the twentieth century had to a
certain extent set aside the terminology of *ständisch* monarchy. Yet, the
basic idea of gramota conforms to the old traditions. In my view, furthermore, the term *korennye zakony* derives from the seventeenth and eighteenth centuries' ideas of natural law. *Korennye zakony*, at least in Speranski's
papers, has the meaning of *leges fundamentales* from the 17th century. And
quite probably Speranski was the first to use the term *korennye zakony* in
Russia.

Chapter 9

THE FIRST MIGRANTS' MINER ASSOCIATIONS IN THE RUHR

John J. Kulczycki

In accounts of the formation of a working class among miners in the Ruhr, historians rely heavily on the corporate tradition that existed among miners as well as on their extensive network of voluntary associations. Thus, a leading historian of the Ruhr miners claims that the miners' experience of membership in a corporate body aided them in organizing the miners' first mass strike in the region in 1872 and in maintaining a high degree of discipline during the strike.[1] Also, his elucidation of the origins of the mass strike of 1889, which led to the creation of the first enduring miners' trade union, begins with a chapter on the miners' voluntary associations.[2]

This approach to working class formation has focused almost exclusively on native miners even though migrants flooded the Ruhr and entered the mines in large numbers in the decades before World War I, eventually forming more than a third of the work force.[3] Migrants lacked the experience of the miners' corporate status, which a series of laws culminating in the General Mining Law of 1865 abolished well before any large number of them arrived in the Ruhr. Moreover, a majority of the migrants in the last two

1. Klaus Tenfelde, *Sozialgeschichte der Bergarbeiterschaft an der Ruhr im 19. Jahrhundert* (Bonn–Bad Godesberg: Verlag Neue Gesellschaft GmbH, 1977), p. 482.

2. *Ibid.*, pp. 345–396.

3. See Christoph Klessmann, *Polnische Bergarbeiter im Ruhrgebiet 1870–1945: Soziale Integration und nationale Subkultur einer Minderheit in der deutschen Industriegesellschaft* (Göttingen: Vandenhoeck & Ruprecht, 1978), p. 265, for statistics on the number of migrants in the work force. Tenfelde, *Sozialgeshichte*, pp. 383–386, included some information on the migrants' associations, but his account and conclusions did not give them the same importance as the associations of native miners.

decades before World War I came from among the Polish-speaking inhabitants of eastern Prussia and as such constituted a "foreign" element that seems to have no place in the history of the formation of the *German* working class.[4]

In the early 1870s, when Polish–speaking migrants had just begun to arrive in the Ruhr, native miners played an important role in the Christian–social movement, with its militant advocacy of a Christian, rather than a liberal (*laissez–faire*) or socialist, solution to workers' issues.[5] On the initiative of the Catholic clergy, at the begining of 1871 old miner associations (*Knappenvereine*) in the region of Essen were transforming themselves into Christian–social associations. The organization of new Christian workers' associations followed, with miners forming a major part of the membership. Their goals included material as well as religious–moral betterment through educational programs and mutual aid.

"Possibly the greatest achievement" of German workers in the period before World War I was "the creation of their own highly–developed network of associations. The importance of club life and club culture for the workers of the nineteenth and early twentieth century [sic] can hardly be imagined today, when numerous possibilities for entertainment exist, the radio, television, cinema, mass spectator sports, and so on. . . . Membership in a voluntary organization was, together with family and employment, often one of the three main factors . . . defining the workers' social identity."[6] Religious workers' associations, benefit societies, and a host of sociocultural organizations including "singing, educational, theatrical and sports clubs" proliferated. By sponsoring festivals or participating as a group in church or communal festivals, they fulfilled "the need of the worker and his family to escape from the burdens of everyday life, to find social contact and enjoyment."[7] Amateur theater performances and *tableaux vivants* representing historic scenes had a tradition dating from the 1860s, especially at

---

4.   According to Kathleen Canning, "Gender and the Politics of Class Formation: Rethinking German Labor History," *American Historical Review*, Vol. 97, No. 3 (June 1992), p. 739, the "process of rethinking class, of exploring its cultural dimensions, of analyzing it in relation to gender, race, and ethnicity, which characterizes recent British, French, and American labor historiography, has had little impact thus far on German labor history."

5.   Tenfelde, *Sozialgeschichte*, pp. 464–470.

6.   Gerhard A. Ritter, "Workers' Culture in Imperial Germany: Problems and Points of Departure for Research," *Journal of Contemporary History*, XIII, No. 2 (1978), 172.

7.   *Ibid.*, pp. 172–175.

workers' festivals, which often included lectures, choral singing, and gymnastic displays as well, and usually closed with a grand ball. These associations of workers "made an essential original contribution to the emancipation of the proletariat. By taking part in club activities members learnt to express themselves and accept responsibility," and thus "the clubs were also a training ground for workers' leaders." Moreover, such organizations and their festivals helped in "the formation of common beliefs and patterns of behavior and in particular created their own proletarian code of solidarity in the political and trade union struggle."[8] Hence, these ostensibly 'unpolitical' associations had decidedly political effects. Excluded from bourgeois associations or isolated from social intercourse with their members, the workers "in their societies and clubs . . . experienced, perhaps more intensely than in the political and economic organizations, that sense of 'belonging' and of integration into a real spiritual home. This made bourgeois society's political and social discrimination somewhat more bearable and at the same time, through their consciousness of belonging to a collective, strengthened their hopes for a better future." The workers' associations "thus served a dual function, 'partitioning' the workers from the bourgeoisie while at the same time acting as an 'agent of social integration' in terms of the social system as a whole."[9]

Despite the changes that occurred in the mining industry in the third quarter of the nineteenth century, "the miners' desire for representation as an estate of their own" with "a distinct festive culture" persisted, "even manifesting itself in attempts to revive earlier practices."[10] These included ceremonies surrounding the burial of a comrade, festivals, particularly on the feast of the patroness of miners, St. Barbara, and participation in church processions as a group with its own banner. In the Ruhr, however, rural customs prevailed over attempts to develop a separate miners' festival culture. In the Catholic western areas, the church calendar set the pattern with festivals and processions on local saints' days and important holy days, in which miners generally did not participate as a distinct group. Festive gatherings developed in the Bochum and Essen mining districts out of the cus-

---

8. *Ibid.*, p. 173; on the following, pp. 174–175.

9. Dieter Dowe, "The Workingmen's Choral Movement in Germany before the First World War", *Journal of Contemporary History*, XIII, No. 2 (1978), 269, 272, 274.

10. Klaus Tenfelde, "Mining Festivals in the Nineteenth Century," *Journal of Contemporary History*, XIII, No. 2 (1978), 386–387; on the following see pp. 386–401; also Tenfelde, *Sozialgeschichte*, pp. 349–396.

}

toms of the miners' corporate body, the *Knappschaft*, through which miners formed a professional entity. In all its ceremonies, the corporate banner played a special role as "the visible expression of the Knappschaft, of its unity, its exclusiveness, and its devotion to state and monarch."[11] Originally, the king might confer it; later, miner associations had to fund their own, at considerable expense. It usually depicted symbols of authority, such as a Prussian eagle, together with the tools of the trade, such as a pick and a hammer. The dedication of a new banner provided the occasion for a grandiose celebration.

When new mining regulations transformed the *Knappschaft*, a new institutional framework, that of a voluntary association, adapted some of these old symbols and forms. But the new organizations "followed the lines of social stratification within" the mines. "Now the workers, the management and the entrepreneurs each began associating with people of their own kind in societies, club and informal gatherings."[12] Along with other groups, miners took part in local festivals and marched in processions under their own association banner. Thus, for the older miners the new societies replaced the old community they had lost, while for the many new miners the traditional rituals "cloaked harsh everyday existence in a semblance of dignity" and offered a substitute for customs they had known in their homeland. "Induction into industrial existence now became one of the main functions of the acceptance and spread of the associations and their culture."[13]

Bourgeois associational practices served as a model for the miners' associations as well as for other workers' associations. Thus each association had its own elected officers, even in the Catholic ones, which the local priest formally headed. It often had its own choir, theatrical group, and library. It provided its members with "an opportunity for secluded social intercourse with people of like mind" and the means to satisfy their desire for amusement among themselves.[14] Catholic miners' associations also took a prominent part in parish life, with special services on the feast day of the association's patron saint and group participation in the annual Corpus Christi procession. In keeping with the old customs, members would march behind their association banner wearing miners' caps and insignia. Also aping the

---

11. Tenfelde, "Mining Festivals," p. 388.

12. *Ibid.*, p. 391.

13. *Ibid.*, pp. 395–396.

14. *Ibid.*, pp. 396–397.

past, associations would mark a banner dedication by organizing a festival, but one that followed the bourgeois model copied by other workers' festivals. Whereas in the 1870s during the *Kulturkampf* a demonstrative Catholic element in festivals and processions expressed at least latent defiance of the authorities, later symbols of loyalty, such as the laying of a wreath at a war memorial, toasting the emperor, or singing nationalist songs, became part of the ceremonies organized by miners' associations.

Catholic clergymen played a leading role in the organization of workers' associations in the Ruhr, but Protestant activists did not follow their example until 1882. Thus, in the predominantly Protestant eastern areas of the Ruhr, the first religiously affiliated workers' associations came into existence under Catholic sponsorship, though the more hostile environment than in the predominantly Catholic western Ruhr caused them to band together. They held a joint meeting in 1867, which eventually in the early 1880s led to the organization of an annual festival of all the associations in the area of Dortmund. Even earlier, in 1871, 'free' or non–denominational associations, which were "among the most important predecessors of the organized miners' movement in the Dortmund area" and which like the Catholic associations borrowed from the traditions of miners, held their own joint festival.[15]

These and other organizational activities centered around Dortmund, particularly within its Catholic community, suggest that it was more than a coincidence that the first migrant association, one for Catholic Polish–speaking workers, should have been founded in that same city in the eastern Ruhr.[16] In light of the similarities between the practices of this association and those of the German workers' associations we have described above, it seems likely that the latter served as a model for the Polish associations. But if Polish–speaking workers took the forms for their associations from those of the native workers and German–speaking miners, the migrants filled these forms with a content familiar to them from their homeland. They built on the tradition of social gatherings on Sunday afternoons in Polish villages. When the migrants met on Sunday afternoons to sing "old" songs and converse in Polish, they behaved no differently than in the homeland.[17] This

15. *Ibid.*, p. 401.

16. Jared Edwin Clark, "Industry, Society, and Politics in the Ruhr: National Liberalism in Dortmund, 1848–1913" (Unpublished Ph.D. Dissertation, University of Illinois at Chicago, 1990), pp. 198–200, described the organizational activity of Catholics in Dortmund in these years.

17. Johannes Kaczmarek, "Die polnischen Arbeiter im rheinisch-westfälischen Industriegebiet, eine Studie zum Problem der sozialen Anpassung" (Unpublished Ph.D. Dissertation, Cologne, 1922), pp. 32–33, saw this as the *Urgrund* of the associations; further grounds he saw in language, religion, and very importantly a feeling of wounded pride because of "höhergestellten" Germans.

Polish content set their associations apart from the other workers' associations of the Ruhr, just as the latter stood apart from the bourgeois associations from which they had borrowed forms. If the German miners' associations played such a significant part in the development of a miners' movement and community, the migrant associations had the potential of playing an analogous role in the formation of a working class in the Ruhr.

The oldest migrant organization in the Ruhr, the "Unity" (*Jedność*) Educational Association of Polish Workers and Artisans, originated in Dortmund probably at the end of 1876.[18] According to the statute, membership was open to Polish-speaking Catholics of irreproachable morality. The "Unity" Association had as its main goal the lifting of the educational and general cultural level of its members by means of "educational-political" reading material. The next year, the members succeeded in funding a banner for the association. On one side below the inscription "The 'Unity' Polish Association in Dortmund 1878," it bore a Christian cross in the middle and, at the foot of the cross, the Polish eagle on the left and the Lithuanian charging knight on the right.[19] The obverse presented the image of Our Lady of Czestochowa, the most revered icon of the Catholic Church of the Polish-Lithuanian Commonwealth, with the words, "Queen of Poland pray for us."

This blend of religious and national symbols typified the Polish national movement in Prussian Poland, particularly during and after the *Kulturkampf*, and therefore it seems characteristic that the founder and first president of the association, Hipolit Sibilski, should be a migrant from Poznań, the center of that movement. A miner but also a book peddler and later, at the end of the 1880s, owner of the first Polish bookstore in the Ruhr (in Bochum) as well as a co-founder of the Polish Trade union in 1902, Sibilski had ties with the so-called populists led by the editor of the Poznań newspaper *Orędownik* (Advocate), Roman Szymański.[20] In defense of the faith and the

---

18. A German translation of its statute filed with the authorities bears the date 7 January 1877, Jerzy Kozłowski, *Rozwój organizacji społeczno–narodowych wychodźstwa polskiego w Niemczech w latach 1870–1914* (Wrocław: Ossolineum, 1987), p. 76. One may assume that the name "Unity" stemmed from the attempt to unite Polish-speaking migrants from various regions of the Prussian East at the same time that it sought to separate them from native workers.

19. *Ibid.*, p. 76; Hans Jürgen Brandt, ed., *Die Polen und die Kirche im Ruhrgebiet 1871–1919: Ausgewählte Dokumente zur pastoralen und kirchlichen Integration sprachlicher Minderheiten im deutschen Kaiserreich*, (Münster: Aschendorff, 1987), p. 52, reproduced a drawing of the banner.

20. Klessmann, *Polnische Bergarbeiter*, p. 225; Krystyna Murzynowska, *Polskie wychodźstwo zarobkowe w Zagłębiu Ruhry w latach 1880–1914* (Wrocław: Ossolineum, 1972), pp. 70–71; Wojciech Chojnacki, "Księgarstwo polskie w Westfalii i Nadrenii do 1914 roku," *Studia Polonijne*, IV (1981), 204.

nation, Szymański promoted education and economic development among the Polish-speaking urban population which the landed nobility at the head of the Polish national movement had largely ignored.[21] The activities of the "Unity" Association embodied Szymański's views. It established its own library. At its weekly meetings, members read from Polish newspapers from Poznań. In addition to *Orędownik*, which kept members up to date on political developments, the association subscribed to the religious weekly *Niedziela* (Sunday), which during the *Kulturkampf* tried to assist those deprived of clergy by printing the Sunday gospel, a sermon, and other religious material along with some historical tales and practical advice.[22] As a measure of economic self-help, the association established a "fund for the sick" (*kasa chorych*). For an enrollment fee and a monthly payment, members who fell sick—not through their own fault, for example, because of heavy drinking—received financial assistance after the third day of an illness. In case of death, a payment went to the nearest relative. A financial penalty threatened those who did not participate in the funeral service for a fellow member.[23]

Further evidence of contact between the "Unity" Association and the Polish nationalist movement in Poznania came in 1881 when the Society for Folk Reading Rooms, *Towarzvstwo Czytelni Ludowych* (TCL), established the first of its libraries in the Ruhr with the association, which already had its own book collection.[24] Founded only the year before in Poznań, the TCL took up the activities of a predecessor organization that the Prussian authorities had dissolved, something the TCL avoided by carefully staying within the law.[25] It had as its goal the provision of Polish books for the broad masses of the population, particularly where Germanization threatened them. Between 1881 and 1884 TCL founded 390 rural and 85 urban libraries in Prussian Poland and other parts of Germany, distributing 78,784

21. On Szymański and the populists in English, see Richard Blanke, *Prussian Poland in the German Empire (1871–1900)* (Boulder, Colorado: East European Monographs, 1981), pp. 101–105; William W. Hagen, *Germans, Poles, and Jews: The Nationality Conflict in the Prussian East, 1772–1914* (Chicago: University of Chicago Press, 1980), pp. 149–150.

22. Kozłowski, *Rozwój*, p. 77.

23. Murzynowska, *Polskie wychodźstwo*, p. 71.

24. Kozłowski, *Rozwój*, p. 86.

25. On the library movement, see Witold Jakóbczyk, *Studia nad dziejami Wielkopolski* (Poznań: Państwowe Wydawnictwo Naukowe, 1959–1967), II, 35–89; III, 60–89.

books free of charge. While excluding books forbidden by the authorities, the TCL's reading material promoted Polish national consciousness along with religious and moral values.

Despite these ties with the Polish national movement, it is typical of this period that the "Unity" Association had the support of a German clergyman in Dortmund, who even took care of the TCL library.[26] As mentioned, the Catholic clergy took the initiative in founding workers' associations and therefore served as agents for the transfer of the practices of these associations to migrant organizations. It was natural for a German priest to concern himself with the Catholic migrants who settled in his parish, and he typically served as patron for their religiously affiliated associations. Especially during the *Kulturkampf*, German and Polish Catholic leaders closely cooperated in defense of the common faith. As for the migrants, finding themselves in a strange land, they looked to the local German parish priest for guidance and orientation, as a sailor without instruments at sea at night would look to the stars.[27]

Not all migrant associations thrived as well as the "Unity" Association. Those founded in Bochum in 1877 and in Essen in 1878 did not survive long.[28] Others may have similarly faded away without leaving a trace. In 1882 an article in the German press spoke of attempts to form "Polish associations" in "Bochum, Dortmund and elsewhere," but cited a Polish newspaper as saying that one existed only in Dortmund.[29] Then in January 1883 the St. Barbara Association came into existence in Gelsenkirchen. According to its statute, "every reputable Pole of the Catholic faith who lives in Bochum county" could join the association.[30] It took as its aim "to support the spirit of order and of good customs among workers who speak Polish and to protect these same workers from all dangers and offenses against

26. Kozłowski, *Rozwój*, p. 86.

27. On clerical influence among Polish peasants, see William I. Thomas and Florian Znaniecki, *The Polish Peasant in Europe and America* (New York: Alfred A. Knopf, 1927), I, 105, 285, 287; II, 1261, 1262, 1331; Jakub Wojciechowski, *Życiorys własny robotnika*, I (Poznań: Wydawnictwo Poznańskie, 1971), 232, 233.

28. Kaczmarek, "Die polnischen Arbeiter," p. 32; Stanisław Wachowiak, *Polacy w Nadrenii i Westfalii* (Poznan: Nakładem Zjednoczenia Zawodowego Polskiego, 1917), p. 99. A Polish newspaper reported on a meeting held in Essen in 1880 to organize the "Polish Circle," but no other evidence confirms its existence, reprinted in Witold Jakóbczyk, ed., *Wielkopolska (1851–1914): Wybór źródeł* (Wrocław: Ossolineum, 1954), pp. 69–70.

29. Reprinted in Brandt, *Die Polen*, pp. 54–57.

30. Kozlowski, *Rozwój*, p. 79.

morality. Political matters are completely excluded from the Association." In keeping with this emphasis on moral improvement, which suggests clerical involvement as well as concern over the migrants' reputation among the native population, meetings included the reading of the gospel and a homily in Polish. Within a year, its membership grew to about 300. By then it had a library of 182 books, some of them supplied by the TCL in Poznań. Also in 1884 it established a fund to assist sick members and, in case of death, their families.[31]

Since the association took the name of the patron saint of miners and mining dominated the industry of the area around Gelsenkirchen, the Prussian authorities probably erred in claiming that most of the association's members worked at factories or above ground at the mines rather than underground.[32] Its founders included a migrant who apparently had been a school teacher and one, born in Poznania, who later owned a bookstore in Gelsenkirchen. A firm in Poznań printed the association's statute, which indicates members had contacts there. Nor was a Polish nationalist accent missing: the association banner bore a Polish eagle, until it was replaced—perhaps because of official pressure—by a cross with the inscription "Queen of Poland pray for us."[33] But some evidence also hints at the involvement of a German clergyman. The association first came to the attention of government officials in Berlin when *Germania*, the organ of the German Catholic Center party (*Zentrum*), carried a positive report about it, and the Bochum *Landrat* believed that party could count on the support of association members in elections.[34]

The St. Barbara Association in Gelsenkirchen served as a model for other associations, but the first to follow it proved to be a rival that illustrated the divisions among the migrants. Before the end of 1883 a group of "Silesian–Polish miners" established their own Upper Silesian St. Barbara's Association in Schalke, where some of the members of the Gelsenkirchen association resided. It copied its namesake's statutes but limited membership to "Upper Silesian workers of the Catholic religion residing in Bochum county whose conduct is irreproachable." The initial membership of 51 eventually

31. *Ibid.*, pp. 79–80, 86.

32. Valentina-Maria Stefanski, *Zum Prozess der Emanzipation und Integration von Aussenseitern: Polnische Arbeitsmigranten im Ruhrgebiet* (Dortmund: Forschungsstelle Ostmitteleuropa an der Universität Dortmund, 1984), p. 79.

33. Kozłowski, *Rozwój*, pp. 79–82; Stefanski, *Zum Prozess*, p. 79.

34. Kozłowski, *Rozwój*, p. 82; Stefanski, *Zum Prozess*, pp. 77–79.

exceeded 100. Though they held their meetings in Polish, until 1896 they recorded the minutes in German.[35] In 1884 Polish-speaking migrants formed two more associations, one named after St. Joseph in Wattenscheid and one after St. Stanislaus—the Polish bishop–martyr—in Herne. Most members of the associations worked in the mines, and a miner served as the first chairman of the latter. Local parish priests acted as the patrons of both societies, which the Prussian authorities again saw as an effort to win votes for the *Zentrum* party. But loyalty to the state also marked the activities of the migrant associations, as when in 1885 members of the St. Stanislaus Association of Herne took part in the ceremonies on the anniversary of the Prussian victory at Sedan.[36]

Protestant migrants from the East did not have a religiously affiliated association to join until the creation of an Evangelical Worker Association in Gelsenkirchen in 1882, formed on the initiative of a Protestant miner.[37] But a lack of fluency in German among the primarily Masurian-speaking migrants from East Prussia plus presumably a desire to socialize among themselves prompted Protestant migrants to form their own organizations, the first being the Old-Prussian Association in Elberfeld organized on 17 January 1885.[38] Others followed: the Evangelical-Polish Worker Association in Gelsenkirchen, founded on 31 October 1886, and the Polish-Evangelical Worker Assistance Association in Schalke, created early in 1887.[39]

These Protestant workers' associations modeled themselves after their Catholic counterparts. For example, the statute of the one in Gelsenkirchen, which initially had 85 members, also spoke of moral and educational improvement and of a fund to assist the sick and the families of those who died. But at the same time, it set itself apart by listing as the association's first purpose "the support and awakening of evangelical consciousness among evangelical-Polish workers."[40] The banners of these associations also

---

35. Stefanski, *Zum Prozess*, pp. 78, 80; Kozłowski, *Rozwój*, p. 82. Brandt, *Die Polen*, pp. 60–62, reprinted the association statute.

36. Klessmann, *Polnische Bergarbeiter*, p. 58; Kozłowski, *Rozwój*, p. 83.

37. S.H.F. Hickey, *Workers in Imperial Germany: The Miners of the Ruhr* (Oxford: Clarendon Press, 1985), p. 95.

38. Wojciech Chojnacki, "Wydawnictwa w j̨ezyku polskim dla Mazurów w Westfalii i Nadrenii w latach 1889–1914," *Komunikaty Mazursko–Warmińskie*, 1975, No. 2, pp. 179–180; Franz Krins, "Zur Geschichte der Ostpreussen–Vereine in Nordrhein–Westfalen," *Jahrbuch für Volkskunde der Heimatvertriebenen*, VI (1961), 138.

39. Krins, "Zur Geschichte," p. 138; Kozłowski, *Rozwój*, p. 90.

40. Kozłowski, *Rozwój*, p. 90.

probably emphasized symbols typical of the Prussian Protestant state church: a chalice and a bible decorated the banner of an association in Bochum-Langendreer that dated from 1892.[41] Other differences brought these Protestant associations closer to the views of the Prussian authorities than Catholic associations. To achieve its educational goals, the association in Gelsenkirchen promised lectures in German as well as in Polish.[42] According to an official report to the Arnsberg government district at the end of 1886, "This evangelical–Polish association differs Essentially from the Catholic–Polish associations in that in its statutes, it has fortunately taken as one of its chief objects the fostering of loyalty to the emperor and the *Reich*." Nevertheless, this demonstration of loyalty did not satisfy the authorities. In 1890 the Gelsenkirchen *Landrat* reported that Masurians disavow the Polish nationality with the explanation: "We are German, we merely speak Polish."[43] Still, the authorities persuaded the associations to replace the word "Polish" in their names with "East Prussian," thereby stressing a regional identification similar to that of the Polish-speaking Upper Silesians.[44] Thus in 1889, when Masurian-speaking migrants formed an association in Lütgendortmund, they called it the Evangelical East Prussian Worker-Association.[45]

In 1885 Rev. Józef Szotowski arrived in the Ruhr as the region's first resident Polish clergyman assigned to minister to the region's Polish-speaking migrants. Like the German clergy in the Ruhr who believed that Catholic organizations for workers could play a positive role, Szotowski did not confine himself to purely sacral activity. He also had ties to the Polish populist movement in Poznan and the newspaper *Orędownik*, with its advocacy of the national mobilization of the Polish-speaking urban population. During his pastoral visits to various communities, he would attend meetings of Polish associations where they existed. On the first Sunday of the month he usually said mass, complete with a Polish sermon and Polish hymns, at the Church of Our Lady (*Liebfrauenkirche*) in Dortmund, with the group participation of members of the oldest Polish association "Unity." Afterwards he would attend the association's meeting and give a talk.[46]

41. Krins, "Zur Geschichte," p. 144.

42. Kozłowski, *Rozwój*, p. 90.

43. Krins, "Zur Geschichte," p. 138.

44. See Kozłowski, *Rozwój*, p. 90, on the change in association names.

45. Krins, "Zur Geschichte," p. 137.

46. Anastazy Nadolny, "Polskie duszpasterstwo w Zagłebiu Ruhry (1871–1894)," *Studia Pelplinskie*, 1981, p. 248; Kozłowski, *Rozwój*, p. 78.

Szotowski used the "Unity" Association's statute as a model for establishing others. On 26 July 1885 he took the initiative that led to the founding one week later of the Sts. Cyril and Methodius—the "apostles of the Slavs"—"Unity" Polish Association in Langendreer near Bochum. During his five years in the Ruhr, the number of such organizations grew from five to nineteen with a total membership of some 1600, including associations named for the patroness of miners St. Barbara, founded in Bochum in February 1886 and in Bottrop in November 1886, and for popular "Polish" saints, St. Wojciech (Adalbert) in Rohlinghausen in 1885 and St. Casimir in Baukau in July 1889. Szotowski also had contact with the TCL in Poznań, and during these same years it established about a dozen additional libraries in the Ruhr, including two in Bochum (in 1885 and in 1888), Szotowski's home base.[47]

Yet not all of these organizational developments from 1885 to 1890 owed their origin to Szotowski. Polish associations had begun to form in the Ruhr before his arrival. Although the Upper Silesian St. Barbara Association in Bottrop came into existence shortly after Szotowski's first visit there, its explicitly regional character suggests he had little influence over its founding.[48] After he left the Ruhr, in a speech at a Catholic meeting in Toruń in 1891, Szotowski defended the migrants as industrious but expressed concern over their regionalism, which provided the rationale for his organizational activity in the Ruhr:[49]

In social–national respects, the ignorance that they bring from home characterizes our people generally. Parochialism reigns. Poznanians [*Wielkopolanie*] don't want to know West Prussians, they in turn don't want to know Upper Silesians, though they work together. Even people from one county look unfavorably on those from another county. . . . That which is called national sentiment, that the Polish people of Westphalia in general do not know. That which is called the national question is for them irrelevant, alien, unknown. National sentiment,

47. Kozłowski, *Rozwój*, pp. 78, 84–86, 140; his total of 21 includes two outside the coal mining region of the Ruhr. For not entirely identical listings of early Polish associations, see *Wiarus Polski*, 25 April 1891, No. 46, and Joseph Michalek, "Die polnischen Volksorganisationen in Deutschland. Eine historische Studie zur Polenfrage vor der Wiedererstehung Polens" (Unpublished Ph.D. Dissertation, Cologne, 1923), p. 98.

48. See Richard Charles Murphy, *Guestworkers in the German Reich: A Polish Community in Wilhelmian Germany* (Boulder, Colorado: East European Monographs, 1983), p. 150, for the full name of the association, not noted by Kozłowski, *Rozwój*, p. 84.

49. Murzynowska, *Polskie wychodźstwo*, p. 68.

national consciousness depend on the level of education, which our people acquire. Only in Westphalia, those who read newspapers and get some education develop a conception of nationality and identify themselves as Poles. Such are usually better Poles in Westphalia than they were at home, where they did not think about it at all.

Although Szotowski steered clear of politics in his activities, the Prussian authorities nevertheless concluded that, "without doubt at every opportunity offered, he agitates on behalf of Polishness."[50]

The Prussian authorities manifested no concern over the growing migration from the East to the Ruhr until they became aware of the creation of the Polish migrant association in Gelsenkirchen in 1883. They had trusted in a kind of natural assimilation of the migrants "through the schools, marriages, and constant contact."[51] Therefore the mayor of Gelsenkirchen opposed allowing a separate organization for migrants, believing that they should join German organizations. In a report to the Bochum *Landrat* he claimed that the local Catholic clergymen agreed with him, but their efforts in this direction proved in vain: "Polish workers want to unite only on a national–Polish basis."[52] Thus, although the statutes of migrant associations specifically excluded political matters from consideration, in the minds of Prussian officials the "national-Polish character" of the association in Gelsenkirchen— the emphasis on the Polish language in the statute, the Polish library, and especially the Polish eagle on the association banner—sufficed as evidence of the political nature of the association.[53]

News of the formation of the Polish association in Gelsenkirchen also caused concern in the highest government circles in Berlin, prompting the Prussian Ministry of Religious, Educational, and Health Affairs first to request information about "the establishment, tendency, and development of the St. Barbara Association" and then to request information about other Polish associations and to direct that their leaders and members be watched and their lectures, books, and newspapers be checked. [54] Henceforth Polish associations in the Ruhr came under the scrutiny of the Prussian police,

50. Kozłowski, *Rozwój*, p. 88.
51. Tenfelde, *Sozialgeschichte*, p. 385.
52. Kozłowski, *Rozwój*, p. 80.
53. *Ibid.*, p. 80; Stefanski, *Zum Prozess*, p. 79.
54. Stefanski, *Zum Prozess*, pp. 78, 80; see the ministerial query reprinted in Brandt, *Die Polen*, p. 58.

which however lacked a sufficient number of employees who understood Polish. Also, some officials continued to have doubts about the alleged political nature of the associations.[55] Although the German clergy facilitated the creation of the first associations for Polish-speaking migrants, Rev. Szotowski soon ran into difficulties from the side of the Catholic Church, presumably because of his organizational activities. He later complained that some German clerics obstructed his efforts to minister to the Polish-speaking migrants as well as that the Prussian police spied upon him. Because of delinquent payment of his salary assessed on the parishes where he fulfilled pastoral functions, Szotowski sought the intervention of the diocesan authorities. In 1889 he appealed to a conference of the German episcopate in Fulda for more clergy for Polish Catholics. Shortly thereafter the diocesan authorities of Paderborn had the Polish priest recalled to his home diocese in the East, ostensibly for exceeding his authority by carrying his work beyond the borders of the diocese.[56] Perhaps they simply agreed with Prussian officials who regarded a prolongation of his stay in the Ruhr as a hindrance to the "aim of Germanization" and harmful politically, though they uncovered nothing in his activities that "would indicate prohibited goals."[57] On the contrary, they found that he urged the practice of Christian moral principles and the maintenance of the social order. But his efforts at organizing the migrants plus his probable initiative early in 1889 behind a reported project to publish a Polish–language newspaper in the Ruhr meant that the departure from the Ruhr early in 1890 of the sole resident cleric who could minister to Polish–speaking Catholics in their native language suited Prussian officials.

In the years prior to the 1889 strike, migrants demonstrated the same capacity to form voluntary associations as native miners. The migrants' associations, inspired in part by the native miners' associations, shared many of the latter's attributes and featured many of the same activities. Yet, they also had a distinctly separate character reflecting the traditions and origins of the migrants. If Rev. Szotowski played a key role in fostering their development, so did the German clergy in the associations of native miners. These

55. Kozłowski, *Rozwój*, p. 81.

56. Nadolny, "Polskie duszpasterstwo," p. 249; Hans–Jürgen Brandt, "Das Kloster der Redemptoristen in Bochum und die Polenseelsorge im westfälischen Industriegebiet (1883–1918)," *Spicilegium Historicum Congregationis SSmi Redemptoris*, XXIII, No. 1 (1975), 142.

57. Kozłowski, *Rozwój*, p. 88.

facts suggest a greater similarity of outlook and interests between the native and migrant populations and of their capacity to participate in a working-class movement than if one focuses solely on their differences of language, religious customs, and origins. To dismiss the migrants' associations as merely manifestations of ethnicity rather than as part of the process of class formation is to adopt the view of the Prussian authorities. Yet in looking at the 1889 strike, in which Polish-speaking migrants played an active role, historians have ignored this organizational activity on the part of the migrants and simply assumed that they had a less developed social consciousness than the native miners. Whereas corporate traditions presumably enabled native miners to act in a disciplined and organized way, "deficient social integration" supposedly explains the readiness of migrants to undertake the risky struggle against the mine owners.[58] It is time for German labor historians to reexamine how differences of ethnicity influenced class formation in the Ruhr.

58. Albin Gladen, "Die Streiks der Bergarbeiter im Ruhrgebiet in den Jahren 1889, 1905, und 1912," in *Arbeiterbewegung an Rhein und Ruhr: Beiträge zur Geschichte der Arbeiterbewegung in Rheinland-Westfalen*, ed. by Jürgen Reulecke (Wuppertal: Peter Hammer, 1974), p. 129. For similar views, see Knut Hartmann, *Der Weg zur gewerkschaftlichen Organisation: Bergarbeiterbewegung und kapitalistischer Bergbau im Ruhrgebiet, 1851–1889* (Munich: tuduv-Buch, 1977), pp. 152–159; Tenfelde, *Sozialgeschichte*, pp. 246, 512, 513; S.H.F. Hickey, *Workers*, p. 206. A collection of ten articles published to mark the centennial of the strike did not include any devoted to the role of the migrants, Karl Ditt and Dagmar Kift (eds.), *1889—Bergarbeiterstreik und Wilhelminische Gesellschaft* (Hagen: v.d. Linnepe, 1989); Michael Zimmerman's contribution to the collection, "Parole heisst Sieg oder Todt: Der Bergarbeiterstreik von 1889 im Raume Recklinghausen," pp. 53–68, focused on a region with a high percentage of Polish-speaking migrants and therefore provides valuable information on their role, which, however, was not his main concern. On the role that migrants played in the 1889 strike, see John J. Kulczycki, "Polish Migrants in the Ruhr Region and the Great Coal Miners' Strike of 1889," in *Ideologie, pogl,ady, mity w dziejach Polski i Europy XIX i XX wieku: Studia historyczne*, ed. by Jerzy Topolski, Witold Molik, and Krzysztof Makowski (Poznań: Wydawnictwo Naukowe Uniwersytetu im. Adama Mickiewicza, 1991), pp. 165–177.

Chapter 10

CHICAGO'S PILSEN PARK AND THE STRUGGLE
FOR CZECHOSLOVAK INDEPENDENCE DURING
WORLD WAR ONE

Dominic A. Pacyga

In the 1980s and 1990s Eastern and Central Europe went through convulsive changes that reshaped maps and political alliances as communism lost its grip first among the Soviet satellites and then within the Soviet Union itself. Many of the media images that came out of the "other" Europe were those of crowds pulling down statues, emblems, flags, and other symbols of the old regimes. Clashes between ethnic groups over the use of language also appeared as the Soviet Union crumbled. Symbols and languages have long been important to Eastern Europeans. The desecration of hated political symbols is a long and revered tradition, as is the perseverance of national languages and culture. At the outbreak of World War One such attacks against symbols and the celebration of ethnic languages were also evident. In Chicago's Czech community, pro-Serbian demonstrators pulled down the black two-headed eagle symbol of the Hapsburg Empire and trampled it under foot on the day that Austria-Hungary declared war on Serbia to begin the First World War. The Serbian language was greeted with shouts of approval from a multi-Slavic crowd angered about what they saw as a German attack against all Slavs. As a result, July 28, 1914 saw the movement for Czechoslovak independence take off in as unlikely a place as a Chicago beer garden and dance pavilion packed with Slavic immigrants from the Austro-Hungarian Empire.

Chicago's Czech community dates back to 1852 when the first Bohemian settlers arrived in the city from New York. The original Czech settlement was located just south of the city cemetery that would become Lincoln Park at Dearborn and North Avenue. The Czechs settled near the North Side German community, then making its way along Clark Street. By 1855 the Czechs moved from the neighborhood, and a more permanent Czech settlement appeared on the West Side of the city along Canal Street south from Van Buren to Taylor Street. Here early settlers founded the first Czech Catholic parish, St. Wenceslaus, in 1866. This part of the city became known as Praha named after the capital of Bohemia. After the 1871 Chicago Fire, which began close to Praha, Czechs moved farther south to 18th Street. In 1881 Mathew Skudera opened the Pilsen Inn at Fisk and McMullen Streets. This new Czech settlement quickly took its name from the inn and from the most famous beer producing town in Bohemia.

Pilsen soon developed into a thriving ethnic community as Chicago's Czechs left Praha to newer immigrant groups including their fellow Western Slavs, the Poles. 18th Street ran through the heart of the neighborhood and furnished the mainstreet of Bohemian Chicago. The Bohemian settlement in Chicago became the leading Czech colony in the United States as immigration peaked in the years between 1880 and the First World War. In Pilsen could be found the headquarters of Czech fraternals, Sokol gymnastic groups, and the offices of Czech newspapers. Both Freethinker or Rationalist and Roman Catholic schools appeared, as did Czech Protestant congregations. Pilsen, the largest of several Czech neighborhoods in Chicago, came close to being a self-sustaining immigrant community.[1]

As the Czech community continued to expand, it outgrew Pilsen which provided an entry point for immigrants. Some Czechs moved west of Ashland Avenue were they lived with Poles and other ethnic groups. Still more Czechs began to look farther west to the city's expanding periphery where cheap lots and newer single-family homes beckoned to them. The more successful immigrants and members of the second generation began to create a new Czech community along 26th Street west of California Avenue. This area became known as České Kalifornii or Czech California. The 26th Street settlement soon provided a base for the further expansion of the Czech community even farther westward to the suburbs of Cicero and Berwyn.

České Kalafornii developed as a stable ethnic community, in part because of the location of the Western Electric Company plant in the suburb of Cicero at 22nd and Cicero Avenue in 1903. Western Electric became a major em-

---

1.   Jan Habenicht, *Dějiny Čechův Amerických* (St. Louis: Tiskem A Nakladem Casopisu, Hlas, 1910), pp. 566–567; Alice G. Masaryk, "The Bohemians in Chicago," *Charities* (December 3, 1904), p. 206, Joseph Slabey Roucek, "The Passing of American Czechoslovaks," *The American Journal of Sociology* (March 1934), p. 612.

ployer in the Czech community and was readily accessible from České
Kalafornii. The new district developed as part of Chicago's "bungalow belt"
a series of neighborhoods built up primarily after the turn of the century and
was occupied typically by single-family residences which included front and
backyards. The Czechs with their almost legendary desire to own real estate—in 1922 twenty-five percent of Chicago Czechs owned their own
homes—flocked to České Kalafornii and brought their institutions and culture with them. As the new century proceeded, Pilsen was rebuilt a little less
densely on the prairie between California Avenue and Pulaski Road in what
most Chicagoans called South Lawndale. Certainly by the time of World War
One, and despite the fact that Pilsen remained heavily Bohemian, České
Kalafornii was the more prestigious neighborhood for Czech Chicagoans.
Prominent Czech business and political leaders such as the future mayor of
Chicago, Anton Čermak, called the district home.

Czech California's institutional development occurred quickly. Freethinkers, Protestants, and Roman Catholics brought their organizations with them.
Czech Catholics opened the parish of St. Ludmilla at 24th and Albany and
dedicated the original parish church on September 20, 1891. Eleven years
later a new church was built to serve the expanding Bohemian community. A
second Czech Catholic parish, Blessed Agnes, opened in 1904 at 26th and
Central Park Avenue less than a mile from St. Ludmilla's. Czechs organized
Sokol groups and built a Sokol hall at 2345 South Kedzie Avenue. The Freethinkers opened the Vojta Naprstek School at 2548 South Homan, and Sokol
Havlicek-Tyrs built a hall at 2619 South Lawndale. Czech Protestants organized the Jan Hus Church at 24th Street and Sawyer. At this time it was estimated that there were over five hundred Czech benevolent societies, including independent societies and lodges of the larger national fraternals, and two
hundred and twenty-seven building and loan associations in Chicago alone.[2]

Despite this organizational progress many observers commented on the

2. Eugene McCarthy, "The Bohemians in Chicago and Their Benevolent Societies: 1875–
1946," (M.A. Thesis, University of Chicago, 1950), pp. 8, 55; Rev. Msgr. Harry C. Koenig,
ed., A History·of the Parishes of the Archdiocese of Chicago 2 vols. I: 547–550; Jakub
Horak, "Assimilation of Czechs in Chicago" (Ph.D. Dissertation, University of Chicago,
1928), pp. 24–27; Dr. J.E.S. Voyan, "How the Czechs and Slovaks Helped Build Chi-
cago." (typed manuscript, Chicago Historical Society Clippings File); Vlasta Vraz, ed.,
Panorama: A Historical Review of the Czechs and Slovaks in the United States of America
(Cicero, IL.: Czechoslovak National Council of America, 1970), p. 125; Charles Pergler,
America in the Struggle for Czechoslovak Independence (Philadelphia: Dorrance and
Company, 1926), p. 18.

divisions within the Czech community which ran deep and centered principally on religion. Bohemia had been a center of reformist Christian thought even before Luther. Bohemians regarded Jan Hus, burned at the stake as a heretic by Rome, as a national martyr, and many saw the Catholic Church as an institution imposed on Bohemia by its Hapsburg rulers. In the United States an anti-Catholic movement sometimes called rationalism, but more often referred to as the Freethinker Movement, became very popular among the Czechs in the 1870s. While it corresponded to a similar German movement, the Freethinker Movement became especially popular among Czechs in the United States and provided a nationalist base for the immigrant community. Roughly fifty percent of Czech Americans left the Catholic Church and joined the Freethinkers, many of the original leaders of which were former Catholic clergy. The division of the Czech community into three competing groups, Catholics, Protestants, and Freethinkers led many observers to refer to the Czechs as a divided and contentious community.[3]

Czech immigrants had a good reputation in Chicago as hard working and industrious residents. In the first generation, the Czech population contained a high percentage of skilled craftsmen. Many worked in the tailoring and slaughterhouse trades. Second generation Czech Chicagoans often tended to go into business or office work. Chicago's Czechs also maintained a high literacy rate with only 3 percent being illiterate in 1900. Czech neighborhoods quickly developed a large middle class as part of the institutional and economic life of the city's "Little Bohemia." The Czech community was well known for its sociability. Bohemians had a long cultural tradition, based on peasant village life, of celebrating holiday feasts and picnics with music and a good deal of drinking. Czech entertainment businesses flourished in Pilsen and České Kalafornii. Saloonkeepers, restaurant owners, and others prospered as they catered to their Czech clientele.[4]

On September 3, 1903 a group of Czech innkeepers combined to establish a cooperative brewery, the Pilsen Brewing Company, as an answer to what they regarded as the monopolistic policies of the Schlitz Brewing

3.   Karel D. Bicha, "Community or Cooperation? The Case of the Czech Americans," in Charles A. Ward, Philip Shashko, and Donald E. Pienkos, eds., *Studies in Ethnicity: The East European Experience in America* (Boulder, Colorado: East European Monographs, 1980).

4.   McCarthy, "Bohemians in Chicago," pp. 6–8; Kenneth D. Miller, *The Czecho–Slovaks in America* New York: George H. Doran Company, 1922), p. 69; Thomas Capek, *The Cechs (Bohemians) in America: A Study of their National, Cultural, Political, Social, Economic, and Religious Life* (Boston and New York: Houghton Mifflin Company, 1920), pp. 77–78.

Company then located at 19th and Blue Island in Pilsen. John A. Červenka, a Pilsen innkeeper, was elected president of the new enterprise which was capitalized at $100,000. Červenka had come as a twelve year old child with his parents to Chicago from the town of Svatý Křiž in the Pilsen district of Bohemia.[5] The Pilsen Brewing Company in 1910 had 164 stockholders, each of whom was an innkeeper. The company's modern plant, designed by Adolf Lonek, stood on the corner of 26th and Albany and occupied six acres of land. The brewery employed mostly Slavic workers.[6]

In August 1907 the stockholders of the Pilsen Brewing Company decided to open a beer garden on a lot adjacent to their plant. Previously the company had allowed various Sokol groups to use the empty lot for gymnastic demonstrations. The announcement in 1907 called for the creation of a park, restaurant, saloon, and dance pavilion at a cost of between $20,000 and $25,000. The Czech newspaper *Denni Hlasatel* predicted that České Kalafornii and the entire Southwest Side would now have a facility equal to the German Bismark Park on the North Side.[7] The new facility, called Pilsen Brewery Park or simply Pilsen Park, opened the following spring and soon became a center for Czech cultural and institutional life. The park attracted Czechs from all the various parts of the community. On Sunday May 31, 1908 the Regional Fuegner-Tyrs Sokol held six public gymnastic exercises and contests in the new park. Catholics also came to Pilsen Park on June 7, 1908 when the Bohemian Catholic Organization of Czech California held a large outing. The night before, the first evening event took place at the new park as electric lights allowed the celebrating to continue into the night. On June 14, 1908 the first Sokol Festival in Chicago and Peoples Celebration was held at Pilsen Park, and in August a large meeting to raise funds for the erection of a statue in honor of Karal Havlicek-Borovsky was held by the Freethinkers.[8] The facility provided neutral ground to be used by all the various Czech factions in Chicago. The park was large enough to hold most Czech celebrations and demonstrations. It was also conveniently located along the 26th Street streetcar line and close to the various Czech halls,

5. *Amerikan Národni Kalendář Na Rok 1926* (Chicago: Gerringer Press, 1926), pp. 312–313. Copies of this annual publication are available in the Czech and Slovak Immigrant Archives at the Regenstein Library of the University of Chicago. Hereafter referred to as Czech and Slovak Archives.

6. Habenicht, *Dějiny Čechův*, p. 679.

7. *Denni Hlasatel*, August 7, 1907.

8. *Denni Hlasatel*, May 9, 1908, May 31, 1908.

churches, and schools of Czech California. The park was also used as a site for lectures of interest to the Czechs. In July 1913 over 1,200 people heard Vaclav J. Klofac lecture on the topic of the Balkan War and its meaning for the Slavic nations. Klofac also elaborated on his ideas concerning the exchange of children between Czech parents in the United States and Bohemia.[9]

In 1914 as war clouds gathered over the Balkans, Czech Chicagoans continued to use Pilsen Park for community celebrations. On July 22, 1914 the annual outing of Czech Old Settlers took place at the park. By this time John Červenka was also a well known Chicago Democratic politician tied to Anton Čermak. In the fall of 1914 Červenka ran for Clerk of the Probate Court.[10] Pilsen Park therefore was intimately tied to the most successful residents of Czech California. A week after the old Settlers outing, the park also became tied to the struggle for Czechoslovak independence. On July 26, 1914 a group of Czech Sokol leaders, journalists, and intellectuals met at a small Czech restaurant on the corner of 26th and Trumbull Streets to plan for a response to the expected Austro-Hungarian declaration of war on Serbia. Included in the group were Czech newspapermen, Josef Tvrzicky, Josef Mach, and J.V. Nigrin, along with Sokol leaders Vincenc Sedlak and Frantisek Sustek. The Moravian Slovaks were represented by J. Sala, and the meeting was also attended by a Mr. Votava. As a result of this conversation another council was held the next day to plan a public demonstration. It was during one of these planning sessions that J.V. Nigrin brought up the possibility of the dismemberment of the Austro-Hungarian Empire. The journalist declared: "Let us ferment the fire of enthusiasm in Czech hearts. The new age must bring freedom to Bohemia."[11] With the help of the Bohemian-American Office of the Press, a group of journalists, including Nigrin, dedicated to bringing news of Bohemia to other Americans, the group put together a plan for a rally and protest the following evening at Pilsen Park. It was obvious from the beginning that many among this group hoped for the collapse of the Hapsburg Empire and the resurrection of an independent Czech state possibly combined with the Slovaks. Tvrzicky, a student activist in Prague, had been forced to leave Bohemia in 1911 because of his

---

9. *Denni Hlasatel*, July 30, 1913.

10. *Denni Hlasatel*, September 7, 1914.

11. Pergler, *America in the Struggle*, pp. 21–22.

12. Joseph Jahelka, "The Role of Chicago Czechs in the Struggle for Czechoslovak Independence," *Journal of the Illinois State Historical Society* (December 1938), p. 385.

radical political beliefs. He would work tirelessly for Czech independence during World War One.[12]

The rally the following evening proved to be a huge success. The Austrians' declaration of war on Serbia that morning electrified Chicago's Czech community. Business was practically suspended in those Chicago neighborhoods where Serbians, Croatians, Dalmatians, Bosnians, and Czechs lived. Men, women and children gathered in small groups to discuss the Austro-Hungarian declaration of war. James Stepina in an interview with a *Chicago Daily News* reporter stated:

> We had expected to memorialize congress, asking that resolutions protesting against war be passed by that body....Austria's act puts another face on the situation and now we shall condemn the dual monarchy for bringing war upon Servia [sic], as well as asking the United States to adopt resolutions against this action.[13]

Officially citizens of Austria-Hungary, Czech sympathies lay with their fellow Slavs, the Serbs. On both sides of the Atlantic Ocean, Czechs empathized with the enemies of the Hapsburgs. In Chicago, however, Czechs could more freely criticize the Austrians than in Prague. The Pilsen Park meeting on the evening of July 28 took on a life of its own and went far beyond the expectations of the organizers. Four thousand Bohemians, Austrian Slavs, Serbians, and Croatians gathered in the Pilsen Park Pavilion the evening of July 28. As the organizers began to call the meeting to order, someone noticed two large metal shields hanging from the pavilion's rafters. On those shields were images of eagles which the crowd immediately identified as the Hapsburg coat of arms.

A cry rose up as the eyes of the crowd looked up to the two shields. A man with a deep voice yelled out in Serbian, "Down with the Austrian eagle." The eagles were perhaps thirty-five feet above the heads of those on the floor. James F. Stepina, a Czech banker and the meeting chairman, banged on the table with a gavel and attempted to call the meeting to order, but no one paid him much attention. At that point several hundred members of the audience climbed onto the roof of the pavilion. From windows near the roof they tried to reach into the hall and snatch the shields, but having neglected to carry axes up with them they could not reach the offending shields. After this failed attempt to knock down the shields, a group of about one hundred trained gymnasts, probably Czech Sokols, stripped off their coats and formed a human ladder. Two climbers finally reached the rafters at the same time

---

13. *Chicago Daily News*, July 28, 1914.

and ran along them in a "monkey-like" fashion. Each grabbed a shield and wrenched it from the wall. They then threw them down to the floor. The meeting did not proceed until everyone had a chance to trample on the Hapsburg coat of arms. The question of why Austrian eagles were fastened to the Pilsen Park pavilion walls immediately presented itself. John Červenka, the head of the Pilsen Brewing Company, later denied that they were Austrian eagles. He claimed that the shields were probably Moravian or Serbian escutcheons, both of which include an eagle, that were mistaken for the hated Hapsburg symbol. The *Chicago Tribune* reporter at the scene, however, described the shields as marked by "black eagles, each with a double head....the national bird of the Austro-Hungarian Empire." Each of the members of the crowd wore a red, white, and blue ribbon on which was printed "To Hell With Austria." Finally Stepina took control of the meeting and restored order. He was assisted by A.J. Psenka of the Chicago Freethinker newspaper *Svornost* and by J.V. Nigrin.

The meeting passed a resolution and sent it to the Austro-Hungarian embassy in Washington, D.C. condemning the empire's declaration of war, as "the act of brutal monster impelled solely by greed and a desire for conquest." The resolution concluded:

> Resolved, that we Bohemians of Chicago extend our heartfelt sympathies to the Servian [sic] nation, and that we commend the honorable and manful attitude it has taken in this horrible crisis at a time when it is weakened after a long and terrible struggle for liberty.

> Resolved, that we deem it our duty to extend to the Servian people such moral and financial assistance as is in our power, and that a fund be raised to be donated to the Red Cross Society of Servia.

Stepina himself started Chicago's Czechs contribution to funds for the Serbian Red Cross with a donation of one hundred dollars. James F. Stepina told the crowd, "Now is the time, let us strike. No people have been oppressed as the Bohemians have. Let us cut off our ties with Austria and ally ourselves with our brother Slavs in their time of need." Stepina further told the crowd to "Write to those who remain at home. Tell them to resist conscription. Tell them if they are forced to serve, to desert and fight on the side of their brothers the Servians." Stepina's call for Czech draft resistance was followed by speeches by Dr. J. Rudis Jicinsky, editor of the *Sokol*, Joseph Tvrzicky, editor of *Svornost*, Arnost Krizan, a Slovak, editor of *Slovenske Slovo*, and Nigrin of the Bohemian American Press Association. Tvrzicky spoke about the possibility of helping the Czechs fighting a political struggle in their homeland. John R. Palendech, editor of *The United Servian and the*

Balkan World, also addressed the crowd. The Serb asked the assembly in Czech, "What tongue should I use?" The crowd in a passionate demonstration of Pan-Slavism yelled back "Serbian!"[14]

While there were similar protests in Czech settlements across the United States, the Chicago demonstration was the largest. The Austrian consul in Chicago, Hugo Silvestri, had his informants that night at Pilsen Park. Reportedly they brought the consul a list of the most prominent people at the meeting whose names eventually ended up in the so-called black book of the Austrian police in Prague.[15]

On the following day the Austrian Consul announced that the empire would be notifying its subjects abroad to report home for military service. Joseph Tvrzicky scoffed at the idea of Czechs returning to the Austrian Empire to fight Serbs. He told a reporter:

> To be sure Chicago is filled with Austrian reservists. That is one reason why they are in Chicago, because they were forced into the army of those they hated. Will they answer the call to go back to fight their brothers? No if they go back at all it will be to fight with the Servian Army. It is Slav against German. Instead of 20,000 going back to the Austrian colors, there will not even be twenty.[16]

Certainly Tvrzicky's sentiments were shared by other Chicago Bohemians. Several days after the Pilsen Park meeting, Peter O. Sticich, editor of *Sokol,* James Stepina, and V.A. Gerringer, representing the Chicago Czech-American newspaper *Svornost,* assured the Serbs of the financial and moral support of the Bohemians. But Gerringer went further: "I hope that this war may be followed by an uprising of the Bohemians against the tyranny of the empire," he declared. "Something I promise you is going to happen when old Franz Josef dies." Earlier Gerringer had predicted a revolution among the Austrian Slavs. He theorized correctly that Czechs would desert to enemy armies and would be of no use to the Austrians in a war against their fellow Slavs.

Most of Chicago's immigrant neighborhoods were in an uproar over the outbreak of the war. In South Chicago, Russian steelworkers began to hold impromptu military drills. Croatians, who also lived in Pilsen, held a mass

---

14. The most complete description of the events at Pilsen Park that evening appeared in the *Chicago Tribune,* July 29, 1914. See also the *Chicago Evening American,* July 28, 1914, July 29, 1914. Jahelka, "Chicago's Role," p. 387.

15. Pergler, *America in the Struggle,* pp. 19–21.

16. *Chicago Evening American,* July 29, 1914.

meeting on August 1, 1914 at Congressional Hall on 18th Street and Racine Avenue. The city's Germans and Austrians also responded with patriotic rallies at Turner Hall at North Avenue and Clark Street in the Lincoln Park neighborhood. Chicago's West Side Irish, meeting at Emmett Hall on the corner of Taylor Street and Ogden Avenue, promised to send troops to fight the British in Ireland. The socialists also responded to the war declaration by calling a mass meeting of immigrant workingmen at Pilsen Park on Monday August 3, 1914 to protest the Austrian action. The meeting was to be organized by the foreign-speaking socialist federations.[17]

The Czechs immediately began to organize their community with an eye on helping Serbia and promoting the idea of Czech independence, and they played a key role in the creation of the Bohemian National Alliance. As early as August 9, 1914 a preliminary organization issued the following statement in the Czech press:

> It is possible that the present storm will uproot the old state system and give rise to a larger freedom and independence. We must think even of this possibility and with opportune help show that we are worthy descendants of the nation and worthy of its former glory.

Josef Tvrzicky conceived the idea to establish a revolutionary organization in America which was to evolve into the Bohemian National Alliance on September 2, 1914 in Chicago. On September 18, 1914 the first manifesto of the nascent Czech organization was issued. It stated that demands for Czech independence had to be taken into account when the war ended. That same month the American Committee for the Liberation of the Czech People was founded in New York City. The following January another conference was held in Chicago. Finally in March 1915 the organization was perfected and the Bohemian National Alliance emerged as an important force in the struggle for Czech independence. The Chicago chapter of the Bohemian National Alliance emerged as the central body of the organization.[18]

While the Czech leadership organized to fight the Austrians, Pilsen Park

---

17. *Chicago Daily News*, July 29, 1914, July 31, 1914; *Chicago Tribune*, July 30, 1914, August 2, 1914; for the best description of anti–German feeling in Chicago during the World War One era see Melvin G. Holli, "The Great War Sinks Chicago's *Kultur*," in Melvin G. Holli and Peter d'A Jones, eds., *Ethnic Chicago* (Grand Rapids, MI: Eerdmans Publishing Co., 1984), pp. 460–511.

18. Pergler, *America in the Struggle*, p. 22; Jahelka, "The Role of Chicago," pp: 387–394; Joseph Chada, *The Czechs in the United States* (Washington, D.C.: Czechoslovak Society of Arts and Sciences, 1981), pp. 43–47.

remained undiminished by the war as an important center for Bohemian social activity. On August 12, 1914 as war clouds engulfed all of Europe, Ferdinand Zhotaka conducted a concert of "artistically sensitive numbers" as well as American music and union songs at Pilsen Park. The event marked the Third Annual Garden Concert held for the benefit of the Czech shelter and orphanage. Admittance was fifty cents. Ten days later the Klub Česky Lev held an outing that organizers promised "will make you forget your worries and the controversies surrounding the war...." Weekend after weekend saw Pilsen Park filled with Chicago's Czechs attending an outing or festival.[19]

Soon these festivals turned to the serious business of supporting the war effort, especially after the Czechoslovak demand for independence made in Paris on November 15, 1915. Many Czech Americans took part in this declaration.[20] Czech sociability and their propensity to organize into clubs and fraternals served the cause of independence well. By the winter of 1916/1917 the Czechs were well on their way raising funds for Czech organizations. In February 1917 the *Bohemian Review*, an English language publication dedicated to the spreading of news about the Czech struggle for independence, stated:

> This winter will be remembered among the Czechs in the United States as the season for big bazaars. In almost every large city the Bohemians either held their own bazaars or participated in the Allied bazaars as one of the races ranged on the side of the ten nations.

A bazaar given by Bohemians in New York netted $23,000 for the cause of Czech independence. In January Chicago's Czechs and Slovaks took part in the Chicago Allied Bazaar held at the Chicago Coliseum, and sold $7,000 worth of goods donated by their community. The Bohemian National Alliance sold nearly ten thousand advance tickets to the rally. On the last day of the bazaar, "Slav Day," Czech artists furnished the greater part of the musical and cabaret program.

After this event the Chicago Czech community began to prepare for their own bazaar to be held from March 3 to March 10, 1917 at Pilsen Park. Organizers hoped to exceed the amount of money collected in New York, but cautioned that this would be difficult as each of the Bohemian settlements in Chicago had already held local bazaars and all took part in the Allied bazaar at the Coliseum.[21]

---

19. *Denni Hlasatel*, August 12, 1914; August 14, 1914; August 22, 1914.

20. Pergler, *America in the Struggle*, Prefatory Note.

21. *The Bohemian Review* (February 1917), p. 17.

The eight day March 1917 bazaar at Pilsen Park was a huge success. Billed as the biggest event in the history of the community, it raised $40,000 for the Czech cause. Bohemian National Alliance organizers claimed they could have raised even more money, but they could not get a bigger hall than the Pilsen Park Pavilion. The cause of Bohemian independence was obviously uniting the fragmented Czech-American community. That year saw more mass meetings at Pilsen Park and across the country, especially after the American declaration of war in April.[22]

On June 12, 1917 the gap between Freethinker and Roman Catholic was finally overcome as representatives from all parts of the Bohemian community promised their full cooperation in a mass meeting at Pilsen Park. More rallies followed. In August the Russian Commission visited Chicago representing the new Kerensky government in Moscow. A rally was organized by the Bohemian National Alliance in honor of the Czech regiment which had fought so bravely on the side of the Russians at Tarnopol. Professor George Lomonossov of the Russian Commission addressed the meeting of some 6,000 Bohemians who had waited nearly three hours for his arrival at Pilsen Park. A Czech flag was presented to Lomonossov with the request that he deliver it to the Czechoslovak regiments. Lomonossov kissed its folds upon receiving the standard, and the crowd responded with great enthusiasm for the Russians and the Czech regiments. The following Labor Day the Bohemian National Alliance held another rally at Pilsen Park drawing 30,000 participants. The festival was preceded by a parade in which members of the Catholic Workmen's Association, the Bohemian-American Foresters, the Bohemian-American Union, the Bohemian National Alliance, the Union of Catholic Sokols, the Czech Butcher Employees' Educational Club, the American Czech Sokol, and the Slovak League took part. The parade was particularly colorful because the Sokols were on horseback and wore their blue shirts.[23]

As Charles Pergler, a Czech-American activist who later became an important member of the Czechoslovak government, stated the general movement for Czechoslovak independence was not only a European idea, but also an American one. Certainly the Chicago Czech community played a vital role in this movement that led to the famous Pittsburgh agreement concerning the creation of a Czecho-Slovak state on May 31, 1918, and the

22. *The Bohemian Review* (March 1917), inside cover; (April 1917), p. 15.

23. *The Bohemian Review* (July 1917), p. 15; (September 1917), p. 16; (October 1917), p. 13; McCarthy, "Bohemians in Chicago," p. 76.23.

eventual creation of Czechoslovakia on October 28,1918.[24] Pilsen Park had provided a physical space where much of the drama of this movement was played out.

24. Pergler, *America in the Struggle*, p. 19. For a discussion of the Slovak community's role in the creation of the new state see M. Mark Stolarik, *Slovaks in Canada and the United States, 1870–1990* (Ottawa, Canada: University of Ottawa, 1992), p. 13 and M. Mark Stolarik, *The Role of Slovaks in the Creation of Czecho–Slovakia, 1914–1918* (Rome: Slovak Institute, 1968).

Chapter 11

THE IRON GUARD: ITS PLACE IN ROMANIAN HISTORY

Stephen Fischer–Galati

The Iron Guard, perhaps the most notorious fascist organization of interwar and wartime Eastern Europe, has had the fewest historians. The reasons for this seemingly abnormal situation are easy to find: the Iron Guard is still among the most active of contemporary fascist organizations in the world. It is also, and has always been, among the most secretive political organizations and for good reasons. The rulers of interwar Romania, and for that matter even of wartime Romania after the destruction of the Guard, were determined to ferret out the leaders and infiltrate the units which comprised the Iron Guard. Of course, the mystical–fraternal pattern of organization and behavior expected of all members of the Guard precluded divulgence of data to anyone but the most trusted members of the hierarchy. After World War II, the legionaries of the Guard whether in Spain, or in Germany, or in Argentina, or in the United States have, as a matter of course, declined to reveal any information to researchers or other individuals concerned with the study of the fascist movement in Romania.

Unavailable from members or ex-members of the Guard data is similarly unobtainable from non-Guardist sources. Except for standard newspapers and periodicals devoted to dissemination of standard political theology and anti-Semitic polemic such as *Porunca Vremii* (Commandment of the Times) or *Buna Vestire* (Glad Tidings), no reliable sources are to be found. The Romanian archives are closed on that subject, also for good reasons. Aside from the danger that investigation of the materials would reveal the previous history of converts to the national socialism of the left, systematic research in what is still considered to be a "non-topic" would *de facto* legitimize the historic existence of the Iron Guard and its program whose actual character, not to mention validity, are denied even by the post-communist Romanian regime. The main, well-supplied repository of information accessible to students of the Romanian fascist movement is located in Israel. However, the value of that material is limited by its almost exclusive concern with the Jewish Question. Important as that question is for understanding fascist activities in Romania in the interwar and wartime years and, for that matter, even for the postwar work of the exiled Guardists, it is not the only question which must be considered by students of the Guard and of Romanian fascism. In sum, the researcher cannot at this time, nor most likely in the foreseeable future, hope to secure access to materials which would allow investigation of any but the most basic problems connected with the fascist movement in Romania.

This is not to say that certain historians and political scientists working in Romania and abroad have not attempted to write accounts of varying merit on one or another aspect of Romanian fascism. Yet, with the notable exception of work by non-Romanian historians, primarily by Eugen Weber[1] and Nicholas Nagy-Talavera[2], little of any major significance has been produced. It should be noted, however, that not even Weber or Nagy-Talavera have been able to come to grips with numerous unclear, unknown, and unresolved relevant issues albeit for lack of reliable source material. Only the most fragmentary data are available on membership, past and present. The social composition of the membership, the age structure, the educational level, and other essential sociological data are obtainable only through extrapolation and educated guesswork, hardly a scientific basis for nonhistorians. Equally sketchy are the data pertaining to specific motivations for individuals' joining the Iron Guard although intelligent assumptions can, and have been, made on the basis of fragmentary materials and personal acquaintance with members of the Guard. Similarly, very little is known about the current status of former members of the Guard, except for those members who have flaunted their perennial status and longevity as Guardists, since few are those who would willingly identify activists, converts, or proselytizers.

This rather lengthy, negative, and pessimistic foreword should normally

1. Eugen Weber's studies on Romanian fascism are numerous. The most significant is "Romania" in *The European Right*, Hans Rogger and Eugen Weber, eds. (Berkeley: University of California Press, 1966), pp. 501–574.

2. Nicholas M. Nagy–Talavera, *The Green Shirts and the Others*. (Stanford: Hoover Institution Press, 1970).

act as a deterrent to serious scholarship. *A faute de mieux*, and for the sake of stimulating discussion through reaction to probably questionable assumptions and hypotheses, the present writer has been forced to limit his discussion of fascism in Romania to an analytical description of what is known about the Guardist movement as such and within the broad framework of national socialism in Romania. The essay does not pretend to be a definitive statement; at best it is a tentative introduction to a fascist movement and to a series of questions, mostly unanswered, related to that movement.

Henry Roberts, the eminent student of interwar Romanian politics, has distinguished four elements of international fascism that were in one form or another recognizable in the Romanian movement.[3] In order of growing significance, Romanian fascism represented the "death rattle of capitalism," a national chauvinist manifestation, a form of dictatorship plus hooliganism, and an expression of anti-Semitism and racial glorification. Of these, the first element is the least significant. Capitalism, identified in Romania with urban, Jewish-dominated ownership or control of the banking, commercial, and industrial network was roundly attacked by the followers of Romanian fascism. But historically the target of their attacks has been the Jewish "arendas"—the *locum tenens* of the absentee landlord of pre-World War I years. The forerunners of the anticapitalist fascists of the interwar era were the agrarian, anti-Semitic populists of the early nineteenth century, the followers of Constantin Stere.[4] As glorifiers of the peasant and opponents of his exploitation by the then most powerful capitalist figure, the Jewish "corporation," the populists assumed the role of friends of the masses and defenders of their interests. But the masses were generally equated with the peasantry even after the "second emancipation" of 1917-21 and the socioeconomic reorganization of the village after World War I. The industrial masses never enjoyed the same privileged position as the rural in fascist ideology. The distinction between agrarian and industrial capitalism remained valid throughout the interwar years: Guardists were friends of the peasant, and their anticapitalism bore that stamp. Industrial capitalists were tolerated perhaps because they were the principal financiers of the fascist movement whose doctrines had little effect on their industrial empires. Guardist anticapitalism combined the populist and the anti-Semitic strands. The success of Romanian fascism was as much a consequence of mass reaction to

---

3. Henry L. Roberts, *Rumania: Political Problems of an Agrarian State*. (New Haven: Yale University Press, 1951), p. 223.

4. On populism and Stere's ideology consult Roberts, *Rumania*, pp. 142–156.

134 ESSAYS IN RUSSIAN AND EAST EUROPEAN HISTORY

socioeconomic proposals by the Guardist leadership as of popular acceptance of anti–Semitic slogans and policies.

It is noteworthy that all Romanian "fascists" advocated populist doctrines at one time or another albeit in varying degrees. Populism was vociferously expounded by members of the Iron Guardist movement led by Corneliu Zelea Codreanu, but even the exclusively anti-Semitic LANC (League of National Christian Defense) headed by Professor A.C. Cuza initially sought the support of the peasantry in its struggle against the Jewish entrepreneur and merchant—the League's whipping boy and alleged exploiter of the Romanian peasantry. Cuza abandoned the peasants in the twenties—he considered them satisfied by the agrarian reform—and concentrated on the Jew, now the enemy of all Romanians. For Cuza the very presence of Jews in Romania was intolerable. The Jews had to be isolated, their activities boycotted by Romanians, and acts of violence against the Jewish population were condoned if not necessarily encouraged. Codreanu shared Cuza's crude anti-Semitism but only within the framework of a complex socioeconomic and political philosophy which in the early thirties became the doctrine of "pure" Romanian fascism.[5]

In this doctrine anti-capitalism was a cornerstone. But since the peasants were unresponsive to Codreanu's appeals as long as the National Peasant Party was regarded as the representative of their political interests, Codreanu's men concentrated temporarily on the Jew and his alleged friend and the peasant's enemy, the communist. It was during the early years of King Carol's reign that the Guardist "anti-Judaeo-Communist Christian crusade" assumed clear expression. To Codreanu and his associates the King stood for betrayal of true Romanian values as evidenced by his association with Magda Lupescu, his Jewish mistress, appeasement of Jews in general, a search for reconciliation with the Soviet Union, and a basically unfriendly attitude toward Mussolini's fascism. The replacement of the Prime Minister Iuliu Maniu by men of lesser nationalist orientation and particularly the appointment by the King of the "pro-Jewish" Duca regime, which eventually outlawed the Legion, provided a basis for testing the strength of nationalist anti-Semitic and anti-communist sentiments among the population at

---

5. Codreanu's political philosophy is contained in Corneliu Zelea Codreanu, *Pentru Legionari*. (Bucureşti: Editura Mişcării Legionare, 1937). The program of the Legion of Archangel Michael is available in an English translation in Stephen Fischer–Galati, *Twentieth Century Europe: A Documentary History*. (Philadelphia: Lippincott, 1956), pp. 137–140.

large. Duca's assassination by the Guard and the minimal consequences of that criminal action convinced Codreanu that his was not a lost cause.[6] It is a misrepresentation of the events of the early thirties to equate the Legionaries' actual power with the results of popular elections held in that period. Official tallies reflected a falsification of actual results and the continuing allegiance of voters sympathetic to Codreanu's cause to more established parties offering programs superficially similar to the Guard's. Any meaningful appraisal of the actual strength and following of the Legion of Archangel Michael became possible only after the establishment by Codreanu of a formal political party, *Totul Pentru Tară* (All For The Fatherland) and publication of its program in 1934. The Guardists' power was by no means negligible.[7]

That power in 1934 was intimately related to the broad dissatisfaction with existing economic conditions which was prevalent among the Romanian peasantry, the unemployed or frustrated urban intelligentsia, the bureaucracy, and the working class. It would be erroneous, however, to assume that economic problems alone accounted for the success of Codreanu's legionaries. It is true that *Totul Pentru Tară* promised palliatives and even solutions for the general *malaise* that engulfed Romanian society. It is also true that Codreanu attacked the traditional corruption, inaction, and ineffectualness of the political establishment and the prevalent social injustice and immobility with exceptional vigor and determination. However, it was the populist, anti-Semitic doctrine, which constituted the very essence of the political philosophy of the Iron Guard, which accounted for the success of Codreanu and his followers. That doctrine was elementary.[8] It may be summarized as consisting of a political crusade for the regeneration of true Romanian values by Romanians and for the benefit of oppressed Romanians, primarily the Romanian peasant. According to Codreanu and his fellow ideologues these Romanian values, incorporated in the Romanian Orthodox Christian tradition, faith, hard work, devotion to the country, cleanliness, spiritual purity and the like had been corrupted by alien elements—the Jews and Jew-like politicians. The Jews were sucking the lifeblood of the Romanians through domination of the country's economy, free professions, edu-

---

6. See in particular Weber, "Romania," pp. 547–548.

7. Very revealing are Codreanu's own statements contained in Corneliu Zelea Codreanu, *Circulări și Manifeste 1927–1938*. (București: Editura Mişcării Legionare, 1941). See also note 5 above.

8. Notes 5 and 7 above provide the basic bibliography on doctrinal matters.

cational system, and by penetration of Romania's political life through the buying of politicians and securing the protection of the political establishment. The Jews, loud, greedy, dirty, uncouth, lovers of pornography, and possessors of other vices, were poisoning the Romanian spirit. These leeches on the Romanian body politic and the physical and spiritual values of the Romanians had to be removed from Romanian life by isolation, boycott, and physical violence. Their wealth was to be confiscated and redistributed among the needy Romanian masses. They had to be driven out of Romania.[9] In the last analysis Codreanu held out national rejuvenation, moral rearmament, and above all a national Christian social and moral crusade against all betrayers of what the Legionaries believed to be the true national historic legacy. That legacy was ultimately identified with the supremacy of the Christian Romanian peasant and his supporters and friends. The peasant, led by the Guard, would develop a Romania for the Romanians over the dead bodies of Judaeo-Communists and all other exponents of non-Christian, non-Romanian, political and socio-economic philosophies.

Thus, in terms of Roberts' criteria and definitions, only a specific brand of anti-Semitism could be identified as an integral component of Guardist fascism in 1934. The Legionaries had no monopoly on chauvinism, hooliganism, and notions of dictatorship. Chauvinism was not an indispensable part of their political philosophy; their ideas on dictatorship were still poorly defined; hooliganism was kept within bounds. Idealism and mysticism pervaded the movement. But this was to change under the impact of domestic political reaction against the potentially explosive doctrine of the Guardists and of the rapid progress recorded by fascism in Germany, Italy, and Spain.[10]

The strength of the Legionaries in 1934 has never been determined with any degree of accuracy. The most reliable estimates indicate the existence of approximately 4,000 basic political units—the so-called "cuiburi" (nests)—with a total membership not in excess of 50,000. It is also estimated that the overwhelming majority of the members of the Guard came from the ranks of university students, white collar workers, and intellectuals located in Bucharest, Iaşi, and other urban centers. Be this as it may, the

9.   A modern restatement and justification of these arguments was provided by Horia Sima in *Osservazioni sull' articolo del R.P. Angelo Martini S.I. "La Santa Sede e gli ebrei della Romania durante la seconda guerra mondiale"* published in 1963 in the "Colecţia Omul Nou."

10. The basic work on this question remains Andreas Hillgruber's *Hitler, König Carol und Marschall Antonescu: Die deutsch–rumänischen Beziehungen, 1938–1944.* (Wiesbaden: Steiner, 1954).

effectiveness of the preachings of rural reform and anti-Semitic doctrine by an increasingly larger number of adherents assumed alarming proportions between 1934 and 1937.[11] During these years the proselytizing focussed onto the village where the response of the masses was generally responsive and frequently enthusiastic. The Guardists, however, were also welcomed by the clergy, anxious to participate in Christian reform, by school-teachers, and by an ever growing number of students, intellectuals, and bureaucrats who for one reason or another believed in moral rejuvenation and, in any event, were anti-Semitic. By the beginning of 1937 the size of the Guard had apparently tripled, yet the danger it posed to the ruling establishment and to the country as a whole was still underestimated by all political parties except those concerned with the attitude of the peasantry.[12] The Legionaries' slogan "Omul şi Pogonul" (Man and his Land) threatened the stability of the village because of the radical solutions to the agrarian problems which it propounded. This was clearly recognized by the National Peasant Party and by the Plowmen's Front and its ideological ally, the disorganized Communist Party. The dominant wing of the National Peasant Party, headed by Iuliu Maniu, favored an *Ausgleich* with the Legion in the common political struggle against the ruling National Liberal Party and its patron, King Carol II. And it was precisely the conclusion of an electoral pact between Maniu and Codreanu prior to the national elections of December 1937 which alerted the King and his allies to the dangers posed to the ruling establishment by the ever enlarged scope of Codreanu's activities.

1937 was the crucial year for the Iron Guard. It was the year of intensification of financial and political contacts with Mussolini's Italy and Hitler's Germany, the year in which the number of financial contributors derived from the Romanian industrial and financial community increased dramatically, the year of stocktaking of the lessons gained by activists in the Spanish Civil War and, in the last analysis, the year in which the Guard hoped to gain a share of political power by legitimate means at the polls in December. It is true that these activities, changes, and expectations were limited in scope in that not even Codreanu envisaged the establishment of a Legionary state in the foreseeable future. But it is significant that the political crisis which was triggered off by the activities of the Guard prior to and by

---

11. Nagy–Talavera, *Green Shirts*, pp. 292–293.

12. Stephen Fischer–Galati, *The New Rumania: From People's Democracy to Socialist Republic*. (Cambridge, Mass.: The M.I.T Press, 1967), pp. 10–16.

King Carol after the elections of 1937 was ultimately a function of the actual strength of Romanian fascism.

The official results of this last so-called "free" Romanian election of December 1937 resulted in the defeat of the National Liberal government, which was unable to muster the minimum 40 percent of the vote required to insure its continuation in power.[13] The defeat was ascribed to the unexpected size of the Guardist vote, reported at approximately 16 percent of the ballots cast. It is conceded by contemporary political observers that the actual fascist vote was well above that percentage. In fact, the King's decision not to proclaim the National Liberals winners but instead to hand over the government to the right-wing coalition of Octavian Goga and A.C. Cuza was a clear reflection of his realization that the country was leaning toward the extreme right. The appointment of the Goga-Cuza cabinet was a stopgap measure in anticipation of the establishment of an outright royal dictatorship. The King's maneuver of December 1937 revealed his great political acumen and also his shock over the extent of Guardist penetration into the society at large. It would be erroneous to assume, as some of the analysts of the Romanian fascist movement have done, that the size of the Guardist vote merely reflected the anti-Semitic sentiment of the Romanian population. That this was not the case was amply proven by the failure of the Goga-Cuza electoral coalition to obtain more than 9 percent of the total popular vote or to stay in power for more than a few weeks on the basis of their purely nationalistic and specifically anti-Semitic program. The success of the Guard, as Carol realized, was based on the broad support it received from the village and the urban bureaucracy and intelligentsia. To counter this trend and to secure the neutrality, if not necessarily the outright cessation of support by the foreign and domestic sponsors of the Guard, Carol decided in February 1938 to substitute monarcho-fascism for legionary-fascism and in the process to destroy the power base of Codreanu and his followers. After February 1938 a life and death struggle began between the King and the Iron Guard during which the very character of Romanian fascism was profoundly altered.

The royal dictatorship, "monarcho-fascist" as it has been characterized by its detractors, had few of the characteristics ascribed by Roberts to fascist movements. It was not anticapitalistic, it was only moderately anti-Semitic and chauvinistic, and it contained no elements of racial glorification and hooliganism. It was, however, a dictatorship that "borrowed" the

---

13. Roberts, *Rumania*, pp. 191–192.

essential tenets of Guardist philosophy: nationalist socio-reformism and national renaissance. It did lack, however, the crusading spirit directed, particularly after the end of the Spanish Civil War, by Guardist activists against the "Judaeo-Communist conspiracy" in all its manifestations. The abolition of political parties and the establishment of "collective democracy" under the leadership of the King in the *Frontul Renaşterii Naţionale* (The Front of National Rebirth) was designed to provide a substitute for the militant idealism and reformism of Codreanu and his associates. His failure to attain this goal was ultimately due to the monarch's inability to destroy the Guard as a political force in Romania. By 1938 the membership of the outlawed Guard was estimated at some 350,000 men and women dedicated to Codreanu and his cause.[14] Carol's ultimate solution, arrest and execution of Corneliu Zelea Codreanu and his closest associates in November 1938 and mass extermination of Legionaries in the months immediately following Codreanu's death was also a failure in that it merely strengthened the determination of the Romanian right to rid itself of Carol at all cost. And, for the first time, the Guardists secured meaningful support from Nazi Germany which heretofore had merely extended moral encouragement and token financial assistance to the Legionaries, especially to those who had fought in the Spanish Civil War. Forced underground, the survivors of the purge assumed the role of martyrs and avengers of the dead. Between 1938 and 1940 they became the executioners of Carol's "accomplices," hooligans and assassins dedicated to the physical annihilation of their mortal enemies: Jews, communists, and royalists. In the process they abandoned their idealism and plans for nationalist social reform in the village, the factory, and the bureaucracy. The Romanian fascists lost their original political identity and with it their political *raison d'être*, between the fall of 1938 and the summer of 1940, when the Guard defeated its archenemy, Carol II, and finally gained power.

The struggle for power between Carol and the Guard was deceptively uneven before 1940. If Carol had the upper hand in 1938 it was because the Germans were not ready, before Munich, to impose their dictates on Romania. Their interests were sufficiently safeguarded, although superficially and temporarily, by the Carolist dictatorship and the efficiency of the King's major-domo, Armand Călinescu. Nevertheless, the Germans and their sympathizers in Romania were not out of touch with the remnants of the Legion, which to them represented a lever and alternative to the "monarcho-

14. Nagy–Talavera, *Green Shirts*, p. 293.

fascists." Throughout 1939 the Nazis supported the rejuvenation of the still illegal Guard. By September 1939, as Poland's defeat was recorded, the Guard assassinated Călinescu in cold blood. And as Germany's military and political achievements became increasingly more spectacular and detrimental to Romania's national interests, the Guard reappeared as the defender of the interests of Romania against bolshevism and Judaism, as champion of true militant Romanianism, as avenger of treacherous royalism, as rectifier of all ills afflicting Romanian society and politics. The Legionaries hour came in September 1940 when after the Vienna Diktat Carol was forced to abdicate and monarcho-fascism came to an inglorious end. As the King fled the country his son, Michael, entrusted power to the Iron Guard and the proGuardist military leaders who forced Carol's abdication headed by General Ion Antonescu. A new crusade, anti-communist, antiSemitic, and anti-all opponents of the Guard were initiated by the "new" Iron Guard led by power-hungry men like Horia Sima and other betrayers of the original legionary goals.[15] The triumph of legionary-fascism was short lived not because the National Legionary State which was set up in September 1940 did not correspond to the interests of the Romanian population. In fact, the number of "Green Shirts" worn with pride and arrogance by uncountable men and women from all walks of life in 1940 bore testimony to the popularity of Antonescu's and Sima's regime. But the "new Guard" was so disruptive to the country's economy and engaged in such extreme acts of hooliganism and crime against their enemies that it had to be forcibly removed from power by the unlikely coalition of General Antonescu and the German High Command after a bloody revolt by militant Guardists in January 1941. Still, the decimation of the Guardist revolutionaries did not mark the end of fascism or of the Guardist movement.

Antonescu ruled Romania as a fascist military dictatorship after January 1941.[16] His dictatorship, however, differed from that of his predecessors and of contemporary European counterparts in significant respects. He adopted many of the corporatist features characteristic of Carol's regime and sought the support of traditional conservative political groups and of responsible Legionaries for the pursuit of an anticommunist and nationalist crusade of his own. It is noteworthy that Antonescu rooted out all manifes-

15. An excellent discussion of these problems in Roberts, *Rumania*, pp. 223–235.

16. Antonescu's views are clearly expressed in his public statements contained in Ion Antonescu, *Generalul Antonescu către țară, 6 Septemvrie 1940–22 Iunie 1941*. (București: Luceafărul, 1941).

tations of hooliganism and did not claim the racist and anti-Semitic Guardist legacy. His reformist tendencies were closer to Carol's than Codreanu's concentrating, albeit for military purposes, on the modernization of industry and agriculture. His crucial error, inherent in the *raison d'être* of his dictatorship, was in focusing the national effort onto the pursuit of an anti-Russian, anti-communist, military campaign. He thus was the forerunner of the explicitly anti-Bolshevik orientation that became the fascists' trade-mark after World War II. Antonescu's de facto repudiation of anti-Semitism and hooliganism was not endorsed, however, by the Guardist leaders in exile in Germany, or Spain, or Argentina until after the final debacle of the Third Reich. It was only at that time that Sima and his retinues, old and new, reassumed the role of social reformers bent on "liberating" Romania from communism.

The revamped fascists enjoyed more than a modicum of success, even though their political successors, the Romanian communists, assumed anti-Russian positions themselves and carried out, as Romanian national communists, social reforms that had been anticipated by Codreanu and initiated by Carol and Antonescu. And since the collapse of Ceausescu's regime they continue to enjoy more than a modicum of success among Romanians in exile and in Romania proper as champions of anticommunism, and as true nationalist social reformers rooted in the history of twentieth century Romania. In truth, however, their primary historic significance rests in their assumption of the role of promoters and defenders of Romanianism.

Chapter 12

EDOUARD BENEŠ ET LA FRANCE, 1918–1938

Bernard Michel

Beneš n'a cessé de manifester sa passion pour la France et son attachement à la politique française et à ses hommes d'Etat. Homme de conceptions claires, il avait gardé de ses années d'enseignement un goût affirmé pour la pédagogie: il aimait expliquer, justifier, prévoir, dans de vastes tours d'horizon qui sont très proches de la tradition française. Ses adversaires, surtout allemands, hongrois, italiens cherchaient en vain à le faire passer pour tortueux et hypocrite. Son arme principale fut toujours au contraire d'expliquer sa politique sur la place publique.

I – Les liens personnels avec la France.

Il a eu une formation française. Jeune étudiant, il est arrivé à Paris en 1905 pour y faire d'abord des études sur la langue française. Après avoir suivi avec passion des cours d'histoire et de droit, il s'est tourné vers la science politique. Sous la direction de Louis Eisenmann, il a soutenu en 1908 sa thèse de doctorat à Dijon sur *le problème autrichien et la question tchèque.*

Il a évoqué dans ses *Souvenirs de guerre et de révolution* ces années de formation:

> Jeune étudiant, venant d'un milieu qui connaissait les difficultés de la vie, n'ayant pu mener à bien mes études qu'au prix de rudes efforts, supportant avec peine le régime politique et social qui pesait sur ma patrie, je fus très vite et complètement enveloppé par l'atmosphère de la France et de Paris. Je subis très fortement l'influence de toute la tradition révolutionnaire française et parisienne, je fus séduit par les formules révolutionnaires et radicales des syndicalistes français ainsi

que des autres partis de gauche. Je m'intéressai aux doctrines extrémistes, syndicalisme révolutionnaire, socialisme, antimilitarisme et anarchisme français: j'étudiai les révolutions française et russe jusque dans leurs ramifications extrémistes.[1]

Ces années de travail acharné, d'ouverture sur la vie politique française l'ont profondément marqué. Ensuite de 1915 à 1918, il est revenu à Paris pour y fonder le Conseil National tchèque et lutter pour l'indépendance. D'abord exilé modeste, tenu en marge, il n'a cessé de pénétrer patiemment dans la vie politique française pour devenir, au printemps 1918, un interlocuteur officieux, puis officiel des pays alliés.

Dans le livre d'hommages publié en 1934 pour son 50e anniversaire, les journalistes Pierre Quirielle et Etienne Fournol, le professeur Eisenmann et Madame Boas de Jouvenel ont évoqué son action à Paris avant et pendant la guerre.[2]

Il a noué des liens personnels avec le personnel politique français. Homme de gauche, il a eu des relations privilégiées avec les dirigeants de ces partis. Franc–maçon, il a été l'interlocuteur du Grand Orient de France. Dans les années 1920, il est très lié à Aristide Briand et au secrétaire général du Quai d'Orsay, Philippe Berthelot. Il est reçu sans rendez–vous par le ministre des Affaires Etrangères, tout comme le ministre de Tchécoslovaquie à Paris, le Slovaque Stefan Osusky. C'est seulement en 1920, lorsque Paléologue fut un temps secrétaire général, que son influence subit une courte éclipse de quelques mois.

Dans les années 1930, une partie de la gauche française, socialistes, radicaux, francs–maçons, furent touchés par le pacifisme. Pragmatique, Beneš trouve alors des appuis solides dans des gouvernements de droite, auprès de Tardieu en 1932, et de Barthou en 1934. Comme en témoigne Léon Noël, ministre de France à Prague: "En 1932, peu aprés mon arrivée, alors qu'Herriot était président du Conseil et ministre des Affairs Etrangères, il ne me cacha pas qu'il regrettait André Tardieu 'parce qu'il sait ce qu'il veut.' Maintes fois, il me répéta en 1933 et avant le 6 février 1934 que la formation, en France, d'un gouvernement d'union nationale lui semblait indispensable."[3] Après l'affaiblissement de la politique française en 1933,

---

1. Beneš (Edouard). Souvenirs de guerre et de révolution. 1914–1918. Paris, Leroux, 1928. I p. 3–4.

2. 50 let Eduarda Beneše (les cinquante ans d'Edourd Beneš). Prague, 1934. p. 323–354.

3. Noel (Léon). La Tchécoslovaquie d'avant Munich. Paris Institut d'Etudes Slaves, Sorbonne, 1982. p. 97.

avec l'arrivée d'Hitler au pouvoir et la négociation du Pacte à Quatre, il est optimiste au début de 1934. A la réunion de la Petite Entente à Zagreb, le 22 janvier 1934,

Monsieur Beneš informe ses collègues des impressions de son voyage à Paris. Il constate que la ligne générale de la politique étrangère française est redressée et que l'on s'est rendu compte de ce que représente la Petite Entente. Il estime que même une crise éventuelle du Gouvernement actuel, même s'il devait être remplacé par un Gouvernement des gauches ou de concentration nationals ne pourrait porter atteinte à cette ligne.[4]

Ses relations avec Delbos, de 1936 à 1938, furent chaleureuses, mais limitées par l'absence d' initiatives de la politique extérieure française. Il semble avoir jugé sévèrement l'action du Front Populaire. Mais il gardait des illusions sur Léon Blum. A Louise Weiss, il déclara en mars 1937: "je suis sûr de Léon Blum. Il défendra la Tchécoslovaquie, me répeté Beneš obstiné."[5]

En dehors de ses contacts personnels avec les milieux politiques français, Beneš utilisait des envoyés personnels: Hubert Ripka, journalists, dans les milieux de gauche, radicaux et socialistes; le chanoine Dvornik dans les milieux de la droite catholique.[6] Lorsque Beneš, en 1935, devint président de la République, ces contacts indirects complétèrent les informations que recueillait Kamil Krofta, son successeur au poste de ministre des Affaires Etrangères. Lors de la crise de septembre 1938, il envoya en mission à Paris auprès de Léon Blum et des socialistes français Jaromir Nečas, ministre des Affaires sociales et membre influent de la Social-Démocratie tchèque.[7]

Par ailleurs, Beneš contrôlait une partie de la presse française, grâce à la section de la presse du ministère des Affaires Etrangères que dirigea durant toute l'entre deux guerres Jan Hajek. Il versait des sommes considérables

---

4. Procès verbal de la 3e session ordinaire de la Petite Entente, tenue à Zagreb au Palais de la Banovine le 22 janvier 1934. Archiv Ministerstva Zahranicných věci (AMZV). Archives du Ministère des Affaires Etrangères. Prague, Carton 21, Malá Dohoda (Petite Entente).

5. Weiss (Louise), Mémoires d'une Européenne, III. Paris, Payot. p.153–156.

6. Par exemple, rapport de Ripka sur ses conversations à Paris en septembre 1933. AMZV. Kroftuv Fond (Fonds Krofta). Carton 26, rapport de František Dvornik, 2 mars 1934. Idem carton 13, conversation de Ripka avec le Président Beneš, 25 mai 1936. Ibidem.

7. Sur la mission Necas, voir mon article: l'action de Stefan Osusky, ministre plénipotentiaire de Tchécoslovaquie à Paris et le dossier Jaromir Necas, présenté par Antoine Mares. Munich 1938. Mythes et réalités. Revue des Etudes Slaves, Paris 1979.

au *Temps* (160.000 francs par an en 1925 et 200.000 francs en 1927), au *Petit Parisien*, à des agences de presse et à du nombreux journalistes, dont Pierre Quirielle, Lapradelle, Milioukov. Le budget total représentait 698.000 francs en 1925, mais, en 1938, 1 million 1/2 de francs.[8] Beneš s'assurait donc une opinion publique favorable pendant presque toute la période. Mais en 1938, la pression intérieure du pacifisme et extérieure de la propaganda allemande neutralisa l'influence tchèque en France.

Beneš entretint avec les diplomates français en poste à Prague des relations confiantes. Lorsque Beneš fut menacé en Juin 1926 de perdre ses fonctions de ministre, pour des raisons de politique intérieure, le ministre de France Joseph Couget lui accorda ouvertement son soutien. S'il quittait son poste: "son pays perdrait au moins cinquante pour cent de l'influence et de l'autorité qu'il a obtenu pour lui en Europe."[9]

Charles-Roux (1926–1932) apprécia l'efficacité de Beneš. Mais il était parfois agacé de découvrir que la presse française recevait directement ses informations de la propaganda officielle tchèque, sans esprit critique et sans passer par la légation. Le zèle des journalistes français lui paraissait même excessif.[10]

Léon Noël (1932–1935) porte sur Beneš un jugement très favorable.

> On s'est plu à accuser Beneš de fourberie et de duplicité. J'ignore ce qu'il pouvait être avec d'autres mais durant des années difficiles, je l'ai constamment trouvé, envers la France et envers moi-même, parfaitement loyal.

> Mon prédécesseur, Charles-Roux, fit la même constatation. Les représentants de la France ont toujours trouvé en lui un partenaire franc et fidèle. Son comportement envers eux était aussi différent que possible de la méfiance réticente et malveillante d'un Beck, comme de la tumultueuse indiscrétion d'un Titulescu.

> Beneš aimait sincèrement notre pays. Il gardait un souvenir reconnaissant des années de jeunesse pendant lesquelles, à Paris et à Dijon, il s'était nourri de notre science, pénétré de nos idées.

> En réponse au toast qu'il m'adressa, avant mon départ de Prague, au

---

8. Le livre de Urban (Rudolf). Demokratenpresse im Lichte der Prager Geheimakten. Prag, 1943, donne une documentation de première main, p.16–80.

9. Lettre de Couget à Briand, 22 juin 1926. Ministère des Affaires Etrangères. Tchécoslovaquie 69, p. 177–178.

10. Wandycz (Piotr). The Twilight of French Eastern Alliances, 1926–1936. French-Czechoslovak-Polish Relations from Locarno to the Remilitarization of the Rhineland. Princeton University Press, 1988, p. 84–85.

déjeuner que sa femme et lui nous offrirent au palais Černin, je lui dis, sans flatterie aucune que ma longue fréquentation avec lui m'avait démontré qu'un homme d'Etat pouvait unir, à une extrême habileté, une loyauté sans faille. Il se montra ému de ce qui n'était dans ma bouche que la simple constatation d'un fait.[11]

II – La fidélité à l'alliance avec la France.

Il convient de rappeler qu'entre les deux guerres, il existe des systèmes d'alliances entre les peuples, fondés sur des intérêts communs et des affinités mutuelles. Il n'existe pas de blocs idéologiques, comme après 1948. L'alliance avec la France n'exclut pas une diplomatie multilatérale. Beneš joue aussi sa propre carte à la Société des Nations, se présente en médiateur entre les Grandes Puissances. Son influence dans la Petite Entente lui donne une liberté d'action qu'il a su utiliser, en 1925 lors de Locarno ou en 1933, lors du Pacte à Quatre.

Les bases de l'alliance sont simples. Sortie victorieuse de la Guerre mondiale, la France apparait comme la première puissance militaire et diplomatique. Paris, centre financier pour les emprunts d'Etat et les investissements privés, apparait comme un appui essentiel pour renforcer l'indépendance économique de la Tchécoslovaquie, en prenant partout la relève des capitaux allemands d'Autriche.

Dans ses discours devant les commissions des Affaires étrangères de la Chambre des Députés et du Sénat, Beneš n'a pas cessé de présenter comme de tranquilles certitudes ses relations avec la France.

En 1928, il déclarait:

> Sur mon séjour en France et en Belgique, je n'ai rien de particulier à mettre en relief. Nos rapports sont fixés, inchangés, solidement amicaux et définitifs.[12]

En 1934, rendant hommage à Barthou, il parlait de ses entretiens à Paris avec le Président Gaston Doumergue et le nouveau ministre des Affaires Etrangères, Pierre Laval.

> Nous avons examiné toutes les questions actuelles de la politique européenne de façon très approfondie et précise pour l'avenir des lignes de notre collaboration. Ce qui nous unit à la France dans tout cela, ce ne sont pas seulement les sympathies séculaires et l'amitié de nos deux

---

11. Noel (Léon). La Tchécoslovaquie d'avant Munich. Livre cité p. 74–75.

12. La situation internationale et la politique étrangère tchécoslovaque, 6 juin 1928. Sources et documents tchécoslovaques. No 6, Orbis. p. 19.

peuples, leurs intérêts communs politiques et spirituels; c'est avant tout notre absolue unité de vues sur l'avenir de l'Europe, Le communauté de nos idéals de liberté et de démocratie, l'identité de nos luttes pour un idéal de paix et d'humanité.[13]

En 1933, lors de l'adoption du nouveau pacte d'organisation de la Petite Entente, il faisait l'éloge de la politique française:

> C'est un simple fait historique que la France conserve encore aujourd'hui dans sa politique internationale les souvenirs et les principes de la Grande Révolution qui a donné naissance au principe des nationalités des jeunes peuples de l'Europe. C'est un fait que ces derniers ne l'oublient pas, qu'ils voient encore dans la France le représentant naturel de ces idées. C'est un fait que la France, au cours de son histoire, même après la Révolution, a fait dans d'innombrables circonstances la politique des petites nations et que pendant la Grande Guerre depuis 1917, elle s'est mise consciemment et résolument à la tête du mouvement de libération des moyens et des petits peuples de l'Europe.
>
> Ayant ainsi agi pendant la guerre, elle ne pouvait pas ne pas continuer cette politique des hostilités finies non seulement parce qu'elle est conforme à la tradition nationale et aux fondements de sa doctrine politique actuelle mais encore parce qu'elle correspond aux intérêts politiques réels de la France dans l'Europe d'après guerre.
>
> Est-il quelqu'un qui puisse imputer à crime à la France ce beau rôle: aider les jeunes nations de l'Europe à acquérir de nouvelles forces, à se donner une nouvélle organisation, à reprendre l'accomplissement de leur mission historique?...
>
> C'est encore un fait que, dans les durs moments d'après guerre, la France s'est toujours trouvée à leur côté, que ce fût dans la lutte contre les Habsbourg, dans celle qui se déroula à la Conférence de Gênes, dans leurs travaux à la Société des Nations, dans la question du révisionisme, dans les difficultés économiques et financières, dans la solution du problème des Réparations et des dettes de guerre, etc., etc. C'est aussi un fait que, dans le plus grand nombre des cas, les intérêts de la France ont été identiques aux leurs. Nos traités d'alliance avec la France, de même que notre convention d'amitié avec l'Italie, n'ont toutefois été mis en vigueur qu'en 1924 et ils n'ont fait que sanctionner un état de fait né de la simple marche des choses. Même sans ces accords, nos

---

13. Vers un regroupement des forces en Europe, 6 novembre 1934. Sources et documents tchécoslovaques. No 26, Orbis. p. 30.

14. Le pacte d'organisation de la Petite Entente et l'état actuel de la politique internationale, 1 mars 1933. Sources et documents tchécoslovaques No 20, Orbis. p. 34–37.

rapports envers la France ne seraient pas différents. C'est ce qu'on ne saurait jamais oublier des ces discussions.[14]

Ainsi, l'alliance française apparait comme une évidence que l'on ne pourrait discuter qu'en remettant en cause "la simple marche des choses." À la Conférence de la Petite Entente à Bucarest, du 2 au 5 mai 1931, Beneš proclamait fermement: "Je ne trahirai jamais mes amis, la France."[15] Il n'existe aucune alternative possible.

Qui dirige l'alliance? A premiere vue, c'est la France qui devrait en assurer la direction. Mais cela était contesté par Anatole de Monzie: "J'espère que nous changerons enfin de ministre des Affaires Etrangères. Nous avons le même depuis 1920: Beneš."[16]

Cette boutade avait une apparence de réalité. Les ministres français qui auraient dû donner une constante impulsion à l'alliance exercèrent souvent de manière relâchée leurs responsabilités. Lors des conférences internationales, au lieu de donner des instructions précises à leurs alliés, ils eurent souvent tendance à s'informer des intentions de Beneš.

Celui-ci répondait en 1933 aux critiques de sa politique, surtout à l'opposition de la droite tchécoslovaque, la Démocratie nationale:

> Le plus souvent, quand on parle des rapports entre la Petite Entente et ce pays, on se plait à dire que les Etats de la Petite Entente sont les vassaux de la France et que, grâce à eux, cette dernière établit son hégémonie sur l'Europe centrale, prêtant de l'argent à ces Etats et leur procurent des armes. Permettez de qualifier ces assertions comme elles le méritent: c'est un bavardage superficiel et vide de sens.

> Avant tout, je voudrais donner le coup de grâce à une légende qui est devenue une sorte de contre–vérité historique: la Petite Entente aurait, paraît–il, été créée par la France ou sous sa pression.

Et il rappelait comment, en 1920, la Petite Entente était née en réaction contre la politique du secrétaire général du Quai d'Orsay, Paléologue:

> Nous ne nions pas que certains milieux, en France même, n'ont pas toujours eu des vues justes sur les relations de la Petite Entente et de la France. Il y a eu ça et là des gens qui, attachés aux conceptions politiques d'un autre âge, avaient effectivement tendance à voir dans ces relations une sorte de rapport de subordination. Ils étaient dans l'erreur. Cela ne servirait ni les intérêts de la France, ni ceux de la Petite Entente. Et je puis dire que depuis quatorze ans que notre République fait sa politique

---

15. Compte rendu des entretiens du ministre Beneš à Bucarest lors de la conférence de la Petite Entente du 2 au 5 mai 1931. AMZV. Carton 21, Malá Dohoda (Petite Entente).

16. Noel (Léon). Livre cité p. 79.

17. Texte cité note 14 p. 32, 33, 39.

indépendante, il n'y a pas eu un seul cas où quelque chose de semblable se soit produit dans les rapports mutuels de nos deux Etats.[17] Recevant Barthou à Prague en avril 1934, Beneš soulignait qu'il n'avait jamais senti une hégémonie où domination de la France. Parlant de la Petite Entente, il affirmait: "Nos nations sont et veulent être vos jeunes 'soeurs' en Europe centrale."[18] Cela correspond à la réalité. Beneš n'a jamais hésité à dire clairement ses objections à certains tournants de la politique française, en 1920, en 1925, en 1933. Chaque fois, il a été entendu. A l'inverse, la France n'a pas toujours montré fermement sa volonté. Par exemple, elle n'a pas clairement imposé un accord militaire entre la Pologne et la Tchécoslovaquie qui aurait fermé le triangle de ses alliances orientales. C'est une des lacunes les plus éclatantes de sa politique dans l'entre deux guerres. Inversement, très souvent, Beneš conseille la France, même lorsque le ministre est une personnalité forte. Ainsi, dans un entretien à Genève le 15 mars 1932, Beneš s'attribue—comme il le fait très souvent—le rôle de mentor. "Je lui ai exposé comment je me représente la procédure; Tardieu approuva." Et ce dernier, au début de l'entretien, lui citait un discours qu'il venait de prononcer à la Chambre des Députés à Paris pour soutenir le projet d'emprunt tchécoslovaque. "Vous allez voir comment je me serai servi de votre aide–mémoire; cela a eu de l'effet."[19]

Même si Beneš montre souvent une certaine vanité dans ces notes, nous sentons constamment que les rapports entre les ministres français et le ministre tchéque sont empreints d'une grande liberté.

Même si le poids de la Tchécoslovaquie dans l'Europe de l'entre deux guerres était important, la réussite de la politique extérieure tient aussi à l'habileté personnelle de Beneš. Une petite puissance ne peut jouer un rôle que si son représentant à l'étranger jouit d'un fort prestige international. Jusqu'en 1938, les rapports entre les deux pays restent un modèle équilibré de coopération entre une grande et une petite puissance. Mais en 1938, quand les grandes puissances démocratiques cessent de remplir leurs fonctions face à l'Allemagne, le système cesse de fonctionner. Malgré Beneš, la Tchécoslovaquie ne pèse plus que son poids réel: celui d'une petite puissance qui ne peut seule s'opposer au déferlement de la puissance allemande, le jour où l'alliance française ne peut plus la protéger.

---

18. Texte de l'agence Havas, 26–28 avril 1934. Wandycz. Livre cité p. 351.

19. Compte rendu de l'entretien du ministre Benes avec Monsieur le Ministre Tardieu, 15 mars 1932 à 10 h, à l'hôtel des Bergues à Genève. AMZV Kroftuv Fond (Fonds Krofta) Carton 16.

Chapter 13

THE RUSSIFICATION THEME IN RECENT LATVIAN HISTORY

Andrejs Plakans

The scholars who under Edward Thaden's leadership cooperated in producing in 1981 the book *Russification in the Baltic Provinces and Finland 1850-1914* were writing during a time when the Soviet Union seemed a permanent fixture on the world scene.[1] Since then, as hardly needs stating, much has changed: the Soviet Union has disintegrated and the peoples dealt with in the book—Estonians, Latvians, Finns, Russians, and Baltic Germans—are all coping with the consequences and byproducts of that collapse. The Estonians and Latvians now govern sovereign states, the Finns have to deal with the economic impact of an evaporated Soviet market, and those citizen of Germany who identify themselves with a Baltic German heritage are feeling the costs created by German reunification. The Russians, residing in the Russian Federation and in erstwhile Soviet republics, are witnessing in their midst the growth of a political movement that has announced itself as seeking to revive the territorial borders of the pre-World War I Russian Empire and has even mentioned Finland as one of the territories to be returned to Russian control. In Latvia and Estonia, many among what are now minority Russian populations are having to adjust to a new status and would like to have dual citizenship in Baltic states and in the Russian Fed-

---

1. Edward C. Thaden, Michael H. Haltzel, C. Leonard Lundin, and Toivo Raun, *Russification in the Baltic Provinces and Finland, 1855-1914*. Princeton: Princeton University Press, 1981.

eration.[2] One need not wonder, therefore, why the term "russification" and the fears that term engenders have continued to inform political debate in Latvia even after 1991, when the country regained its independence. The coincidence of the political transformation of the Baltic area and the appearance of a *Festschrift* for Edward C. Thaden presents an opportunity for revisiting the theme of russification in Latvian history after 1914, the year to which *Russification in the Baltic Provinces and Finland* took the story. In retrospect, the Tsarist period russification policy examined in that book has turned out to be only the first phase of a much longer history. The fact is that ever since Alexander III's russification measures clashed with the growing consciousness of nationality among the Baltic peoples, the Latvians have been in the grip of a powerful metaphor vis–à–vis the Russians.[3] They have repeatedly contrasted their own small numbers with the immensely larger Russian population, portraying the latter as a "sea" and the Latvian territories as a beachhead periodically inundated, in a tide-like fashion, by "waves" of Russians and Russian influences. The russification policies of the governments of Alexander III and Nicholas II, in this view, were the first period of high tide when the Latvian language and national culture were threatened. The tide ebbed for a time during the interwar period of Latvian independence, but flowed onto the Latvian "beachhead" again during the Second World War, when the USSR occupied and then incorporated Latvia. The tide ebbed briefly during the German occupation between 1941 and 1945, having been temporarily replaced by germanization plans, but returned after the War's end. The Soviet period (1945-1985) witnessed four decades of near-inundation, with the waters receding during Mikhail Gorbachev's *perestroika* years. Though the post-1991 period of independence appears to have allowed the creation of institutions to control and perhaps reverse the "tide" of Russian influence; geography, of course, has not changed and the grip of the metaphor still remains strong. In the figurative language with which Latvians have described the Soviet era of their history, a frequently used term for Moscow's population policies that by 1989 had increased the Slavic-language population of the Latvian SSR to almost half of the total is *iepludināšana*, that is, the deliberate act of flooding a space with water.

2.   Dzintra Bungs, "Latvia: Transition to Independence Complete," *RFE/RL Research Report.* Vol. 3, No. 1(January 7, 1994), pp. 96–98.

3.   The reference here is to those Latvians who have been able to express themselves on the subject freely, i.e. Latvians during the 1918–1940 and post–1990 periods, and the Latvian emigrés living in the west.

It is not the intent of this essay to explore the extent to which russification policies and Russian influences actually threatened Latvian national culture with extinction. The questions of what conditions have to exist for such a threat to be real in this sense—is there a numerical population minimum for sustaining a national culture? which instruments of cultural reproduction are the most vulnerable? when is learning the language of a larger national culture followed by assimilation? is there inevitability of outcome in the interactions among large and small national cultures?—have to await later analysis. Rather, the present essay looks at the ways the russification theme resurfaced in Latvian political attitudes in the post-1914 period and suggests some ideas for future comparative research.

Interwar Independence

By 1914 the Latvian populations of the Baltic provinces of Livland (Livonia), Kurland (Courland), and of the westernmost districts of Vitebsk had long ceased to be "merely" peasantries. The processes of industrialization, urbanization, and socio-economic differentiation had given them an urban component and a nationally conscious but also strongly divided intelligentsia.[4] Russification decrees, enacted from the mid-1880s onward, had required several generations of Latvians to undergo primary education that had a strong Russian-language component taught frequently by Russian teachers, and also had brought the Latvian population into frequent contact with an expanding Russian officialdom in the Baltic area. Yet as the internal history of Latvian intellectual life in the pre-World War I decade makes abundantly clear, the russification policy had failed as an instrument of denationalization.[5] Indeed, it could be argued that this policy had the reverse effect. During the 1870s and 1880s a number of Latvian nationalists—such as Krišjānis Valdemārs and Fricis Brīvzemnieks—had looked to the Slavophile movement to help reduce Baltic German power in the Baltic provinces, hoping that at least greater *cultural* autonomy for the Latvians would follow. This flirtation—which had never grown into a love affair—

---

4. For a short history of pre-war Latvians see Andrejs Plakans, "The Latvians," in Edward C. Thaden, Michael H. Haltzel, C. Leonard Lundin, and Toivo Raun, *Russification in the Baltic Provinces and Finland, 1855–1914* (Princeton: Princeton University Press, 1981), pp. 207–284.

5. There is some ambivalence among Latvian historians about how much a real threat Tsarist russification policies were to the Latvian nation: see Arveds Švābe, *Latvijas vēsture 1800–1914* (Stockholm: Daugava, 1958), pp. 474–478.

was long since over by 1914, and Latvian intellectuals—nationalists and non-nationalists alike—were wont to think as badly of Russian autocracy as they did of Baltic German sociocultural hegemony. After the events of 1905 most Latvian political activists (with the exception of the most extreme conservatives such as Fricis Veinbergs) were looking for various formulas for Latvian separatism precisely on the grounds that Latvians now constituted a separate, culturally developed nation. Whatever doubts were exhibited by the politically active generations between 1905 and 1914, fear of russification was not prominent among them.

Understandably, the dangers posed by russification were rendered innocuous by the success Latvians had in creating an independent state after 1918. The 1914 German invasion of Russia had brought the German army to the Daugava River and had resulted in the military occupation of Kurland during the entire period of hostilities. The flood of refugees from Kurland, heading northeastward into Livland and east into Russia proper had the effect of bringing into being a strong network of Latvian refugee relief organizations that functioned with grants from the Russian crown but also became the organizational base of an embryonic Latvian government. The participants of these organizations were quite adept at living a double life: interacting on a daily basis with Russian officialdom in the Russian language while generally using Latvian among themselves as their organization efforts gained momentum. Memoir literature of the period testifies to this progressive distancing of the Latvian activists from the Russian language culture within which they were moving, and, though there was not as yet a Latvian state, there was also a growing desire among these activists for separation.[6] By the early 1920s, when the embryonic Latvian government had succeeded in creating a Latvian army and expelling from the Latvian territories both the Latvian Bolsheviks and the armed forces of the Bermont-von Goltz alliance, the desire to build a state with a Latvian cultural content was overwhelmingly the preference of the Latvian political elite, regardless of other ideological positions. The only Latvian subpopulation that did not share in this enthusiasm were the Latvian Bolsheviks and their family members, some 200,000 of whom had taken up residence in what was to become in 1922 the Soviet Union.

During the interwar decades the Latvian state functioned as a protector of Latvian-language culture and worked assiduously to render all institu-

---

6. A recently reprinted memoir of this genre is J. Seskis, *Latvijas valsts izcelšanās pasaules kara notikumu norisē 1914–1921* (Riga, 1997; original 1937).

tions more Latvian. Some of these efforts required a considerable length of time, particularly legal reform. In many of those aspects of everyday life in which the law played a role, Latvians continued to move in a context created before independence had arrived. The desire to be Latvians, however, was understandably strong, and educational and cultural institutions were the principal arenas in which this desire was exercised. The Latvian language—now the language of the state—became of course the language of instruction at all levels of the educational system.[7] The language itself was standardized with respect to spelling, punctuation, and orthography. Though the Latvianization movement was already fairly strong during the parliamentary period (1918-1935) it gained considerable momentum after Karlis Ulmanis established presidential rule and the call of "Latvia for the Latvians" became something of a slogan for all of cultural life. Surnames were changed if they sounded too German, and considerable doubt was expressed about whether it was healthy for the country to have such large portions of its commercial enterprises and professional positions "in the hands" of non-Latvians. Though the Latvian constitution guaranteed to non-Latvian national minorities educational and cultural autonomy and the government in fact subsidized minority schools and cultural organizations, the attitudes of the Ulmanis government and its acolytes left no doubt that the preference was for even further Latvianization of Latvian society.[8]

Finding themselves fully in control of the national state, Latvian political and cultural elites during the interwar period fully believed that russification was a dead issue. Little attention was paid to and relatively little was known about those Latvians who had migrated to, or chosen to stay in, the Soviet Union, in spite of the fact that until the mid-1930s the "Soviet" Latvians led a relatively brisk cultural life in Leningrad and Moscow. Germanization—another pronounced fear during the pre-1900 "national awakening" period—was an even deader issue, because with the agrarian reforms of the 1920s, the "ancient enemy"—the Baltic German landowners—had lost their landed power base and had become just another national minority. The proportion of Russians in the total population of the state in the in the interwar period did not rise above 10% and, among them, assimilation processes worked in favor of the Latvian-speaking population.[9]

7. M. Sosāre, "Valodas likumdošanas jautājumi Latvijas republikas pastāvēšanas sākuma posmā," Latvijas Zinātņu Akdēmijas Vēstis, No. 4, 1992, A: Humanitārās zinātnes, pp. 40–42.

8. Adolfs Šilde, Latvijas Vēsture 1914–1940 (Stockholm: Daugava, 1976), pp. 589–602.

9. P. Zvidriņš and I. Vanovska, Latvieši: statistiski demogrāfisks portretējums (Riga: Zinātne, 1992), pp. 24–44.

The vast majority of the Latvian population was Lutheran and there was little expectation that proportion would change.

The Double Occupation 1940-1945

Because continued Latvianization during the interwar years seemed to have become an inevitable process, the dramatic events of the World War II period were especially traumatic for the Latvians. The establishment of Soviet military bases on Latvian soil in the fall of 1939 seemed to foreshadow the return of a threat that was widely believed to have been extinguished, and with occupation of the country by the Soviet army in June, 1940, the "Russian" presence became a part of everyday life once again. Although the government succeeding Ulmanis was composed of Latvians, the belief was widespread that these new political leaders were puppets and that the puppetmaster resided in the Embassy of the USSR. With the incorporation of Latvia into the Soviet Union in August, 1940, all safeguards against Russian pressures were eliminated and the following twelve months showed that these pressures would only increase. Everyday life and all institutions were systematically subjected to sovietization, which, to most Latvians, was another word for russification, since the central directives for sovietization arrived in the Russian language and the persons supervising the process frequently spoke no Latvian and therefore introduced the need for the use of the Russian language (in addition to Latvian) at all levels of public affairs. The increased presence of the Soviet military was a continued reminder that in some sense the clock had been turned back to the pre-1918 period, when Latvians had been peripheralized by a Russian-speaking officialdom and a Russian-speaking military presence.[10]

Hitler's decision to invade the USSR in June of 1941 quickly brought to an end for the time being the russification threats lurking within sovietization but at the same time revived another traditional threat—germanization. During the weeks immediately following the occupation of Latvia by the Wehrmacht, Latvians hoped that the Third Reich would be more receptive to their national aspirations, and the German military and civilian authorities took initial steps to keep this illusion alive. National symbols were permitted and a number of pre-1940 institutions allowed to function under Latvian leadership. But as time wore on, it became increasingly clear that the Third Reich had its own plans for the country, which had been included

---

10. Ro Mald J. Misiunas and Rein Taagepera, *The Baltic States: Years of Dependence 1940–1980* (Berkeley: University of California Press, 1983), pp. 29–44.

administratively into a new geographical component of the Third Reich called *Ostland*. *Ostland* was a temporary arrangement until the defeat of the USSR; thereafter, Latvians were to be expelled from their traditional territories to points further east, the Latvian area resettled with German farmers, and those Latvians who remained in Latvia were to be germanized. How widely these plans were known is not clear, but by 1942 it was patently obvious that all major decisions were going to remain in German hands.[11] To the Latvian leaders who had quickly emerged after the departure of Soviet authorities, the German occupation and its call for the formation of a Latvian Legion at least provided some instruments for doing battle against the return of Soviet power. But even those who chose to utilize these opportunities were not fundamentally persuaded that in the long run the country could return to a *status quo ante*. This became increasingly clear by the fall of 1944, as the German armies began the process of withdrawal and tens of thousands of Latvian refugees began to leave the country in a westwardly direction.

Neither the Soviet nor the German occupation were long enough to make a direct impact on the Latvians' consciousness of national identity. But their consequences for Latvian life were traumatizing nevertheless. The all but complete disappearance of the pre-1940 Latvian political elite, the physical destruction of some 150,000 of the country's citizens, the dispersion of another 300,000 because of flight and participation in the German military effort, and the complete destruction of pre-war civil society meant that in most respects life in the post-war decades would have to start from scratch. Yet those Latvians who would now be enveloped by a renewed Soviet Latvian Republic revealed in a number of ways that among them a sense of national identity had remained intact. Some 30,000 immediately entered a partisan movement, which continued to do battle against Soviet authorities until the mid-1950s. Moreover, even to some fervent Latvian Communist leaders the policies dictated by the Moscow government all seemed to have the disturbing result—regardless of their stated motive—of unnecessarily enlarging the number of Russians and other Slavic speakers in the republic. While the term "russification" does not (and could not) appear in the written sources of the period in Latvia, descriptions of the situation among Latvian emigrés used the term literally.[12] While in the last decades of the

---

11. Haralds Beizais, *Latvija kāšu krustu varā* (N.p.:Gauja, 1992), pp. 13–37.

12. The popular three–volume *Latvju enckilopēdija* (Stockholm: Tris Zvaigznes, 1952–53) described the historical origins of Tsarist russification policy (*pārkrievošanas politika*) and suggested that such policy had been introduced in the Baltic area after World War II (pp. 1860– 1862).

nineteenth century russification had been an explicit and above-board policy, now everyday changes seemed to be resulting from a hidden agenda that used the terminology of Marxism-Leninism to disguise its true nature.

The Period 1945-1959

After 1945, the sovietization process in Latvia could continue without major hindrances because the basic steps of integrating the country into the USSR had been taken in 1940-1941. Formal incorporation had taken place in August, 1940, the Latvian Communist Party had become a constituent part of the CPUSSR in the fall of that year, the substitution of Soviet for Latvian law had occurred by the end of 1940, and the introduction of the Russian ruble had been concluded by the spring of 1941. In the immediate post-war years, the Baltic area was reorganized into the Baltic Military district with Riga as the site of the headquarters, and substantial number of properties in the country were requisitioned for military use. An estimated 3000 private persons were displaced through these actions. The economy was placed on a five-year planning basis starting with 1946. The Latvian Communist Party, now the country's new political elite, grew in size rapidly, with the non-Latvian component of its membership increasing with every year. The position of Second Secretary in the Latvian Party from 1945 until well into the 1970s was always an ethnic Russian, as were a considerable number of other high officials in the new government. The structure of government itself was patterned on the Soviet model, so that the political-institutional terminology of the interwar period disappeared completely.[13]

The deportation, arrest, and emigration during the war years of large segments of the professional intelligentsia had left large holes in the ranks of those "experts" who were now essential for the tasks of rebuilding. Moreover, Latvians with the required expertise, having been trained in the independence period, were suspect, and therefore the Party in the immediate postwar years devoted much time recruiting Party members from other parts of the Soviet Union. While knowledge of the Latvian language was sometimes specified as desirable, it was by no means mandatory, and thus the recruitment action brought into Latvia a host of party officials, administrators, bureaucrats and experts with the most varied backgrounds. Some had Latvian names and came out of that Latvian subpopulation that had resided in the USSR from 1919 onward and had survived the Old Bolshevik purges of the 1930s. Others were of Slavic origin with no familial or linguistic

13. Odisejs Kostanda, ed. *Latvijas vēsture* (Riga: Zvaigzne, 1992), pp. 284–401.

connection to Latvia at all. The latter, rather than seeing themselves obliged to learn the local language, were more likely to view Latvia as recently acquired Soviet territory the inhabitants of which should now learn Russian as quickly as possible.

What is being called here the "Russian presence" increased in less direct ways as well. A complete transformation of instructional materials in the school systems now highlighted the good fortune of Latvians in having been able to join the Soviet system and in being forced to learn the Russian language, which was the language of communication not only for many millions of people, but also, allegedly, the language of the future as the world became more communist. At a different level, historians worked at rewriting Latvian history to highlight the benefits for Latvians of having lived through the ages close to the "protective" Russian people, who had repeatedly exerted themselves—most recently during World War II—to protect Latvians from predatory westerners. The independence period was portrayed as an anomaly, as a time when with the help of western capitalists the Latvian bourgeoisie had seized power and temporarily removed the Latvian nation from the beneficent influences of their Russian neighbors.[14]

Though until 1953 and Stalin's death the Latvian Communist Party assented to this reorientation and in fact helped to bring much of it about, there was evidently a growing resentment among many party activists over the growing presence of both Russians and the Russian language. This can be inferred from what happened during the end of the 1950s, when a younger generation of Party leaders, those born during the independence period in independent Latvia, used the period of Khrushchev's "thaw" to try to control and diminish the influx of Russians and the increasing role of the Russian language. A set of regulations promulgated in the 1954-58 period sought to reduce immigration into Latvia from other parts of the USSR and to restore the primacy of Latvian in the school system. These, however, were actions that Moscow could not tolerate, and in 1959 there took place a sizable purge of the Latvian Party, with several thousands of officials dismissed from the positions and the "leaders" of the "opposition"—notably Edvards Berklavs—being forced into administrative exile in the eastern part of the Russian Federation. They were all accused of "bourgeois nationalist" tendencies, and the purge served as a warning to the intelligentsia about where Moscow was drawing the line.[15]

---

14. Heinrichs Strods, "Die Geschichtswissenschaft Lettlands in den Jahren 1945–1990," *Acta Baltica*, Vol. 23 (1990), pp. 9–18.

15. Misiunas and Taagepera, *The Baltic States: Years of Dependence*, pp. 134–141.

The Brezhnev Years

After 1964, when Leonid Brezhnev ascended to the position of General Secretary of the CPUSSR, the growth of the Slavic component of the Latvian population continued to increase, as the Moscow government pursued its policy of building state enterprises without regard to the structure of the local labor force. Recruitment of laborers from outside Latvia brought into the country many persons who had little interest in the local culture and language and no incentive at all to integrate with the local population. The average stay of these immigrants tended not to be very long, but there is evidence to suggest that in each decade there was a portion of in-migrants who decided to make Latvia into their permanent home. These stayers increased with each half-decade, gradually forming a permanent and growing subpopulation of non-Latvians. Perceiving themselves "at home" in Latvia insofar as Latvia was a constituent part of the USSR and believing that their Russian language should permit them free access to the benefits of Soviet society no matter what the language and culture of their republic of residence was, this subpopulation, just by virtue of its permanent presence, was changing the nature of Latvian public life. The Latvian language became increasingly privatized and peripheralized, as governmental and economic institutions shifted to Russian as the language of government and economic transactions. The growing proportion of non-Latvians in service occupations meant that everyday life for Latvians was punctuated by more frequent episodes in which they were required to use the Russian language in order to communicate at all. Adapting to this situation, Latvians tended to learn Russian, whereas the non–Latvians had no new situation to adapt to. The proportion of non–Latvians who learned to speak and use Latvian more than likely emerged from the growing incidence of intermarriage between Latvians and non–Latvians as well as from the small number of in-migrants who no doubt felt a moral obligation to speak the language of the republic of their residence. These trends, begun in the 1960s, continued unchanged until the mid-1980s.[16]

Among the intelligentsia, similar trends were developing and forcing similar adaptations. In the higher education system, Russian became increasingly the language of scholarship, in part because of the growing component of non-Latvians on the university staffs and the institutes of the Academy of Science. The use of Russian in academic and research publications meant a much larger audience for one's work as well as a connection to the language being used by the Academy and university intellectuals "at the center"—Moscow and Leningrad. Mature intellectuals, of course, could use Russian while maintaining Latvian as a second language, but the language dynamics in grade schools was a different question. There was from the early 1960s a generalized pressure to increase the sum total of time school-children would be using Russian, punctuated by "campaigns" to popularize the use of Russian beyond ordinary levels. These campaigns were accom-panied by new regulations on the use of Russian in the school system as well as by extensive articles in the press, written by linguists and other specialists, pointing out the disadvantages of monolingualism (when the sole language was Latvian) in a Soviet society in which upward mobility and opportunities were all linked to a knowledge of Russian. These cam-paigns were far more sophisticated than their analogues in the later nine-teenth century, when russification had the appearance of the exercise of naked power–replacing Latvians with Russians in the classroom and in school administration. In the Soviet period, the pro-Russian-language campaigns tended to appeal to individual self-interest and emphasized the advantages of knowing a "world" language such as Russian (by contrast with a provin-cial language such as Latvian).[17] Opposition to these policies and campaigns could not be direct. Though punishment for "bourgeois nationalist" senti-ments was no longer as harsh as it had been, overt questioning of the al-leged natural superiority of the Russian language and culture could result in reduced career opportunities. By the 1970s the Latvian Communist Party also had to contend with a much more vocal Latvian emigré population in Western Europe and North America. The emigré communities — formed by the refugees of 1944-45—had not assimilated to their host cultures and, indeed, had maintained a lively cultural life and emigré literature, which, to Latvian authorities, was anathema because of its continued insistence on the desirability of a Latvian national culture.[18]

The Gorbachev Era

Surprising though it is in retrospect, an official campaign to trumpet the superiority of the Russian language was going on in Latvia even as the first

---

16. Zvidriņš and Vanovska, *Latviesi*, pp. 44–67.

17. Eduards Silkalns, "Latviešu valodas problēmas trimdā un okupētajā Latvijā," *Archivs* (1986), Vol. 26, pp. 29–52.

18. For a general survey of the Latvian emigré communities see Edgars Dunsdorfs, *Trešā Latvijā* (Melbourne: K. Goppers, 1968).

signs of General Secretary Gorbachev's new policies were being felt, and this no doubt contributed to the speed with which Latvians seized the opportunity presented to them by *glasnost'*, *perestroika*, and *demokratizatsiia*. The enlarged meeting of the Latvian Writer's Union, which brought together representatives from a large number of the so-called "creative" organizations in June, 1988, became the first decisive public event in which the accumulated frustrations of the intelligentsia were given voice. For the first time, the 1940 events were called an "occupation," and the decades-long nonresistance by the Latvian Communist Party to increased Russian presence in the country was condemned as complicity in the gradual destruction of the Latvian nation. All those who had slavishly reiterated the Party's line about the dependence of Latvian culture on Russian culture, about the parochial nature of the Latvian language and the "international" nature of Russian, and about the great benefits Latvians obtained from being members of the Soviet Union now stood condemned. The term "russification" thereafter became one of the milder words for referring to the processes that had transpired during the past forty years; the preferred word was "genocide."[19] From the fall of 1988, when the Latvian Popular Front was formed, during the next three years, demonstrations, declarations, and a steady stream of publications attacked the economic, demographic, and cultural policies which were said to have brought the Latvian nation and its culture to the brink of extinction. Although the Popular Front recognized that in calling for autonomy and, later, for independence, it was seeking to extricate Latvians from the political structures of a federation of republics—the USSR—the arguments about how this was to be done were scarcely distinguishable from a deeply felt desire to escape from the presence of Russians and from the influence of their culture and language. Inevitably, as this drama unfolded and as the Popular Front became the sole leader of the Latvian cause against Moscow, the Russian population of the country—both the military and the civilian—increasingly came to be seen as an alien presence. Support by the majority of the non-Latvian population for Latvian independence in the referendum of 1990 was not sufficient to transform the image Slavic-speakers had come to have in Latvia—an image of persons who would not be there had it not been for the deliberate half-century long efforts by the Moscow government to bring them to Latvia. Much of the legislation of the Supreme Soviet which from March of 1990 was dominated by the Popular

---

19. See, for example, the proceedings of the conference on *Komunistiskā totalitārisma un genocīda prakse Latvijā* (Riga: Zinātne, 1992).

Front was meant not only to recreate in the republic the institutions of statehood, but also insure that the Latvians, at least initially, would be politically and institutionally the dominant nationality. Symbolic of all these efforts was the proclamation of Latvian as the language of the state, a measure which, in fact, was passed in 1988, even before the spring elections of 1990 brought into the Supreme Soviet the Popular Front majority.

The Restoration of Independence

The coup of August, 1991, the subsequent disintegration of the USSR, and the reestablishment of Latvia as an independent state should have been received as the ebbing of the russification tide and the start of the rebuilding of cultural security. Yet in the following three years the popular mood in Latvia has not reached the high level of cultural self-confidence that was visible in the early 1920s, immediately after the beginning of the first independence period. Institutionally, the Latvian nation now appears to be fully in control of the Latvian state, with non-Latvians having virtually disappeared from the political elite and the Latvian language having reassured primacy status as the language of the state. In other respects, however, the threat still seems to be looming. Demographically, the population of the Latvian state contains only a bare majority of Latvians (53.8%), with the proportion rising very slowly, mainly through emigration of non-Latvians. The rate of Latvian population growth remains below replacement levels. The likelihood of massive emigration of non-Latvians is not great, and the Latvian government is under considerable internal and external pressure to regularize the status of non-citizens in Latvia and to permit opportunities for their eventual naturalization. Although Latvian political attitudes have resisted the idea of a "two-community state" (*divu kopienu valsts*), the "integration" of the different language communities is not likely to proceed very quickly.[20] After the status of non-Latvians is regularized by means of a citizenship law and treaties with the Russian Federation and other interested parties, there is a strong possibility that some modified form of the two-community state will have become indirectly a *fait accompli*. Though the new Latvian legal system that started to take shape even before August 1991 is scrupulously non-discriminatory with respect to ethnicity and national origin, wide segments of popular political opinion continue to see

---

20. For a thorough discussion of this question see Rasma Karklins, *Ethnopolitics and the Transition to Democracy: The Collapse of the USSR and Latvia* (Baltimore and Washington: Johns Hopkins and Woodrow Wilson Center, 1994).

Russians (a term that oftentimes covers all resident Slavs) as potentially a "fifth column" standing ready to enact the wishes of a future neoimperialist Russian government. The reiterated claims among political leaders of the Russian Federation of their "right" to intervene in the "near abroad" to protect the "rights" of Russians there and the rise of imperial-sounding populists such as Vladimir Zhirinovsky have kept alive the idea that the ebb of the russification threat is illusory and that, given the weight of numbers, Russians could easily inundate the fragile institutions of the new Latvian state.

The prospect of having to live in a "two-community state" is far more disturbing to Latvians than to the western democracies among which Latvia wishes to be counted.[21] In the latter, political philosophies of cultural pluralism and multiculturalism are in ascendancy, and cultural diversity is perceived, certainly among elites, if not as a positive than at least as an inevitable development. The Russian population in Latvia, however, is not perceived as looking forward to the loss of its own "national" identity through integration with or assimilation to the barely majoritarian Latvian population. Moreover, individual Russians in Latvia have quickly taken advantage of opportunities in the developing private sector, and Latvian popular opinion perceives most of new small business enterprise as being "in Russian hands." During the 1920s, the new Latvian government was able through the Agrarian Reform Law of 1920 to severely reduce the power of the pre-World War I dominant class—the Baltic German landowners—through nationalization of their landed properties and redistribution of them to Latvian farmers. The laws of the 1991 Latvian state prohibit such targeted "reforms" and there is every reason to believe that a large portion of the new business elite in Latvia will continue to be composed of Russians who are Latvian citizens. The observation of Rein Taagepera that the Russians in Estonia have difficulty adapting to "non-dominant roles" also describes a prominent attitude among Latvians toward the Russian population, and this belief easily becomes the view that Russians in Latvia will not be satisfied with being merely citizens of the Latvian state.[22]

---

21. Indeed, western countries are more likely to worry about the destabilizing effects of unhappy Russians in the former Soviet republics than about the sensibilities of the titular nationalities of these republics. See William D. Jackson, "Imperial Temptations: Ethnics Abroad," *Orbis* 38 (Winter 1994), pp. 1–18.

22. Rein Taagepera, *Estonia: Return to Independence* (Boulder: Westview Press, 1993), p. 220.

Russification As a Perennial Theme

Earlier analysis of Tsarist-era russification policies from the mid-1880s onward suggested that by the time of their appearance the development of Latvian national consciousness was in full swing and that therefore the policies had no chance of realizing their stated goals. Preordained failure did not stop Latvians then from developing a deep fear that such policies might be successful and that the numerically small Latvian nation and its culture was under threat. Although the 1918-1940 independence period reassured Latvians that their national language and culture could accomplish far more than simply survival, the speed with which the threat to them was renewed after 1940 reinvigorated the fear as well. The reestablishment of the Latvian state in 1991, with a state population having a far smaller proportion of Latvians than was present in the new state of the 1920s, suggests that the russification theme will not soon disappear from Latvian history.[23]

---

23. One aspect of a full history of this theme in the post–1945 period will have to be the reorientations toward the phenomenon of russification that took place at the individual level in the Latvian intelligentsia after 1988. Thus, Anatolijs Gorbunovs, the president from 1990 of the Popular Front-dominated Supreme Council that led Latvia out of the Soviet Union in August, 1991, wrote in 1987, when he was a secretary to the Central Committee of the Latvian Communist Party, the introduction to the proceedings of a conference on *Latvijā un Krievija: vēsturiskie un kultūras sakari* (Riga: Zinātne, 1987), and observed that "the leading place in the Latvian nation's friendship with other nations is occupied by our friendship with the Russian nation" (p. 6). Ļubova Zile, director of the Central Committee's Institute of Party History from 1977 to 1990 and currently the chair of the board of editors of the new journal *Latvijās vēsture*, offered in the first issue an article entitled "Latvijās rusifikācija 1940–1990" (*Latvijās vēsture*, No. 1, 1991, pp. 31–36), which argued cogently for the primacy of the russification theme in the entire Soviet period of Latvian history.

Chapter 14

UKRAINIAN–GERMAN RELATIONS:
BACKGROUND AND PROSPECTS

John A. Armstrong

Since the abortive coup of August 1991 precipitated dissolution of the Soviet Union, an assertive Ukrainian Republic has emerged as an independent factor–the most important apart from the Russian Republic–in Eastern Europe. Simultaneously, it has become apparent that the major outside force affecting this large region will be reunited Germany, both because of its decisive economic importance and its historical geographic relation to the lands of the former Russian Empire. Reexamination of earlier German-Ukrainian relations is urgent as a foundation for projecting the future of this connection.

I

The 1917–1944 interval is the only period, prior to the last two years, when relations between Ukrainians and Germans constituted a major force, not only for the destinies of the two nations, but for European politics in general. During the Tsarist centuries as well as the period of Soviet ascendancy from 1944 through 1990, German-Ukrainian relations were vestigial. Several exhaustive recent investigations of German policy in East Europe during the two World Wars, supplemented by earlier publications, constitute an adequate factual background for the analysis. This essay focuses not on the foreign policy of the two nations but on the effects of geopolitics and ideology. In contrast to relationships where either the geopolitical situation or ideological considerations dominate, the Ukrainian-German relationship during the first half of the twentieth century involved both factors to a generally comparable extent. Thus, while many contemporaries thought the interaction derived entirely from "objective" geopolitical factors, today one can perceive the crucial effect of a hidden agenda, notably Social Darwinism, upon the two nations. Moreover—contrary to frequent assumptions—this ideological agenda motivated Ukrainian as well as German actions, for Ukraine, although surely far weaker, was never a passive object of German policy.

II

During the interwar decades, Western observers—especially British, French, and Americans—appeared to be almost as strongly influenced by geopolitical interpretations as were publicists in East and Central Europe. To all, Ukraine appeared to be a potential fulcrum for the competing levers of European power. Retrospective scrutiny of the policies and goals in both World Wars suggests that this view was, nevertheless, exaggerated.

Short-range policy goals in the Ukrainian-German interaction can be treated almost entirely from the German perspective, however; they were, indeed, predominantly strategic and economic. Although far from passive, Ukrainian reactions, in view of the fragility of their political and economic institutions, could not develop to the point at which Ukrainians could act as partners of the German military machines. As Winifred Baumgart concludes succinctly, the main German objective, even after the Brest-Litovsk Treaty, was a German occupation to obtain raw materials and food for the Central Powers.[1] This view coincides with Erich Ludendorff's softer initial assessment (before he embraced his own version of Social Darwinism) that the utility of the occupied territories reflected the following priorities: "First order and quiet had to be secured behind the army. The land had to support itself and contribute to the maintenance of the army and the home country and, furthermore, to be made useful for the equipping of the troops and for our war economy."[2] From the Austrian side, General Arthur Arz von Stauffenburg was convinced that his Berlin ally regarded Ukraine as the special object of its exploitation and a staging area on the road to Baghdad.[3] But Vienna's own policy was even shorter-range: to obtain food for its starving cities and prevent a reunification of the Russian Empire.

Whether or not these military objectives should be characterized as a determination to treat Ukraine as a colony is another matter. A primary con-

1. Winfried Baumgart, *Deutsche Ostpolitik, 1918* (Vienna: Oldenbourg, 1966), p. 369.

2. Erich Ludendorff, *Kriegführung und Politik*, 2nd ed. (Berlin: Mittler, 1922), p. 146.

3. Baumgart, p. 123.

cern, graphically expressed by the German second-in-command in Ukraine, General Wilhelm Groener: "What is the Ukrainian government? A nebulous illusion. And the State? Chaos... Beyond the reach of our bayonets this artificially put together government exerts no power."[4] Consequently, Groener resisted efforts of the Auswärtiges Amt to take a longer-range view of the Ukrainian-German interaction.

One can find parallels (at the end of World War II in the impatient demand of British and American commanders for a free hand on the territory of shaky allies like Belgium or Greece) wherever wartime authorities confront a very difficult situation in occupied territories. Often insistence on drastic action is followed, years or even months later when strategic interests have shifted, by military demands for withdrawal from the territories to take on other assignments. In the Ukrainian case, German commanders, moved primarily by short-range strategical objectives, might have quickly abandoned Ukraine if the theater of operations had shifted elsewhere. This is especially likely because the actual contribution of Ukraine to the German war effort was much lower than anticipated. One can, it is true, argue that some tens of thousands tons of grain squeezed from the Ukrainian peasants averted starvation and chaos in Austria. The broader Prussian–German objectives in World War I did not even attain that limited fulfillment. In principle, the timber and mineral resources of Ukraine should have eased strained German supplies; in fact German authorities had to ship coal *into* the Donbas to maintain minimal activity.[5] Economic achievements of the World War II occupation were not much higher. Ruthless confiscation failed to produce much food. Efforts to exploit Ukrainian industrial and energy resources were still less successful. Pit props for coal mining were obtained (with great difficulty due to partisan interference) from the northern forests, but most coal went to domestic Ukrainian uses. Only procurement of Nikopol manganese was relatively successful and vital for the German war effort. The Ukrainian territory constituted, of course, an indispensable transit area to the battle fronts. This limited utility was quite different from the image of a "Tor zur Weltmacht" which Rolf-Dieter Müller has analyzed so well.[6] On the surface, the position of military commanders in World War II differed from the earlier occu-

---

4. *Ibid.*, p. 124.

5. *Ibid.*, p. 369.

6. Rolf–Dieter Müller, *Das Tor zur Weltmacht: Die Bedeutung der Sowjetunion für die deutsche Wirtschafts–und Rüstungpolitik zwischen den Weltkriegen* (Boppard am Rhein: Boldt, 1984).

pation because Nazi totalitarianism required them to express their objectives in more ideological terms. In addition, some military officers and most occupation officials were consciously or unconsciously influenced by the fanatical ideological climate to express their short-range objectives in a more ruthless manner—e.g., Field Marshal von Reichenau's order for draconic treatment of Ukrainian peasants who merely failed to oppose the partisans.[7] In the final analysis, military concern with achieving victory or at least a compromise peace, made officers on the spot concentrate on economic and strategic objectives rather than dreams of colonization.

In sum, short-range military goals implied that German military authorities would treat Ukraine as an object, not necessarily as a colony. Since Ukrainian organizations were not in a position in either war to become real partners in the short–run economic exploitation the military demanded, they were shunted aside without any German efforts to enhance the Ukrainian organizational capacity. One result was widespread passive resistance to German exactions. Up to 1917 Ukrainian elites had usually cooperated unenthusiastically with the Tsarist and the Provisional governments. After 1917, these elites confronted the very difficult choice of aiding the German war effort or siding with the Soviets. The quandary was far more acute during World War II, but in both instances notable bodies of articulate Ukrainians did side with the Bolsheviks, and therefore directly opposed the Germans. Most of the Ukrainian leaders who refused to assist the Soviet system nevertheless resisted the German mobilization effort at times, while reluctantly returning to cooperation with the German military when the only alternative appeared to be complete Communist Russian victory. The history of elites in small nations caught between conflicting great powers demonstrates that a bitter dilemma always arises—as witness the position of the Rumanian and the Greek regimes in World War I, Belgium and Scandinavia prior to World War II, and many "non-aligned" countries today. For Ukrainian elites the dilemma was made even crueler by the fact that the choice had to be made under harsh military occupation. What made the psychological as well as the physical wounds of German occupation immensely more painful was the dominant ideological current of the early twentieth century.

---

7. John A. Armstrong, *Ukrainian Nationalism*, 2nd ed. (New York: Columbia University Press, 1963), pp. 148–49.

III

Half a century ago William Langer demonstrated, in his masterful two volumes on *The Diplomacy of Imperialism*, that the style of world politics drastically changed during the 1890s because the new doctrine of Social Darwinism invaded the international sphere. Space precludes analysis of this pervasive but vague notion, but two quotations from key German leaders will suggest its flavor. Shortly after World War I began, Wilhelm II asserted that "Either the Prussian-German-Germanic *Weltanschauung*—Justice, Freedom, Honour, and Morals—will be respected, or the Anglo-Saxon *Weltanschauung* will triumph, and that means sinking into the worship of Mammon. In this struggle one *Weltanschauung* is bound to be destroyed."[8] Admiral von Tirpitz put the matter in less high–flown terms: "The war has developed into a life and death struggle between two world philosophies: The German and the Anglo-American. The question is whether we must sink down and become mere manure for others (*Völkerdünger*)."[9] It should be emphasized that even more sweeping expressions of the "struggle for survival of the fittest" can be found in the writings of Americans, French, and British; for example in the prominent London *Nineteenth Century* shortly after war started: "efficiency in war, or rather efficiency for war is God's test of a nation's soul. By that test it stands or by that it falls."[10] Still, a variety of factors, above all Germany's physical and intellectual isolation, combined to make Social Darwinism appear more evident to German elites during World War I, with the mastery of East Central Europe the "test" of the German soul. "If the Ukraine, the Baltic Provinces, Finland, etc., really fall away from Russia permanently...then what is left of Russia is simply a Great Siberia. If Russia is reborn, our descendants will probably have to fight a second Punic War..." wrote Georg von Wedel, German ambassador to Vienna.[11]

Along with this negative goal of eliminating a major competitor in the ruthless struggle for survival, German spokesmen became more preoccupied, as the war became more costly, with postwar objectives. "If we succeed in having troops in Ukraine after conclusion of peace, the economic

---

8. Martin Kitchen, *The Silent Dictatorship: The Politics of the German High Command under Hindenburg and Ludendorff, 1916–1918* (London: Croom Helm, 1976), p. 204.

9. Fritz Fischer, *Germany's Aims in the First World War* (New York: Norton, 1967), p. 432.

10. H. W. Koch (ed.), *The Origins of the First World War: Great Power Rivalry and German War Aims* (London: Macmillan, 1972), p. 343.

11. Fischer, p. 500.

side would be very valuable."[12] Together with the presumed riches of Ukraine itself, control of the region promised access to sources farther east. In other words, the short-range objective of providing economic and strategic assets to fight the war had become a long-range goal of acquiring permanent assets to aid Germany in the incessant struggle for survival. Such a perception of Germany's inescapable requirement for expansion at the expense of other nations in the international arena logically implied that the short–run military exploitation of Ukraine must be perpetuated by colonization in times of nominal peace.

These implications continued to affect German schemes for regaining a dominant position in Europe temporarily lost in 1918.[13] Ukraine as a colony remained central in German expansionist planning, as some Ukrainian émigré leaders (especially those who sought to collaborate with France and Poland) fully understood. For most émigré leaders, however, the actuality of mass deprivation and starvation in Soviet Ukraine outweighed the bugbear of future German colonization. A major reason why suspicions of German domination were relegated to a secondary level of Ukrainian consciousness was the émigré leadership's realization that German elites—unlike themselves—possessed two plausible alternatives to expansion and direct colonization in East Europe. The first alternative, undoubtedly popular in German intellectual circles of the 1920s before the Locarno system collapsed, envisaged a conservative European union at least at the economic level. As will appear later, such a development might have held much promise for Ukrainians. In the actual conditions of the late 1920s and early 1930s, however, implications of European unity were remote and uncertain. Far more evident in its effects on Ukraine would be Germany's choice of the second alternative—close alliance with Russia.

A conservative alliance with Tsarist Russia had, of course, been the cornerstone of Prussia-Germany's foreign policy throughout the nineteenth century. It had intermittently attracted governing elites of the Austrian branch of the German nation as well. For the Austrians, the "Ukrainian card," on the other hand, was primarily part of the Dual Monarchy's domestic policy of balancing ethnic elements rather than a way to weaken the Russian empire. Much later, as Austrian officers with earlier Ukrainian experience were assigned positions in Third Reich occupation forces, the old Galician connections were conducive to more sympathetic emphasis on the Ukrainian

---

12. Report to Ober–Ost of November 16, 1918, quoted in Müller, p. 17.

13. Müller, p. 238.

factor. For Weimar Germany (and even some Nazi circles) the Prussian preference for an alliance with Russian central authorities against the Western powers persisted as a hindrance to German support of "separatist" forces in the USSR. As long as this tendency prevailed, national Ukrainian leaders found little room for maneuver in Berlin. Increasingly, however, as extreme nationalist, and subsequently National Socialist elements, came to predominate in Berlin, the Russian alternative ceased to appear as a traditional alliance of equal great powers and became instead a neo-Machiavellian scheme for subjugating all Slavs through manipulating Moscow. Superficially, the basis for a Bolshevik-German alliance appeared to exist, for Stalin's 1925 analysis of the global dichotomy strangely echoed Wilhelm II's:

> Two basic but opposed centers of attraction are created and at the same time two directions of currents to those centers throughout the whole world: Anglo-America for the bourgeois states and the Soviet Union for the workers of the west and the revolutionists of the east. Anglo-America attracts with its wealth. The Soviet Union attracts through its revolutionary experience...[14]

By that time Stalin had tacitly adopted the position argued by Trotsky at the Brest-Litovsk conference, that "separatism" was only a ploy for revival of reactionary Russian centralism, which (by implication) Germany should fear more than Communist "federalism."[15] Perhaps these vague Bolshevik overtures were designed to play on the illusions, common in German technocratic and business circles, that a Bolshevik regime could provide the vehicle for German talent to create a semicolonial sphere of penetration and development throughout the new USSR. During the mid-1920s influential bank and industrial circles proposed, in a memorandum to the Reich government, to regard Russia "as an undeveloped colony" which only German penetration could fructify.[16] These ideas contained an unmistakable suggestion that Slavs were generally inferior, that a "plasticity" in the identity of the Eastern peoples kept them from attaining the clear, strong consciousness the Germans had. As early as 1916 a wartime correspondent wrote:

> They have little changed over the centuries. For them it [national identity] is much less a matter of clear consciousness than of unclear feelings....There can be no thought of the cultural superiority of the

14. Stalin, *Sochineniia*, VII, 281–82.

15. United States, Department of State, *Proceedings of the Brest–Litovsk Peace Conference* (Washington: Government Printing Office, 1918), p. 135.

16. Müller, p. 59.

Russians. But the Russians were the first to work out unmistakable [national] characteristics. However, in fact the different ethnic groups (*Stämme*) greatly overlap, and in general it is scarcely possible to set definite boundaries.[17]

Fourteen years later an address to the Weimar Reichstag hinted at the same susceptibility of "undeveloped" East Europeans to "manipulation." "There live peoples who are favorable toward us as we toward them, who live far from the sea, who are not industrialized but agriculturally developed.... There is Europe's *Lebensraum*."[18]

Under different circumstances, such condescension might have moved in harmless, even benevolent directions. In Hitler's unsophisticated mind, the vague doctrine of Social Darwinism combined with the notion of "Eastern" inferiority and the chimera of immense, exploitable wealth. For him, the concept of East Europe, especially Ukraine, as a German sphere of exploitation and basis for world power became an overriding political objective, tenaciously maintained throughout various tactical shifts. In an apparent indiscretion, he prematurely advanced the idea in his speech of September 12, 1936:

> If we had at our disposal the incalculable wealth and stores of raw materials of the Ural mountains and the unending fertile plains of the Ukraine to be exploited under National-Socialist leadership, then we would produce, and our German people would swim in plenty.[19]

Five years later, at the start of his invasion of the USSR, Hitler's fixation was demonstrated by his insistence, contrary to all military science, that conquest of the resources of Ukraine and the Caucasus have a higher priority than strategic positions which would eliminate Soviet military power.[20] This priority permeated the entire German occupation. For a relatively well-trained *Ostministerium* official like Otto Bräutigam, the vision of German world power through expansion in East Europe meant that Ukraine must become a "colonial land for settlement and economic exploitation."[21] Even for "moderate" Nazis, such attitudes, based on the belief that Ukrainians were incapable of self-government, became almost ineradicable. In January 1953, the present writer interviewed Alfred Eduard Frauenfeld, wartime

---

17. Paul Michaelis, *Kurland und Litauen in deutscher Hand* (Berlin–Steglitz: Würtz, n.d. ca. 1916), p. 193.

18. Müller, p. 235.

19. Max Beloff, *The Foreign Policy of Soviet Russia*, II (London: Oxford, 1949), p. 58.

20. Müller, p. 348.

21. *Ibid.*, p. 347.

chief of the "Taurid" (extreme southern Ukraine) administration. Convinced that a Soviet-American war was imminent, Frauenfeld gratuitously preferred the advice that a U.S. occupation force should, for many years, rule Ukrainians with a just but iron hand. To the demurral that such protracted colonial domination did not accord with American traditions, Frauenfeld replied: "But you can learn."

For Ukrainian elites, the learning experience under German occupation in World War II was different, but traumatic. In June 1941 the newly appointed Ukrainian mayor of Lviv telegraphed Hitler as follows: "As the Free Ukrainian People it is our duty to make our contribution to the New Order of Europe along with our friends the German people."[22] At a less formal level, innumerable spontaneous expressions of attachment to the German cause appeared. Within months, the brutal exploitation of Reichskommissariat Ukraine under East Prussian Gauleiter Erich Koch (who had been an early proponent of German expansion in Ukraine) turned Ukrainian elites and masses alike against the colonial occupation regime.[23]

Considering the harshness of German rule and the monstrosity of its poorly concealed aims (as early as May 1939 *Der Stürmer* had demanded that millions of "superfluous" East Europeans die in order to provide agricultural surpluses to render Germany and Europe blockade–proof) any other Ukrainian reaction would have been fatuous.[24] But Ukrainian concern that the struggle between Berlin and Moscow not end with a complete Soviet victory was not unrealistic. Consequently, Ukrainian leaders' efforts, puny as they appear in retrospect, to exert some influence on the military balance reflected a real national interest. Unfortunately for them, many Ukrainians' proclamations and tactics reinforced German prejudices about "Slavic immaturity." The *akt* of June 30, 1941, in which the Bandera faction precipitately proclaimed an independent Ukrainian state alarmed sober officers of Austrian background like Hans Koch, who genuinely feared for the safety of their Ukrainian associates as well as for their own positions. Subsequent fratricidal conflicts within the Organization of Ukrainian Nationalists disgusted relatively sympathetic Germans.

Partly because of these fiascos, Ukrainian efforts to evolve a more balanced program in 1943 (particularly the assertion that Ukraine was in a

---

22. Geheime Feldpolizei Gruppe 711, 454 Sicherungsdivision, Microfilm T 315, Roll 2215, U. S. National Archives.

23. Armstrong, pp. 101ff.

24. Müller, p. 238.

position to act as natural leader of East European nations) did not impress German observers as much as they should have.[25] Instead, stereotypes of Slavic fanaticism and inefficiency were confirmed. Thus SS Obergruppenführer Gottlob Berger reported to Himmler (June 10, 1944) that Stephen Bandera was so convinced of an Anglo-American victory, followed by Western assistance to Ukrainian nationalists, that he had not even considered the possibility of a Soviet-German separate peace. Berger concluded that Bandera was an "adroit, ardent Slav, intent on his own ideas, hating Great Russians as well as Germans, useful but dangerous."[26] Military liaison officers in actual contact with Ukrainian guerrillas (UPA) at this late state of World War II had a distinctly less stereotyped view, but the purely tactical cooperation which followed was kept at arm's length. In any case, it was much too late for Germany to play the Russian card, to acquire a Ukrainian ally, or to hold a Ukrainian colony.

IV

Brief and schematic though it is, the overview of the historical record just presented suggests ways in which the post 1991 relation between the restored German and Ukrainian states can develop. An elementary lesson is that concentration on the material wealth of Ukraine is an unsatisfactory way of assessing its importance to Germany. Like the intermittent American fascination with the "billion-strong Chinese market," German visions of "swimming in plenty" by exploiting Ukrainian resources always turned out to be chimeras. During the last four decades, both economic theory and world opinion have emphatically moved away from autarchy as a method for achieving long–range economic goals. A great accomplishment of the postwar period has been the triumph of liberal economics at the international level as well as domestically, notably in Germany. Both raw materials and labor (in the form of free if not entirely satisfied *Gastarbeiter*) are attainable through normal exchange relations. Markets, if not quite as open, have been sufficient for highly industrialized powers to attain undreamt of standards of living. Hence there are no evident economic reasons why the German nation as a whole *requires* a Ukrainian relation.

Indeed, very recently Germans have learned from experience with absorbing the former German Democratic Republic that the short-range costs

25. Text of the Third conference of the Organization of Ukrainian Nationalists, February 17–21, 1943, in *Za Samostiinu Ukraïnu*, No. 9.

26. Reichsführer SS, Chef des SS Hauptamtes, CD SS HA 7, BE/Steg VI–Tgb, No. 189/44, Microfilm T 175, Roll 125, U. S. National Archives.

of intimate relations with a potentially rich but economically disorganized area may entail immense strains. For the time being, therefore, rather than the specter of German economic domination, the problem is for Germany to find sufficient funds for the investment which Ukraine badly needs. From the geopolitical standpoint, it is almost inconceivable that the reunited German nation would wish to pursue a Ukrainian relation as part of a strategy of military expansion. With a frontier on the Oder far to the west of the borders maintained by either the Second or the Third Reich, such a strategy would be absurd. Even more telling, probably, is the declining German demographic base. Although for the moment the eighty million Germans are more numerous than any other European nation except the Russians, demographic trends will almost certainly reduce such ascendance even at the European level, to say nothing of the overall world balance. Quite apart, therefore, from the overwhelming consensus that Social Darwinist expansionism is foolhardy, the sober aversion of contemporary Germans to adventurism in foreign policy constitutes another powerful restraint.

To the outside observer, the real danger for this decade is that Germany will be *too* restrained in its concern for Ukraine and other East European countries. A core of truth in geopolitical speculations—that Germany is inevitably involved in the course of East European events—cannot be ignored. Either chaos or renewed expansionist dictatorships in the region would inevitably have serious implications for the safety of Central Europe. Fortunately, during 1991–92, violent upheavals in Yugoslavia forced this consideration upon German attention. In Croatia and Slovenia the most extensive military operations in Europe since the 1940s proceeded for months virtually at Germany's doorstep. Ultimately, pressure by the German government produced European intervention to curb the Serb-dominated Yugoslav army and recognize independence of smaller republics. But the lesson of the physical vulnerability of nations seeking independence from more powerful neighbors was once again emphasized. Nowhere was this lesson more effective than among Ukrainian leaders who gained independence just as the Yugoslav conflict was starting. A sober estimation of requirements for defense forces, able to hold off potential aggressors until a response by the dilatory international community could be aroused, became intertwined with exaggerated conceptions of the need for separate Ukrainian nuclear, naval, and land contingents.

To avoid armaments which would be economically burdensome and politically risky, Ukraine required concrete assurances that European countries will take strong measures if the Yugoslav army adventure is repeated on a far larger scale in the former USSR. Obviously, association of Ukraine with the European Community would facilitate preventive measures. From the economic standpoint, Germany, an almost irreplaceable support for all former Soviet republics, would, as in the Yuvoslav crisis, act as prime mover. If—as is all too likely—sterner intervention became necessary, a concert of nations would be required, but Germany would be the principal base. To avert a crisis, steady German support for Ukrainian economic development is essential: Such support should not be confined to aid, or even to mutually advantageous commerce. To avoid even a hint of colonial dependence, Ukrainians will prefer to draw on the experience (in law, public administration, and military organizaticn as well as economics) of a range of European powers rather than on any single national source. Nevertheless, experience in Ukraine and other East European regions has provided German industrialists with exceptional skills in management counseling suitable to economies emerging from Soviet socialism.

In contrast to earlier decades, in Europe at the close of the millennium, close German-Ukrainian cooperation has a strong chance of becoming one of the cornerstones of peace. Both sides, however, must firmly grasp the parameters of a relationship which can never again be that of occupier to a colony. Germans must not merely welcome this change, but accept responsibility for assisting Ukraine to become a strong, stable element of the European community. Ukrainians must recognize their inexperience as a new governing elite, while receptively exploring a wide range of special relationships with the European powers. If these conditions are met, the two nations can fulfill together their most promising vocation—to help build, in the words of one of the greatest Europeans, a "Europe from the Atlantic to the Urals."

Part Three:
Historiography

Chapter 15

SWISS MIGRATION TO IMPERIAL RUSSIA: A REVIEW ESSAY

Leo Schelbert

Carsten Goehrke et al., *Schweizer im Zarenreich. Zur Geschichte der Auswanderung nach Russland.* Zürich: Verlag Hans Rohr, 1985. Pp. 519.

Urs Rauber, *Schweizer Industrie in Russland. Ein Beitrag zur Geschichte der industriellen Emigration, des Kapitalexports und des Handels der Schweiz mit dem Zarenreich (1760 – 1917).* Zürich: Verlag Hans Rohr, 1985. Pp. 460.

Gisela Tschudin, *Schweizer Käser im Zarenreich. Zur Mentalität und Wirtschaft ausgewanderter Bauernsöhne und Bauerntöchter.* Zürich: Verlag Hans Rohr, 1990. Pp. 328.

Rudolph Mummenthaler, *"Keiner lebt in Armut." Schweizer Ärzte im Zarenreich.* Zürich: Hans Rohr, 1991. Pp.267.

Roman Bühler, *Bündner im Russischen Reich. 18. Jahrhundert – Erster Weltkrieg. Ein Beitrag zur Wanderungsgeschichte Graubündens.* Disentis/ Mustér: Stampa Romontscha 1991. Pp. 669.

Carsten Goehrke, Professor of Russian and East European history at the University of Zürich, and his team of researchers have published to date five volumes on Swiss migration to Russia which represent an admirable scholarly achievement. A felicitous confluence of interest, expertise, and funding opportunity made an intensive research effort possible; its findings are valuable not only for scholars concerned with the Swiss past, but also with migration in general and with the role and impact of aliens in Imperial

Russia in the context of its massive modernization efforts in conformity with West European patterns. The volume titled *Swiss in the Tsarist Empire* (1985) offers the group's main findings and interpretative assessments, while the four monographs explore the emigration of entrepreneurs (U. Rauber), the activities of cheesemakers (G. Tschudin), the role of physicians (R. Mummenthaler) and, finally, the migration of people from the Swiss canton Graubünden, for whom Imperial Russia was an especially attractive destination (R. Bühler).

The survey volume shows the hand of Goehrke who had accepted an appointment at the University of Zürich in 1971. As an expert scholar of early Russian history he insisted on disciplined methodology, a rigorous critical approach, and interpretative sophistication. At the same time he remained democratically in the background. Although clearly the leading force of the undertaking, he lists himself merely as one among the other researchers whose individual projects he also guided as mentor. Two other factors promoted the enterprise. First, almost by accident, Josef Vögeli, a member of the research team, discovered in a garage the archive of the Association of the Russian Swiss (*Vereinigung der Russlandschweizer*), a group founded in 1918, but defunct by 1980. The archive included a list of some 5,500 names with data such as commune of citizenship (*Bürgergemeinde*), occupation, and wealth; it also contained memoirs, letters, and memorabilia which the research team later enriched by numerous interviews. Second, in the fall of 1979 the Swiss National Endowment (*Schweizerischer Nationalfond*) agreed to fund the research project on Swiss migration to Russia for three years; this allowed the gathering, preserving, cataloguing, and interpreting of a wealth of dispersed and little known data. Thus the situation was ideal: an inspiring expert, a trained and dedicated research team, a core of hitherto unused primary data, and adequate institutional support permitted the reconstruction of a segment of the history of European migration, the significance of which far surpassed the merely Swiss or Russian dimension. The following essay intends to sketch the nature and main findings of each of the five volumes and to assess their historical importance. First the survey volume is discussed, then each of the four monographs in order of publication.

The survey volume represents a group effort. Although individuals had been assigned separate tasks, the results were reviewed and assessed in common, and Goehrke gave the text its final form. Bühler was mainly responsible for quantitative analysis, the creation of graphs, the collection of pictures, for the study of the emigration of pastry cooks, and the Swiss colony of St. Petersburg. Gander-Wolf, author of a pioneering study of the Swiss colony Chabag or Schabo, founded in 1824 at the mouth of the Dniester river, concentrated on aspects of social history in the tradition of European *Volkskunde*. In addition to serving as guide and editor, Goehrke authored an essay on "the importance of Swiss for Russia" and "of Russia for Swiss immigrants" (275–343). As both a German and historian of Russia he combined an empathetic understanding of things Russian and Swiss with an outsider's critical detachment. Rauber concentrated on the extant historiography, which he had previously featured in his master's thesis (*Lizentiatsarbeit*) and on industrial migration including firms, entrepreneurs, and their involvement in Russian and general European economic development. Tschudin explored the migration of cheesemakers and dairymen, Vögeli the response of Swiss immigrants to Russian culture and to Switzerland on their return. Besides contributing to the summary volume, all participants except Vögeli have published monographs on their chosen topics to which Mumenthaler's study of Swiss health professionals active in Russia is a welcome addition.

The study distinguishes seven phases of the Swiss presence in Russia (375, note 36). The decades 1650 to 1700 were a time of "sporadic single emigration of specialists." The next six decades were marked by Peter the Great's intensified Westernization of Russia, which led to an increase in the number of immigrants with specialized skills. The third phase, from 1761 to 1810, included group migrations of Swiss farmers into Southern Russia, that is into lands wrested from Turkish or Tatar suzerainty. The fourth phase, from 1811 to 1860, saw the occupational diversification of Swiss newcomers with artisinal and commercial skills as well as a second wave of peasant emigration of farmers into southern Russia. The fifth phase spanned the years 1861 to 1900 when a quickening pace of industrialization opened opportunities for Swiss who were experienced in the dairy and cheesemaking industry. Swiss immigrants during the sixth phase, from 1901 to 1917, were socio-economically similar to those of the previous phase, but most of them returned to Switzerland during the seventh phase, which covered the years 1922 to 1945. Overall one may therefore distinguish four overlapping and intertwined facets of Russian development that attracted Swiss: The demand for military specialists in the pre–Petrine era; the need for architects, craftsmen, and intellectuals to promote the westernization initiated by Peter the Great (1672–1725); the desire for experienced farmers, artisans, educators, and artists during the mercantile regime of Catherine the Great (1729–1796); and, finally, the need for seasoned entrepreneurs during the late nine-

teenth and early twentieth centuries in the context of intensified industrialization. Russian administrative elites favored immigrants from Switzerland
since they hailed from a neutral and multilingual state at the crossroads of
Western Europe that was only marginally involved in European power politics.

This work skilfully combines anecdotal, biographical, and numerical
data. It explores the emigrants' origins, occupations, and educational status
and focuses on aspects of language, denomination, and wealth as well as on
the interaction of Swiss immigrants with their compatriots, with immigrants
speaking the same language, especially German, and with the people native
to Russia. The study also investigates issues of mobility, the newcomers'
response to Russian culture, and their progressive acculturation as indicated
by changes in language, religion and adoption of Russian customs, and the
choice of marriage partners. As to origins, the researchers found that there
were "veritable emigration communes (*Auswanderergemeinden*)" (81) as,
for instance, Davos in the Canton Graubünden or Diemtigen in the Canton
of Bern. As to numbers, the study suggests a minimum of about 38,000 or a
maximum of 57,500 Swiss immigrants to Russia for the years 1650 to 1917.
As to religion, Swiss Protestants, who in Switzerland counted slightly over
half the population, were overrepresented: until 1771 the proportions were
65.1 percent Reformed, for the years 1818 to 1848 91.2 percent, and for the
time span 1849 to 1872 81.2 percent. Also the linguistic distribution devi-
ated from that of Switzerland: the average for the years 1650 to 1916 was
56.7 percent German-speaking (as opposed to 70.6 percent in Switzerland
for the years 1880 to 1900), 16.8 percent French-speaking (versus 6.2 percent), and 14.4 percent Romansh-speaking (versus 1.4 percent). According
to this study, 90 percent of the emigrants were male; in economic background, 34 percent were well-to do, 38.9 percent of the middling sort, and
26.8 percent of modest means. The study summarizes the occupational distribution as follows:

Table 15 (p. 156)
Most Frequent Occupations of Swiss in Russia 1761 – 1917
(according to phase, in percent)

PHASES OCCUPATIONS	1761–1810	1811–1860	1861–1900	1901–1917
Confectioner	17.6	33.3	6.3	0.8
Farmers	12.6	4.2	2.1	2.9
Architects	7.6	5.0	0.9	0.5
Merchants	5.0	6.5	13.0	13.2
Clergymen	4.7	2.1	1.2	0.8
Painters (Artists)	4.7	1.7	0.3	0.4
Building Trades	4.3	1.1	0.1	0.1
Military Officers	3.7	2.9	0.5	2.2
Teachers	3.0	3.7	3.2	2.7
Cheesemakers	2.0	4.9	14.3	19.8
Physicians	2.0	0.3	0.5	0.9
Plantation Managers	1.7	1.4	4.3	5.0
Educators	1.7	0.7	7.3	4.0
Weavers	1.7	0.6	0.2	0.3
State Officials	1.7	1.4	1.0	0.8
Private Tutors	0.7	1.1	2.0	1.2
Manufacturers	0.3	1.5	2.4	2.9
Diplomats	0.3	1.4	0.9	1.3
Professors	0.3	0.9	0.5	1.2
Engineers	0.3	0.2	1.0	2.9
Winegrowers	–	5.4	1.9	1.2
Bookkeepers	–	0.2	1.4	1.4
Machinists	–	–	1.2	1.0
Cheese Merchants	–		1.1	1.3
Total Cases	N=301	N=956	N= 1,289	N=767

Moreover, an investigation of occupations at departure for Russia with those later pursued in the host country shows "a tendency towards economic upward mobility" (155). Several maps also feature the main places of Swiss activity, which were predominantly the cities of European Russia such as St. Petersburg and Moscow or the agricultural regions of Russia's south.

As measured by change of citizenship, language, and religion as well as by marriage patterns and customs, the acculturation of Swiss was quite rapid and often occurred via Russian and Baltic German connections. The Swiss immigrant elite rather soon adapted to the ways of the Russian nobility; High German replaced the various forms of Swiss German; Lutheran or Russian Orthodox religious practice superseded the Swiss Reformed or Catholic tradition. C. Goehrke, whose essay carefully traces the activities of Swiss and Russian–Swiss in education, scholarship, medicine, art, the military, the church, in agriculture, and industry, warns that Swiss influence on Russian politics and culture should not be exaggerated. Yet he views people like Frédéric César de la Harpe (1754–1838), tutor to Alexander I, or Jeanne Huc-Mazelet (1765–1852), tutor of princess Maria, as important transmitters of European ways of thinking and holds that Swiss influenced more than other foreigners the younger segments of the Russian nobility. The work in mathematics at the St. Petersburg Academy of scholars from the city of Basel such as Nikolaus Bernoulli (1695–1726), Daniel Bernoulli (1700–1782), and above all Leonhard Euler (1708–1783) was of international significance. Others influenced the fields of botany, physics, medicine and public hygiene; noteworthy among them is especially Huldreich Friedrich Erismann (1842–1915), Russia's "greatest scholar of public hygiene" (295) who as professor at the University of Moscow combined scholarship with the translation of his findings into practice. Domenico Trezzini (1670—1734) more than any other architect shaped the original plan and architecture of St. Petersburg, and the clergyman Johann Baptist Cattaneo (1764–1831) influenced not only the Herrnhuters at Sarepta, but also the religious life of the German Volga colonies. Goehrke stresses that Swiss found numerous opportunities in Russia that were unavailable at home. On their return to Switzerland some remained homesick for the vast Russian spaces and found the mountain–ringed Swiss landscape unbearably narrow. Yet most Swiss emigrating to Russia had kept their Swiss citizenship, which proved to be a great asset on their return.

The chapters of this collaborative work deal expertly with the voluminous data, often using quantitative methods. A striving for numerical exactitude and irrefutable conclusions imparts a positivist flavor to some portions of the study. The work remains untouched by the post-structuralist challenge which relegates the 'noble dream' of objectivity to a time and culture–bound Enlightenment tradition. Sometimes, too, the crisis–view of migration seems to dominate; the counterview, centered on the concept of a migratory *oikumene* consisting of a heartland and its constantly shifting outliers, is disregarded and important works in English are ignored as, for instance, James Cracraft, *The Petrine Revolution in Russian Architecture* (1988) which specifically considers the activities of Swiss. Yet the study represents an outstanding achievement, even if the various parts are not fully integrated into a cohesive whole. Apart from presenting invaluable data, it offers an impressive and carefully crafted overview of the topic and an indispensable framework for subsequent studies.

Urs Rauber's sharply focused work deals with Swiss industry in Russia, that is "the beginnings and evolution of 300 industrial firms" (12). He includes "all industrial corporations, establishments, daughter foundations, and branch offices in Russia that were wholly or mainly owned by Swiss citizens." He also considers "Swiss experts in Russian establishments" and "Swiss capital in Russian or foreign firms" and the "financial and commercial relations of Switzerland with Russian industry," indigenous as well as foreign (10). He defines 'Russian' not in an ethnic, but in a political sense, as referring to the 1914 frontiers of the Empire, which included Finland and Congress Poland. He has explored the archives of industrial firms and of Russian-Swiss organizations, perused family histories, memoirs, and travel accounts, corresponded with or interviewed Russian-Swiss living in Switzerland, and studied Russian registers of factories and joint stock companies. In addition, he had access to Erik Amburger's studies—the bibliography lists thirteen titles (pp. 439 to 441)—as well as to his invaluable archival register of over 250,000 foreign specialists in Russia.

Rauber's study is divided into three parts. A first offers a synopsis of the industrial development of Imperial Russia, a second details the activities of the three hundred firms in nine branches (textiles, watch–making, machines and metals, mining, building and wood, paper and printing, chemicals, electricity, and food). Part Three systematically analyzes numbers, locations, and organizational forms, to which are added profiles of entrepreneurs and experts as well as comments on financial and commercial dealings. Sixteen pages of photographs of industrial plants and individuals enrich the text and three appendices offer further significant data. Appendix I features the geographic distribution of manufacturing and commercial establishments, Appendix II the role of Swiss capital in non-Swiss industrial firms in Russia according to size and type of sponsor (private individuals, industrial firms, other enterprises); Appendix III analyzes the "Special Commerce of Switzerland with Russia 1885–1920" and the proportion between exports and imports.

Rauber found that the 300 Swiss firms represented about one percent of all establishments in Russia and paralleled those of German, English, French, and Belgian origin. Sixty percent of Swiss enterprises, about 20 percent each, produced machines, foodstuffs, and textiles; thirty percent, about 10 percent each, manufactured watches, chemicals, and products of wood. The majority of firms were new establishments, small in scale, and independent entities. About 10 percent were large and had more than 500 employees. The dispersal of Swiss firms followed the general distribution of Russian enterprises, and Swiss business leaders were similar in attitude as their West European counterparts. Yet the Swiss, Rauber found, produced mainly for the Russian market and tended to take fewer risks than members of other national groups. They were less autocratic in their management style and seemed to be especially skilled in their dealings with workers and, therefore, rarely had to face strikes. Also, Swiss specialized workers were not only oriented towards the interest of the owners, but also strove to maintain good relations with the semi– or unskilled workers.

Swiss entrepreneurs were especially active in the area of technological transfer. The Glarnese Michael Weber (1777–1839) introduced cylinder–printing and Johann Jakob Blumer (1749–1822), also from the Canton Glarus, mechanical carpet–weaving; Bernard Lerch (1811– 1904), who was specialized in the making of looms, founded the first elastic band weaving establishment (*Gummibandweberei*) in the 1880s and the brothers Jean Fazy (1734–1812) and Marc Conrad Fazy (b. 1740), a watch–making firm. Others brought the first agricultural machines to Russia and, in the building sector, introduced beamless ceilings and standardized construction. Between 1870 and 1920 Russia's dependence not only on foreign technology, but also on foreign capital, intensified. Swiss investment was substantial especially in the areas of electricity, textiles, and machine production, yet did not translate into political influence as it did for French and German finance. Swiss also imported into Russia Swiss products such as watches, cheese, textiles, machines, precision instruments, and chemicals. Swiss commerce with Russia remained strong even after 1917, although the export of Swiss capital to Russia and the activities of independent Swiss firms in Russia came to an end.

Finally, Rauber assesses the advantages and disadvantages to the Swiss of economic activity in Russia. The proximity of raw materials, lower transport and labor costs, and fewer official regulations concerning working hours, child labor, vacations, safety, and insurance proved attractive. The lack of qualified workers, the fluctuations of the currency, and the threat of confiscation represented the negative side. Rauber found that most Swiss firms established in Russia were quite successful. Skilled workers could claim high wages, become entrepreneurs, and count on the "discrete, yet effective support" of Swiss consulates (348). Also the investment market brought at times substantial returns and contributed to Switzerland's own evolution into a social welfare state. The year 1917, however, brought the "ideological face–off between a capitalist small state and the emerging communist world power" (351), although commercial enmeshments remained strong.

This work is a fact–filled, thorough, interpretatively balanced, and well written study that ably interweaves descriptive, anecdotal, and numerical data into a cohesive and lucidly constructed whole. The University of Zurich justifiably awarded the book its main dissertation prize in 1985. Gisela Tschudin's *Swiss Cheesemakers in the Tsarist Empire* is the most personal of the works under review. The author studied not only history, but also theology and Jungian psychology. "Homesickness," she explains, was to her "a well known experience," and she confesses that to emigrate was for her an impossible thought (219). It was only after she faced the emotional dimension in the letters of the emigrants that she "discovered what unites us" and overcame her initial distaste for those "conformist, intolerant, racist," and moustached go-getters (220). She divides her study into four parts. The first presents an overview of the emigration of cheesemakers "from a Swiss perspective" and offers numerous sketches of individuals and families from the Bernese Oberland region and the valley of Glarus who went to Russia to pursue a career as cheesemakers and agricultural entrepreneurs. Part Two focuses on Russia's agricultural traditions and milk industry with a special section on the Caucasus, where Swiss became quite dominant in that economic sector. Part Three features the world of the cheesemakers, who often began as employees, and later became independent entrepreneurs. Tschudin pays attention to their relationship with the various levels of Russian society and devotes a special section to women as independent businesspeople or as spouses of cheesemakers. Part Four is the most fascinating. On the basis of two extended files of correspondence, the author reconstructs with great sensitivity the careers of David Moser (1868–1942) and his wife Marie, born Schneider (1874–1961), who had settled in the Caucasus where David Moser found plenty of opportunity for his restless entrepreneurial spirit. He established several cheesemaking businesses, tried the export of wool, and planned the production of raisins and cider. His letters, segments of which Tschudin builds mosaic-like into a cohesive narrative, are terse, unemotional, and all business. The letters of Walter Alfred Stettler (1869–1908), in contrast, reveal a rich emotionality, shaped largely by a submerged homesickness. Stettler had gone in his mid-teens from Bern to French-speaking Switzerland, then to East Prussia near Danzig, and in 1890 to Moscow in the hope of establishing a business of his own. He then considered joining his two brothers in the United States or moving to Australia, but in 1892 he married Magdalena Schilt (1868–1931), the daughter of a Swiss immigrant. He then rented the farm Volotsok in the district of Sytseka with fair success. In the fall of 1899 the Stettlers lost three of their children to scarlet fever, and Stettler himself died some years later at age 39 due to a ruptured appendix. The family stayed on in Russia until 1919 when Magdalena Stettler-Schilt returned with her three children to Spiez, Switzerland.

Tschudin pays careful attention to detail, yet strives "to define from an anthropological perspective what it means to be human under those specific circumstances of origin in Swiss mountain villages and agricultural pursuits in the empire of the tsars" (13). She found her sources in communal, cantonal, federal and parish archives and balanced consular commercial reports and data from newspapers with the rich holdings of the "Archive of the Russian Swiss," which included letters, official correspondence, memoirs, genealogical material, and interviews given by returnees to Switzerland. Eight maps, 5 graphs, 14 statistical tables, and 32 well–reproduced photographs enrich the text. A list of some 750 names specifies for each the canton of origin, year of birth, date of emigration, place of settlement in Russia, date of return, and year of death. Another appendix lists the location of Swiss cheese–making establishments according to gouvernement and includes the names of the owners and years of activity.

Tschudin also offers some revealing comparative data. On the basis of the averages for the years 1860, 1871, and 1882 she found that of all possible destinations abroad Russia attracted the most Bernese women as governesses and Bernese men as cheese–makers, 37.5 and 46.6 percent respectively. In contrast, France attracted 58.6 percent of domestic servants as well as 64.3 percent of Bernese active in the restaurant business, and the United States 42.6 percent of artisans and 65.9 percent of agricultural laborers. Of the Bernese, 68.7 percent went to regions of Europe and 31.2 percent overseas (Table 3, p.34). The 900 and more Swiss who were active as cheesemakers in Imperial Russia were largely invisible in the empire's economic life and, in Tschudin's view, made their money in a typical colonial fashion. Prices for milk as well as labor were low, yet the price for cheese products was shaped by a global market and generally high. Cheese-making was an economic niche that demanded hard work, especially during the summer and persistent professional endeavor, but also yielded at times a high return, especially since cheesemakers were exempt from taxation. According to Tschudin economic success was their highest priority and the October Revolution for most an unmitigated disaster. The about two hundred returners often had become strongly anticommunist, yet also suppressed their yearning for Russia and its wide open spaces in order not to be viewed as sympathizing with the new regime. Swiss immigrants in Russia in general, Tschudin claims, and the cheesemakers in particular, were thoroughly bourgeois and catered to the wealthy Swiss in Moscow and St. Petersburg. Although Russian hospitality, culinary traditions, and religious customs, especially those connected with Easter, influenced them, they generally kept aloof from the host society and remained alien to its culture and aspirations. In this fine study the author successfully transcends "quantitative balancing," as Goehrke observes in his foreword, and "discovers behind the individually unique the common and typical traits which shaped the lifestyle and mentality" of these Swiss (11).

Rudolf Mumenthaler similarly focuses on one particular occupational group, that is on some one hundred Swiss who were active in the medical field in Russia, of whom thirty-nine were immigrants and sixty-nine born in Russia of Swiss parents. This group, as Goehrke stresses in his foreword, does not represent a peculiar Swiss tradition, as did the cheesemakers. Physicians from Germany and other West European countries were far more numerous, yet the Swiss group may serve as a representative sample that highlights the range of activities of these professionals and their significance for the history of medicine in Russia. Mumenthaler first discusses those who left Switzerland to practice medicine in Russia, then those born and educated there. In a third section he offers a sketch of their social, regional, and educational background, and in a fourth twelve chronologically ordered biographies which highlight the types of medical activity. The author concludes with a brief discussion of the socio-economic status and social life of these physicians and of those who eventually returned to their homeland. Sixteen photographs, a well structured bibliography, a biographical register, and a list of publications by prominent physicians, either written in Russia or closely related to their stay there, conclude the study.

Mumenthaler found that 63 of these physicians entered state service; 29 of these held administrative posts in a gouvernement, district or city, 27 were in the military, 22 worked in public hospitals, and 13 held academic positions. Ninety-one Swiss and Russian-Swiss were active in the public sector, 35 could be identified as in private practice, although there was no strict separation of their activities (89). Among the group were some questionable characters like Samuel Vogel from Mühlhausen as well as personalities who gained international renown. As previously mentioned, Niklaus Bernoulli (1695–1726), his brother Daniel (1700–1782), and Leonhard Euler (1708–1783) from the City of Basel were members of the newly founded St. Petersburg Academy of Sciences which developed into "a paradise of scholars," as Christian Wolff, a German and advisor to the Academy, wrote to Euler in 1727 (92). The fields of mathematics, physiology, and medicine were then not yet sharply separated. Daniel Bernoulli's fame, for instance, rested on his investigations in mathematics and physics (e.g. hydrodynamics, magnetism, and electricity) as well as in medicine (e.g. muscular movements and blood circulation). His statistics of inoculation based on probability calculations made in 1769 "were a turning point in epidemiology" (95). Johann Ammann (1707– 1741) was mainly interested in the collection of plants, many of which had medicinal value. Hans Jacob Fries (1749– 1801) rose to importance as a military surgeon, and Friedrich Huldreich Erismann (1842–1915) concentrated his research and teaching on preventive medicine and hygiene. He led the investigation of 114,000 workers in 1,080 factories, begun in 1879, and edited the 17 resulting volumes, seven of which he wrote himself. His work influenced not only Russian, but also European developments, especially after he had been appointed Professor of Hygiene at the University of Moscow in 1881. His programmatic inaugural lecture on the "Foundations and Tasks of Modern Hygiene" insisted on the inseparable unity of medicine and hygiene and served as an influential manifesto. F.H. Erismann also insisted on the training of women as physicians whom he viewed not only as equal, but in certain respects superior to men in the medical field. Mumenthaler found that social concerns were central to many of the physicians he studied, especially those born in Russia as sons of pastors. The author also briefly discusses Russian physicians active in Switzerland. Konstantin von Monakov (1853–1930), for instance, became the "father of Swiss neurology" (223); Charles Alexander Herzen (1839–1906), the son of the exile Alexander Herzen (1812–1870), the latter a Swiss citizen since 1851, was professor of physiology at the University of Lausanne from 1881–1906. C.A. Herzen's son Nicolas (1873– –1923) was professor of Roman Law at Lausanne, whereas his brother Pierre Herzen (Petr Aleksandrovic) (1871–1947) became in 1917 professor at the University of Moscow; he was a genius in surgery, yet remained holistically oriented (188) and pioneered the treatment of cancer. He wrote over 90 papers on oncology, embryology, gynecology, and traumatology.

This book, although narrow in focus, is a pleasure to read and offers a balanced and insightful view of one professional group in Russia. Only a similar study of French and German physicians working in Russia would, of course, establish whether the Swiss and Russian-Swiss health professionals were typical of that group.

In contrast to Mumenthaler, Roman Bühler concentrated on a single region, the Swiss canton Graubünden. He offers such a wealth of data on those emigrants that his study approaches the character of a compendium. He offers, for instance, a meticulously constructed register of some 1,800 migrants, arranged according to region and place of origin. Seventy tables, 12 graphs, 40 illustrations, and 60 photographs enrich his treatise of nearly 700 pages. It is the fruit of a ten-year effort and, as to the detail offered, will long remain unsurpassed.

After two introductory chapters that specify the study's sources, general approach, and the background of Graubünden, the author offers a quantitative portrait of the emigrants which includes geographic origins, distribution according to sex, language, denomination, and socio–economic status. A special section addresses the causes of emigration and aspects of the journey to Russia. A meticulous, if tedious chapter contains general data on the dispersal of clergymen and colonists, then gives much detail on their places of settlement, buttressed by maps for 15 regions of Russia, including Poland and the Baltic. The next chapter has a more narrative cast; it describes, first, the migratory experience of the confectioners, a major occupational group among the emigrants, by carefully tracing numerous individual careers, the rise and fall of establishments, and their significance for cities like St. Petersburg or Warsaw; it features, second, the activities of merchants, teachers, jurists, physicians, artists, architects, and farmers; the author offers, third, a socio–historical portrait of the Graubünden emigrants in Russia: their religious affiliations, their role in benevolent societies, the role of consuls, marriage patterns, issues of illness and mortality, and linguistic matters. Three final shorter sections feature the end of the migration, the traces immigrants from Graubünden left in Russia, their place within general Swiss migration to that country, and a summary of findings.

Bühler's work is an impressive achievement. He unearthed an astounding amount of information hidden in the archives of the Grisons and of Russia which he presents and analyzes in exhaustive detail. He left hardly a question unexplored, investigated a complex web of interrelations, and kept developments in Europe in general, and in Russia and Switzerland in particular, in clear focus. Yet the reader is at times lost in the overabundance of data and the critical weighing of occasionally insignificant detail, so that broader outlines are difficult to perceive. In part the work is overorganized; the text has too many subtitles and introductions that unnecessarily and somewhat pedantically state what the author is going to do next, what he has just done, and what had been touched upon earlier. Much methodological and theoretical detail would have been better placed in footnotes or brief appendices in order to achieve a less fractured study. The author packed every bit of evidence into his treatise which makes it a goldmine of valuable information, but tedious and fragmented as a work of history. At times percentages are based on too small a sample to be truly significant. The author seems to forget that much chance rules human affairs as well as what survives from people for posterity, and that interpretations always remain tentative. Thus this study is limited as a work of history, but invaluable as a compendium of historical data.

These five monographs greatly advance the study of Swiss emigration in general and add valuable data and insights to the study of immigration to Russia. They show that the migratory dimension of human history defies easy generalization and creates a complex web of interrelations far beyond national boundaries. An example from Rauber's volume may illustrate this point. In 1827 Heinrich Moser (1805–1874), a watchmaker from Schaffhausen in Switzerland, moved to St. Petersburg. There he established a watch-making firm, and two years later opened a branch of his enterprise in Le Locle, Switzerland. His firm manufactured watches and clocks that were sold not only in Russia, but also in the Middle East and China. In 1848 Moser, who had married meanwhile, returned with his wife and four children to his hometown, where he had a stately home called Charlottenfels built by the Russian-Swiss architect Bernard Simon of Moscow. At his death Moser was a multimillionaire. His son Henri Moser (1844–1923) became a noted traveler, art collector, textile merchant, and writer; he also was a co–founder of the Spassky Copper Mines in Siberia, and at his death donated his valuable collection of arms to the Historical Museum in Bern. The oldest daughter became a citizen of Czechoslovakia through marriage and wrote works on natural science and occultism. The youngest daughter Mentona Moser (1874–1971) became a social worker in London, turned radical feminist, joined the Swiss Communist Party, and emigrated with Fritz Platten (1883–1942) to an agricultural commune in Soviet Russia. Later she founded a children's home near Platten's colony in Vas'kino in order to turn back part of her inherited wealth to the workers. After World War II she moved to East Germany where she died at age 97. These few data from the history of the Heinrich Moser family would have to be complemented by the story of his eight siblings and their children who stayed in Switzerland. Only then would the proper significance of Moser's emigration fully emerge. Most people seem to stay within a certain radius of their origin; yet some become enmeshed in opportunities abroad which then also shape the lives of their progeny. The five volumes under review impart a sense of those processes and show that out-migrations are part of a greater migratory web that includes also internal, return-, and in-migrations, all of which are embedded in a country's or region's dominant texture and historical evolution. It is hoped that these studies will be paralleled by works on Swiss emigration to other European countries like Germany and Italy as well as to destinations overseas. The history of any area remains incomplete if its enmeshments with regions and peoples beyond its boundaries remain unexplored. This the impressive series inspired and shaped by Goehrke makes amply evident.

Postscript (September 1993): A recent letter of Professor Goehrke lists the following further projects on Swiss in Russia completed or in preparation:

1. In 1994 Harry Schneider will publish his dissertation on Protestant and Catholic theologians.

2. Jost Soom is reworking his MA–thesis (*Lizentiatsarbeit*) into a doctoral dissertation dealing with military officers and public administrators.

3. Rudolf Mumenthaler, author of the volume dealing with physicians, is writing his doctoral dissertation on scholars active in Russia.

4. Petra Bischof is transforming her MA–thesis dealing with women active in education into a doctoral dissertation.

5. A completed MA–thesis explores emigration to Russia from the cantons of Appenzell Außerrhoden (Protestant) and Innerrhoden (Catholic), a migration which shows structural differences from the emigration of the people from Graubünden.

6. A MA–thesis in process analyzes the social and occupational composition of the some 350 returnees from Russia after 1917 and will highlight aspects concerning the lower socio–economic strata.

Professor Goehrke hopes that by the year 2000 the research project will be completed and its results available in ten volumes, including a final one containing the texts of primary sources.

Chapter 16

WESTERN HISTORIOGRAPHY OF THE RUSSIAN CIVIL WAR

Peter Kenez

Marx may deserve credit for his insights into the nature of modern indus–trial societies and recognition for inspiring hundreds of millions of human beings to revolt against social inequality, but the conclusion is inescapable: on the basis of Marxist principles it is impossible to build a modern society and economy. Marx did not create "scientific socialism," but was only a great utopian thinker.

But even if the social and political order born out of the October Revolu-tion—fought under a Marxist banner—did not survive, there can be no dis-pute about the world historical significance of that Revolution. That revolu-tion not only changed the lives of the peoples of the Russian Empire, but also profoundly affected the rest of the world. People were inspired by the example of what seemed at the time as the victory of socialism; but just as many were frightened by the prospect of social revolution and therefore were willing to respond to demagogues.

The October Revolution, properly understood, was a crisis in authority. The experience of the First World War demonstrated that it was impossible to administer a country in the midst of a modern war on the basis of those principles that formed the ideological core of Tsarism. It soon also became clear that the political ideas of the liberals and moderate socialists were no more relevant at a time of profound crisis than the ideology of Tsarist autoc-racy; the country was heading toward anarchy. The nadir was reached in October. The Bolsheviks easily assumed power, but the difficult task still lay ahead: they had to impose their rule in a vast country in the midst of war, social strife and misery. The moderate socialists who clearly enjoyed the support of the majority of the people, did not possess an ideology that would have enabled them to form a functioning government, and soon they found themselves on the sidelines. The struggle then boiled down to a contest between two forces: the Whites, organized and sustained by officers of the Imperial Army, who, *mutatis mutandis*, wanted to restore the Empire, and the Bolsheviks, who dreamt of creating a new order and a new socialist humanity. If this interpretation of the Revolution is correct, it follows that the Civil War was not merely an appendage of the Revolution, but on the contrary, it was its most significant and decisive component.

Given the importance of the Revolution it is not surprising that historians have produced a vast literature; there is hardly another event in the history of humanity that occasioned a comparable outpouring of books. Soviet historians have produced the most—though not the best—studies. Since the Soviet system derived its legitimacy from a particular interpretation of the revolution, historiography had far-reaching political significance. As a consequence historians from the era of Stalin to the recent past have been severely constrained in their work. The interpretation of Soviet historians can easily be summarized: the Leninists at the same time provided wise leadership and represented the true aspirations of the workers and peasants. The Socialist Revolutionaries and Mensheviks were traitors who, in fact, served the interests of the bourgeoisie. It was the anti-Bolsheviks who ignited the flames of the civil war, and the new revolutionary state fought primarily not against domestic enemies, but against the combined forces of world imperialism. The rebellious sailors of Kronstadt turned against the Bolsheviks not because of their disappointment with the policies of the new state, but because of the machinations of the class enemy. The Party was always united, not counting a few traitors such as Trotsky and Bukharin. The Whites, led by aristocrats, were interested exclusively in the defense of class privilege.

No other period in Soviet history, and no other topic, including collectivization and the purges, has been more poisoned by political intervention than the history of the great revolution. Although after the 20th Party Congress there were attempts to modify slightly the standard interpretation, most notably by E.N. Burdzhalov, revisionism was not long tolerated. Because of this close supervision, it is possible to talk about a uniform Soviet approach to the history of the Revolution.

Western historians have benefited from reading Soviet works from the 1920s. N. Kakurin's *Kak srazhalas' revoliutsiia* 2 vols. (Moscow, Leningrad, 1925–1926), for example, appears in the bibliography of every decent work on the Civil War. Articles from the journal *Proletarskaia revoliutsiia* and from the collection ed. A.S. Bubnov et. al. *Grazhdanskaia voina, 1918–1921* 3 vols. (Moscow, 1928–1930) have been also widely quoted. However, ever since the establishment of Stalinist orthodoxy, Soviet and Western historians have lived in such different worlds that little communication and exchange were possible. Western historians, of course, used some of the archival materials unearthed by Soviet colleagues, but, they—whether sympathetic to the Leninists or not—rarely engaged Soviet arguments. It was not even considered worthwhile to criticize Soviet works. How could you take historians seriously who, by implication, maintained that the entire Bolshevik High Command, with the exception of Lenin and those who had the good fortune to die, were traitors? What is one to say to a historian, for example, who at the same time argued that the regiments in the Imperial army most influenced by the Bolsheviks were both the most revolutionary and also the best fighting forces?[1] Only in the last ten or fifteen years have Western scholarly journals regularly reviewed Soviet works on the revolutionary period and these reviews, almost without exception, have been devastating.

Soviet historians until very recently, at regular intervals have denounced "bourgeois falsificators," by devoting articles and even entire books to the writings of Western historians.[2] It is unclear what the reviewers wanted to accomplish. They obviously did not hope to persuade their opponents. Nor could they possibly have been concerned about the need to combat foreign ideologies since none of the works they denounced appeared in Soviet bookstores. They made no distinctions among Western scholars. They denounced the pro-Soviet E.H. Carr with almost as much ferocity as the bitterly anti-Soviet, indeed, anti-Russian Richard Pipes. Annoyingly, the conclusions of Western scholars, whether correctly summarized or distorted, were usually prefaced: "Historian X was compelled to admit that..." as if the "bourgeois" historian had not searched for the truth according to his own lights. Worst of all, Soviet writers could not or did not want to make distinctions between historians of proven scholarly competence and the writings of ignorant amateurs.

Western historiography of the Revolution has been vast and heterogeneous, and therefore it is difficult to subject it to generalizations. We can,

---

1. N. M. Iakupov, *Revoliutsiia i mir: Soldatskie massy protiv imperialisticheskoi voiny, 1917–mart 1918 gg.* (Moscow, 1980).

2. This phenomenon is discussed in Walter Laqueur, *The Fate of the Revolution; Interpretations of Soviet History from 1917 to the Present* (Revised and updated. New York, 1987) pp. 200–207.

however, safely make some general comments. First of all, in the post Second World War period the bulk of scholarship has been written in English, published by British and American scholars. The contributions of French and German historians have been relatively meager. The passionate debates that took place concerning the Revolution and Civil War took place in English.[3]

Secondly, if we envisage a spectrum from a Leninist position on the Civil War on the one extreme and a monarchist one the other, most Western historians could be placed somewhere in the middle. The characteristic features of the Leninist position could be summarized this way: the Bolsheviks expressed the genuine radicalism of the workers and poor peasants; the Reds fought against the combined forces of world imperialism; the victory of the Bolsheviks was not only justified, but also was inevitable; the Bolshevik victory meant a profound break in world history; the Soviet regime and the Imperial one had no common features. By contrast, the cardinal beliefs of the monarchists have been: the Bolshevik victory was the result of an accident; the Bolsheviks won because of their ability to manipulate and willingness to use terror; the Bolsheviks were subversive, foreign agents, whose victory brought untold misery to the Russian people with whom they had nothing in common; the Tsar was betrayed by cowardly and selfish people who were interested not in the welfare of the Russian people, but exclusively in their own power. There is only one prominent American historian who in the recent past wrote in a monarchist spirit: Richard Pipes *The Russian Revolution* (New York, 1990). Pipes stands outside of the mainstream of the profession: he has neither followers nor ideological comrades.

Thirdly, the historiography demonstrates the old truism that the historian is influenced not by a dispassionate reading of source material, but by the concerns of his own society. In spite of the great heterogeneity and in spite of the obvious exceptions from generalizations, it is possible to talk about general trends and changing intellectual interests. From the late 1950s the center of the historiography moved from right to left. During the Stalinist period, and immediately after, most histories were conceived in an anti-Bolshevik spirit. The field was at first dominated by emigrés, people who had left Russia because of the Revolution. The writings of Miliukov, Melgunov, Kerenskii, and Vernadskii were particularly influential. Undoubt-

---

3. An exception from this generalization is the excellent work of Peter Scheibert, *Lenin an der Macht: Das Russische Volk in der Revolution, 1918–1922* (Weinheim, 1984), so far untranslated into English.

edly, the Cold War played a role: historians in the late 1940s and 1950s saw the Revolution as the moment of birth of a totalitarian society. The great change occurred in the 1960s and it had little to do with new sources, new availability of archives, or events in the Soviet Union. The new approach was the consequence of the ferment in Western societies, primarily in the United States. A new generation of historians came into intellectual maturity in the late 1960s and early 1970s, at a time of civil rights struggles and the anti–Vietnam war movement. These historians took a hostile stance to their own society, for it seemed to them that the talk about "the free world," democracy, and equal opportunity in the West, was nothing but hypocrisy. The defining characteristic of the young generation was the repudiation of the so-called totalitarian model. Writers in the totalitarian school emphasized similarities between fascism and communism, and juxtaposed the two against the liberal, pluralist West. The young historians perceived a self–congratulatory note here and they responded like a bull to a red flag. The disappointment in the American social order made them look on more favorably on the society which at the time seemed as the great "other." Official America was hostile to the Soviet Union, ipso facto the Soviet Union could not have been all bad. From this attitude followed a more favorable reappraisal of the Revolution.

Much of the new writing on Soviet history was done by people who again and again—to their own satisfaction—demolished the "totalitarian" model; never has been a model so often "demolished." At first the intellectual agenda of the young historians was to save the Revolution from the taint of Stalinism, and therefore they emphasized what seemed to them as a great gap between Lenin and Stalin. The young historians were guilty of overkill in their attacks on the works of the previous generation. They rarely acknowledged that that generation never spoke with one voice, and indeed, some of the best and most lasting works, such as the writings of E.H. Carr and Isaac Deutscher never fit into the totalitarian framework.[4]

In the last ten or fifteen years Western historians have published detailed, serious, and valuable studies of various aspects of 1917. Most of these aimed to contradict the idea that the Party prevailed because it was well organized

---

4.   Stephen Cohen, in particular, vastly oversimplified the views of the previous generation of historians. *Rethinking the Soviet Experience. Politics and History Since 1917* (Oxford, 1985). See in particular chapter 1. He plausibly explained the anti–Soviet views of historians by pointing to the needs of the cold war, but naively failed to see that his own generation was also responding to currents in Western societies while writing about the Soviet Union.

and centralized and therefore capable of manipulating working class opinion. Instead, the young historians argued, the Bolsheviks represented genuine working class radicalism.[5] Historians have been more interested in answering questions such as: how did the Leninists come to power? and how did they acquire working class support? than attempting to answer other, more difficult ones: namely how could the Bolsheviks manage to retain power? how did they manage ultimately to put together a more or less functioning administration? Perhaps historians sympathetic to the Revolution found it more congenial to deal with the march to power by the "working class" than examining the not always attractive policies of the victorious revolutionaries.

Although the left-leaning historians' favorite topic has been 1917, the period of the Civil War played an important role in their overall conception of Soviet history. These historians have been attracted by the noble ideals of the Revolution, yet they could not but see that the revolutionary regime soon degenerated into Stalinism. They attempted to answer the difficult question "what went wrong?" in a variety of ways, but most assumed that the Civil War was a crucial turning point. According to this line of thinking the Civil War was a formative experience: the Bolsheviks became accustomed to the use of terror, bureaucratic methods and repression of the opposition. To put it differently, there was nothing inherently wrong with Leninism; the Russian past, wicked anti-Bolsheviks, and grasping foreigners made the Bolsheviks cruel and repressive.[6] Sheila Fitzpatrick in an important article carefully examined this assumption. She came to the conclusion that while Leninists may have acquired many unpleasant habits while fighting their enemies, they were intellectually and emotionally well prepared to take those steps that in fact they did take.[7] Fitzpatrick's arguments

5. See for example, Diane Koenker, *Moscow Workers and the 1917 Revolution* (Princeton, 1981); S. A. Smith, *Red Petrograd* (Cambridge, 1983); David Mandel, *The Petrograd Workers and the Soviet Seizure of Power* (New York, 1984); T. Hasegawa *The February Revolution* (Seattle, 1981); Donald Raleigh, *Revolution on the Volga* (Ithaca, 1986); Alexander Rabinowitch, *The Bolsheviks Come to Power* (New York, 1976); Allan Widman *The End of the Imperial Russian Army* 2 vols. (Princeton, 1980–1987); Rex Wade, *Red Guards and Worker Militias in the Russian Revolution* (Stanford, 1984); D. Koenker and William Rosenberg, *Strikes and Revolution in Russia, 1917* (Princeton, 1989).

6. Most Western historians writing in the last two decades would have agreed with this formulation. I myself made some of the same points in my book, *Civil War in South Russia, 1918; the First Year of the Volunteer Army* (Berkeley, 1971).

7. Sheila Fitzpatrick, "Civil War as a Formative Experience," in A. Gleason, P. Kenez, R. Stites eds. *Bolshevik Culture; Experiment and Order in the Russian Revolution* (Bloomington, 1985).

were not altogether novel, nevertheless her article was influential: she was a woman with impeccable leftist credentials and widely respected as an erudite scholar. In order to understand the character of the Civil War and the policies of both sides, it is essential to use a comparative approach. Whites and Reds followed each other's acts and propaganda carefully, for they were, of course, well aware that they were engaged in a competition. They faced many of the same problems and often learned from one another; each side needed to impose order and create a functioning administration, to build armies and prevent desertion, and to feed the population. Whenever one discusses the topic of Red terror, for example, it is essential to discuss White atrocities. Unfortunately, neither Western nor Soviet historians paid equal attention to both sides in the Civil War, preferring to study the revolutionaries rather than their enemies. The issue which interested most of them—whether they were hostile or friendly—was the development of the Soviet state. Consciously or unconsciously, these historians believed that the defeated deserved little attention. As far as they were concerned, the defeated represented those branches of the tree of history that bore no fruit, and therefore could be safely disregarded. Characteristically, two interesting and recent American collections of articles dealing with the Civil War, written by some of the best known historians of the period, paid not the slightest attention to the Whites. Not a single article was devoted to examining the anti-Bolshevik cause.[8]

The theorist and most conspicuous practitioner of this approach was E.H. Carr. His three volume history, *The Bolshevik Revolution* London, 1950–1953, which is a part of a larger series *A History of Soviet Russia*, hardly even mentions the opponents of the Bolsheviks. It is an extraordinary work, based on vast erudition, and prodigious research, and written with great originality, and yet the reader could get no sense of the Revolution and especially of the Civil War by reading it. Carr devoted an entire volume to Bolshevik state building and constitutional ideas, another to economic policies and a third one to the first years of Soviet foreign relations. He discussed in detail some obscure topics, such as the establishment of minor Communist Parties in Europe and outside Europe, but said nothing about the Volunteer Army, the revolt of the Czechs or Kolchak. Carr did not simply overlook the Whites; he made an ideologically-based and conscious

---

8. *Bolshevik Culture* and D. Koenker, W. Rosenberg and R. Suny, eds. *Party, State and Society in the Russian Civil War* (Indiana, 1989).

choice.[9] Carr identified himself with Marx' historicism: what mattered to him was the understanding how the current system developed. He contemptuously dismissed the defeated as not worthy of interest and as irrelevant. But by dismissing the opponents that the Leninists faced, he deprived his readers from understanding what the Bolsheviks were doing, who they were, and how they saw their tasks. No historian followed consciously Carr's footsteps and attempted to imitate his approach; nevertheless, in their choice of subject matter, many implicitly accepted his principles.

For an overall picture of the Civil War, the English-speaking reader must still turn to William H. Chamberlin's two volume study of the Revolution, the second volume of which is devoted to the post-October period. That remarkable book was first published in 1935 by a journalist, and yet it remained unsurpassed. Many historians have ever since started out their introduction by pointing out how necessary it was to supersede Chamberlin, and yet none managed to do so. Although we have a great deal more primary material available to us than Chamberlin could have had, the accumulation of details necessitated no fundamental reevaluation. His sympathetic, yet sober-minded approach to the revolutionaries, combined with his excellent knowledge of the country and many of the leading figures of the Revolution enabled Chamberlin to produce a well balanced book. After the Second World War he moved away from his moderately sympathetic stance to the Revolution and became a passionate anti-Communist and anti-Soviet ideologue. In his bitterly anti-Communist period he produced no scholarly work, and his fine study of the Revolution stands by itself.

There have been few Western historians who even attempted to write a general history of the Civil War. The best of the studies is by Evan Mawdsley who published *The Russian Civil War* in 1987 (Boston). This is a valuable book, written by a competent and knowledgeable historian, however, the author in a short study could do nothing more than to touch on the many complex issues of the period. As a consequence the book seems more like a brief encyclopaedia rather than a new interpretation based on fresh materials or fresh approach. Mawdsley sensibly but unsurprisingly argued that the Bolsheviks won because the Russian people opposed their policies less passionately than the policies of the Whites, because the Reds were better led, and were able to field a large army.

There are three other books that claim to be general histories. However,

---

9. Carr developed his ideas about history with exceptional clarity in his short, but fascinating book, *What is History?* (London, 1961).

David Footman's brief *Civil War in Russia* (London, 1961) is frankly impres–sionistic and selective. It has some good material on aspects of the Civil War, such as, for example, a good chapter on Makhno, but contrary to the title, the book is not a general history. John Bradley's *Civil War in Russia, 1917–1920* (London, 1975) is superficial and cannot be regarded as a contri-bution to scholarship. Bruce Lincoln's new *Red Victory* (New York, 1989) is aimed at the general reader.

In the not too distant past the great bulk of monographs devoted to the Bolsheviks side in the Civil War were institutional histories or political bi-ographies. Historians made major contributions to the study of the develop-ment of the Communist Party in the years of civil war in particular, and the evolution of the Soviet system in general. One thinks of such important works as Leonard Schapiro, *The Origins of the Communist Autocracy: Po-litical Opposition in the Soviet State: First Phase, 1917–1922* (London, 1955); T. H. Rigby, *Communist Party Membership in the USSR, 1917– 1967* (Princeton, 1968) and *Lenin's Government: Sovnarkom, 1917–1922* (Cam-bridge, 1978); Robert Daniels, *The Conscience of the Revolution: Commu-nist Opposition in Soviet Russia.* (Cambridge, Mass, 1960) and Robert Ser-vice, *The Bolshevik Party in Revolution; A Study in Organizational Change, 1917–1923* (London, 1979) and John Keep, *The Russian Revolution: A Study in Mass Mobilization* (London, 1976). Among the political biographies the most important ones were: Isaac Deutscher, *The Prophet Armed: Trotsky, 1879–1921* (New York, 1954); Robert Tucker, *Stalin as Revolutionary: 1879– 1929: A Study in History and Personality* (New York, 1974); Adam Ulam, *The Bolsheviks: The Intellectual and Political History of the Triumph of Communism in Russia* (New York, 1965) and Stephen Cohen, *Bukharin and the Bolshevik Revolution* (New York, 1974). These books differed from one another in approach and politics. Deutscher and Cohen, for example, were moved by the emancipatory ideals of the revolutionaries. On the other hand, Schapiro and Ulam were sceptical. In spite of these and other differ-ences, these authors still provide us with the most reliable guidelines for the evolution of the Soviet regime during the difficult years of Civil War and war communism.

In the last decade most Western historians turned their interest from po-litical to social history, and works on the history of the Civil War have been part of this larger phenomenon.[10] There have been two major reasons for

10. On this literature see the thorough, generous and intelligent survey by John Keep, "So-cial Aspects of the Russian Revolutionary Era (1917–1923) in Recent English Language Historiography," *East European Quarterly* XXIV, No. 2. June, 1990.

this change of intellectual interests. Political history appeared more or less exhausted: most of the major figures of the revolution, Lenin, Stalin, Trotsky, and Bukharin, had already found able biographers and there was little of significance that could be added. The history of the party and the various oppositional groups within it also have all been discussed satisfactorily.

The political commitment of the new cohort of historians drew them to the study of social history, a topic that they considered both more important and found more congenial. A few of these scholars have worked within an explicitly Marxist—however modern and revisionist—framework, and insisted accordingly on the primary importance of class in analyzing historical events.[11]

Other scholars, though influenced by Marxism, gravitated toward social history because of their interest in and identification with groups that had been disadvantaged. They wanted to write history from bottom up, to reverse—what seemed to them—the bias of all previous historiography. They wanted to depict the simple people, peasants, soldiers, workers, women, as masters of their own fate and not merely playthings in the hands of the Bolsheviks. Taking the side of the oppressed usually, but not always, implied leftist politics. Oliver Radkey, for example, although an enemy of all privileged—nobles, politicians, and especially intellectuals—could not possibly be described as a man of the left. He took the side of the rebellious Russian peasants and wrote one of the most passionately anti–Bolshevik books, *The Unknown Civil War in Soviet Russia* (Stanford, 1976) in which in a utopian fashion he defended the peasants' anarchism and denounced all "oppression."

Social historians have studied classes, social groups, women, demography, and the elusive subject of changing mentality. The most extensive work has been done in the field of labor history. Although much of the work was devoted to the study of the revolutionary year of 1917, recently also a great deal of valuable writing has been published on the period of the Civil War. All labor historians, of course, recognized that following the Bolshevik victory in October 1917, the new government lost much of its working class support. How to deal with this phenomenon occasioned an interesting historiographical debate.

Most of the labor historians, most prominent among them William G. Rosenberg, were unwilling to accept that in 1918 a fatal and complete breach occurred between the proletariat and the Bolsheviks. For these historians there was much at stake. First of all, to concede that the Bolsheviks lost the support of the group that brought them into power would bring into question the legitimacy of Lenin's revolution, and, in effect, justify the central tenet of the Menshevik position according to which Russia had not been ready for a socialist revolution. Secondly, if the historians admitted that the interests of the "working class", however defined, immediately diverged from those of the victorious revolutionaries, they would also have to concede that the rule of the proletariat was in this instance and most likely in all other instances a chimera. In the American context such admissions would have been tantamount to saying that there was not and there has never been an alternative to a capitalist society.[12]

Western historians have paid far more attention to a tiny minority of Russians, the workers, than to the bulk the people, the peasants. This is not surprising. The proletariat, in fact, played a political role out of proportion

---

11. See for example the writings of R. G. Suny, "Toward a Social History of the October Revolution," *American Historical Review* 1983, pp. 31–52. Suny engaged in an interesting exchange with Sheila Fitzpatrick in *Slavic Review*. Sheila Fitzpatrick in her article "The Bolsheviks' Dilemma: Class Culture and Politics in Early Soviet Years," *Slavic Review* 1988, pp. 599–613 wrote that Russian class structure disintegrated in the revolutionary period and therefore class analysis became useless for analytical purposes. Suny took issue with her. "Class and State in the Early Soviet Period: A Reply to Sheila Fitzpatrick." *Slavic Review* 1988, pp. 614–619.

12. Among the labor historians should be mentioned William Husband, *Revolution in the Factory* (Oxford, 1990); William Chase, *Workers, Society and the Soviet State: Labor and Life in Moscow, 1918–1929* (Urbana, 1987); Steven Smith, *Red Petrograd: Revolution in the Factories, 1917–1918* (Cambridge, 1983); Diane Koenker "Urbanization and Deurbanization in the Russian Revolution and Civil War," in *Party, State and Society in the Russian Civil War.* The *Slavic Review* in 1985 contained an interesting discussion where these points were explicitly raised. William Rosenberg "Russian Labor and Bolshevik Power After October," pp. 213–238. Rosenberg accepted that the workers were dissatisfied with the new regime in 1918, however he argued that working class opposition was economic and not political and that the workers would have still preferred the Bolsheviks against all conceivable alternatives. Furthermore, he maintained that it was in error to look at the change of public opinion only in a short duration. In his view the Bolsheviks later regained workers' support. The trouble with Rosenberg's argument is that as Bolshevik rule became increasingly repressive, there were no longer any means of measuring working class support. Interestingly, Rosenberg, an erudite and careful scholar, wrote a book with D. Koenker about strikes in 1917, where they properly described these acts as directed against the government. Rosenberg and Koenker would not make the same evaluation for the strikes of 1918. Vladimir Brovkin "Politics, Not Economics Was The Key," pp. 244–250 argued that it was only limitless repression that kept the Leninists in power. Brovkin developed his arguments in greater detail in *The Mensheviks After October, Socialist Opposition and the Rise of Bolshevik Dictatorship* (Ithaca, 1987). In my view Brovkin was correct.

to its size. Furthermore, researching working class politics is far easier than to make sense of what was happening in thousands of villages. But undoubtedly the main reason for overemphasizing the significance of the workers in the revolutionary events has been an unexamined Marxism. Young American historians, in particular, whether consciously or unconsciously, have regarded the proletariat as "the universal class."[13]

Recently, however, some fine work appeared about the participation of the peasants in the revolutionary events. The most impressive of these studies is by Orlando Figes, *Peasant Russia, Civil War* (Oxford, 1989). Figes, limiting himself to the examination of four Volga provinces, analyzed the role of the peasantry in the revolutionary events. His conclusions were not surprising, however the great deal of archival material examined gave added weight to his judgments. Figes maintained that the peasants, having destroyed the institutions of the old regime in the countryside in 1917–1918, above all, wanted to be left alone. They feared the restoration of the old order more than they resented the alien and urban Bolsheviks, and therefore as long as the White movement existed, and the danger of restoration, peasant opposition to the new leaders in Moscow remained muted. It was only after the defeat of the Whites that the peasants embarked on a series of bloody, bitter, but ultimately hopeless anti-Bolshevik risings.[14]

Anglo-American, but particularly American historians have recently created an entire subfield of social history which has no equivalent in Soviet historiography. As a result of the feminist movement and the creation of feminist scholarship, American historians have done a great deal in the field of women's history. The first to examine the role of women in the revolution was Richard Stites in his *The Women's Liberation Movement in Russia: Feminism, Nihilism and Bolshevism, 1860–1930* (Princeton, 1978). Some feminist-socialist historians would have liked to show that the oppression of women has been a feature only of capitalist societies, however, after

---

13. Although, naturally, the working class and the peasantry have been most often the subject of research, other social groups have also been examined by Western historians. See for example, Kendall Bailes, *Technology and Society Under Lenin and Stalin; Origins of the Soviet Technical Intelligentsia, 1917–1941* (Princeton, 1978); David Joravsky, "Cultural Revolution and the Fortress Mentality" in *Bolshevik Culture*; James McClelland, "The Professoriat in the Russian Civil War," in *Party, State and Society in the Russian Civil War*.

14. On the history of the peasantry see also Lars Lih, *Bread and Authority in Russia, 1914–1921* (Berkeley, 1990). Lih examined the grain requisitioning policies of the Bolsheviks. There are also relevant chapters in Dorothy Atkinson, *The End of the Russian Land Commune, 1905–1930* (Stanford, 1983).

examining the Russian situation most of them concluded that the aims of the Bolsheviks and those of the feminists collided very soon after October, 1917.[15] After Lenin, Stalin and Trotsky, "three who made a revolution"—according to the phrase of Bertram Wolfe—it was Aleksandra Kollontai who has received the most thorough treatment from historians. Her socialist feminism proved to be extremely attractive to female scholars. There are more books and articles written about Kollontai than there are works on Zinovev, Kamenev, Sverdlov and Rykov combined.[16] Recently Western historians have paid increased attention to what might be called the study of mentality and attempted to capture the extraordinary and uto–pian atmosphere of the revolutionary era. The most ambitious and interesting book on the subject was written by Richard Stites *Utopian Vision and Experimental Life in the Russian Revolution.* (Oxford, 1989), who gives a sympathetic account of the utopian mentality.[17] In this context we might also mention books by Zenovia Sochor, *Revolution and Culture; the Bogdanov-Lenin Controversy* (Ithaca, 1988); Lynn Mally, *The Culture of the Future; the Proletkult Movement in Revolutionary Russia* (Berkeley, 1990); Peter Kenez, *The Birth of the Propaganda State; Soviet Methods of Mass Mobilization* (Cambridge, 1985); Nina Tumarkin, *Lenin Lives!; The Lenin Cult in Soviet Russia* (Cambridge, Mass, 1983); Jane Burbank, *Intelligentsia and Revolution; Russian Views of Bolshevism, 1917–1922.*

Although primary materials are available in the United States concerning the anti–Bolshevik side in the Civil War (most importantly at the Hoover Institution and at Columbia University), Western historians have shown less interest in the defeated than in the victors. In particular they have paid relatively little attention to the most serious opponents of the Bolsheviks, the Whites. For example, the extraordinarily important Siberian counterrevolution has not yet found a chronicler. The South Russian movement, led in succession by Kornilov, Alekseev, Denikin and Wrangel, was described in

15. Let us mention only two articles on the topic of women during the civil war. Barbara Clements, "The Birth of the New Soviet Woman" and Beatrice Farnsworth, "Village Women Experience the Revolution," both in *Bolshevik Culture.*

16. The three known works are Cathy Porter, *Alexandra Kollontai; a Biography* (London, 1980); Beatrice Farnsworth, *Aleksandra Kollontai; Socialism, Feminism and the Bolshevik Revolution* (Stanford, 1980); and Barbara Clements, *Bolshevik Feminist; the Life of Aleksandra Kollontai* (Bloomington, 1979).

17. See the perceptive review of this book by Aileen Kelly in *The New York Review of Books* December 6, 1990 in which Kelly points out the dangers of utopian thinking.

my two books, *Civil War in South Russia, 1918; the First Year of the Volunteer Army* and *Civil War in South Russia, 1919–1920; the Defeat of the Whites* (Berkeley, 1976). In these books I attempted to describe the social composition of the White movement, the social policies of the counterrevolutionaries, and their attempts to establish a functioning administration. Although I tried to describe the genuine dilemmas faced by the generals, these books are by no means admiring accounts of the Whites. I concluded that Denikin and Wrangel stood for the recreation of the old order and that this program found little support among the majority of the Russian people, the peasants.

The Western reader today cannot form an informed opinion of the anti-Bolshevik side in the Civil War because important elements are missing from this picture. There is no complete study of the anarchist movement, although there are good studies of the Kronstadt rising.[18] There are two rather unsatisfactory studies of Makhno.[19] Unfortunately, there is also no study of the role of the Cossacks, which is a very significant omission, since even scholars tend to underestimate their role.

The civilian opponents of the Bolsheviks have been better served by Western historians. William G. Rosenberg wrote the definitive study of the Kadets in the revolutionary period.[20] Rosenberg was by no means an admirer of the Kadets. He described them as inept politicians who on the one hand held on to inappropriate slogans in revolutionary times such as *gosudarstvennost'*, and on the other betrayed their ideals by supporting military counterrevolution's often terroristic policies. Rosenberg, on the basis of diligent research, well conveyed the impossible dilemmas faced by liberals at a time of revolution: they had to choose between—as they saw it—two evils and they did not long hesitate. Their hatred of the Bolsheviks was such as to make them tolerate the lawlessness of the Whites.

The foremost historian of the Socialist Revolutionaries was Oliver Radkey, who thoroughly analyzed the history of the party in 1917 and in the first weeks of 1918.[21] Radkey was even less of an admirer of his protagonists

18. Paul Avrich, *Kronstadt, 1921* (Princeton, 1970) and Izrael Getzler, *Kronstadt, 1917–1921: The Fate of a Soviet Democracy* (Cambridge, 1983).

19. Michael Malet, *Nestor Makhno in the Russian Civil War* (London, 1982) and Michael Palij, *The Anarchism of Nestor Makhno, 1918–1921: An Aspect of the Ukrainian Revolution* (Seattle, 1976).

20. William G. Rosenberg, *Liberals in the Russian Revolution* (Princeton, 1974).

21. *The Agrarian Foes of Bolshevism* (New York, 1958) and *The Sickle Under the Hammer* (New York, 1963).

than Rosenberg was of his. In his extraordinarily detailed study he described the Socialist Revolutionaries as politicians who betrayed their followers. The Right wing of the Party ceased to be socialist in anything but in name, while members of the Left helped the Bolsheviks to capture and retain power. In Radkey's description the Socialist Revolutionaries were intellectuals who had little contact with the simple people of Russia. He denied that they ever represented their nominal constituency, the peasantry. The peasants voted for them in November, 1917 because they naively took their protestations of socialism seriously. Radkey wrote from a populist point of view; only his dislike of the Bolsheviks surpassed his distaste for the subjects of his study, the Socialist Revolutionaries. Nevertheless, the Western reader who wants to find out about the ideology, internal struggles, plans, and projects of the moderate socialists can easily do so by turning to Radkey's books.

Among the opponents of the Bolsheviks it was the Mensheviks who have received the most extensive and sympathetic treatment from Western historians because they shared the moderate socialist beliefs of the Mensheviks. Also, among the Menshevik emigré intellectuals there were many who articulately expressed their political point of view, and these writings have made lasting impressions (for example, Sukhanov, Dan, Nikolaevskii and Dallin).

Leopold Haimson, a prominent and influential historian who trained many people of the young generation at Columbia University, made a life–long study of the Menshevik movement. He and his students collected memoirs by Menshevik leaders, interviewed surviving Menshevik politicians, and published books and articles on this topic. Vladimir Brovkin published recently a challenging study of the Mensheviks in the immediate post–October period.[22] Brovkin, unlike Haimson and his students, wrote from a distinctly antiBolshevik point of view. He argued that the Bolsheviks soon after their victory lost support from the workers and that the Mensheviks, as shown by local soviet elections, were able to provide a credible alternative. In his opinion the Bolsheviks turned to dictatorial methods because that was the only alternative to losing power.

By far the best studied aspect of the Civil War is the history of intervention. It is understandable why this is so: archives have been easily available; amateur historians have believed that it was possible to make a contribution to scholarship without knowing Russian; and Frenchmen, Americans and

---

22. *The Mensheviks after October: Socialist Opposition and the Rise of Dictatorship* (Ithaca, 1987).

British naturally were particularly interested in the doings of their own coun-
trymen. Historians, by paying so much attention to this topic, inadvertently
may have overemphasized its significance; after all, writers want to believe
that their topic is important.

However much Westerners may have overstated the importance of foreign contribution to the anti-Bolshevik cause, nevertheless there remained
a vast gulf between Communist and non-Communist scholars. Ever since
the time of the Revolution the Leninists believed that there existed not only
an international solidarity of the working classes, but also that of the impe-
rialists. Lenin and his comrades expected that the leaders of the capitalist
powers would understand their true self-interest and therefore would forget
about their less important differences among one another and combine to
defeat the young revolutionary state. As we know, no such unity ever came
into being. What was a genuine article of faith among the revolutionaries,
came to be a pretense for Soviet historians of later generations. It was essential for the legitimacy of the regime to sustain this argument. Soviet
publicists had to maintain that at the time of the Civil War the Bolsheviks
enjoyed not only the support of the working class, but also that of the poor
peasants, namely, the vast majority of the people. But if that was so, how
was one to explain that the war lasted for three years? It was essential to be
able to argue that the Bolsheviks defeated not merely a motley collection of
domestic enemies, but the combined force of world imperialism. As nationalism became an ever more important component in Soviet ideology, Soviet historians insisted more and more strongly that the "civil war" was in
fact a struggle against foreign interventionists.

No serious Western scholar ever accepted this argument. There has al-
ways been a unanimity of opinion that when all is said and done, the Civil
War was in fact a civil war, fought by peoples of the defunct Russian Em-
pire. It was the correlation of domestic forces that was ultimately decisive.
The leaders of the Western powers, no matter how much they loathed the
Bolsheviks, were in no position to give meaningful help to their Russian
friends. At the end of the World War the peoples of Europe and of the United
States were tired of fighting and resisted being involved in a struggle that
they did not understand, and the outcome of which did not interest them.
This is not to say that the help that the anti-Bolsheviks received from abroad
made no difference. Some historians plausibly argued that the Civil War
would have ended somewhat sooner and the boundaries of Communism
would have been pushed a little further West, had there been no intervention. But other historians claimed that the intervention took place on such a

small scale that it perhaps harmed the Whites more than it helped them, for it enabled the Bolsheviks to identify themselves with the national cause. From each and every account we learn about the bottomless ignorance of Western policy makers concerning Russia, and, especially, concerning the admittedly complex political situation there. We learn how Lloyd George thought that Kharkov was the name a of General, and the French Commander Borius, arrived in Odessa in December 1918 with no more precise instructions than "make common cause with patriotically thinking Russians."

The differences of opinion that have existed among Western scholars of the intervention had to do with motivation of the interventionists. Some Marxist or Marxist–influenced scholars attributed decisive influence on Western decision-making to financial and industrial circles, while others, indeed the majority, explained intervention as the consequence of decisions of bumbling politicians who knew little of Russian circumstances, had an instinctive dislike of Communism, and a desire to help their Russian friends. Of course, the two explanations are not mutually exclusive, and the issue can be regarded as simply a matter of emphasis. It is fair to say that in the last two decades Marxism found many more adherents among Western historians than in the more distant past.[23]

Although U.S. role in the intervention was by far not the most important, nevertheless the largest number of studies have been devoted to it. Most of these books suffer from repetitiousness and from an inability of their authors to put their topic into a larger context.[24] The authors have been satisfied with a description of the suffering of the American soldiers in a strange and hostile environment and in a world where they could not tell their friends from their enemies. These books cannot be regarded as contributions to our understanding of the Russian Civil War.

The best study of American policy at the time of the Civil War is still the two volume work of George Kennan, *Soviet-American Relations, 1917–1920* 2 vols. (Princeton, 1956–1958). Unfortunately Kennan never completed his work, and took his story no further than the Fall of 1918. Kennan, an extraordinary stylist and a scholar of profound knowledge of Russian

---

23. Among those who stressed imperialist motives were W. A. Williams, *American–Russian Relations, 1781–1947* (New York, 1952); Alex Schmid, *Churchill's privater Krieg; Intervention unter Konterrevolution im russischen Bürgerkrieg, November, 1918–März, 1920* (Zürich, 1974); and Michael Carley, *Revolution and Intervention: The French Government and the Russian Civil War, 1917–1919* (Kingston, 1983).

24. See for example a recent study by Benjamin Rhodes, *The Anglo–American Winter War with Russia, 1918–1919* (New York, 1988).

history, was primarily interested in the weaknesses of American policy making. In his books he showed the indecisiveness of Wilson's policies and how the Americans were dragged into this unfortunate affair largely by their allies. Also, he argued that the Americans wanted to limit the expansion of Japanese influence in the Far East. Kennan's two volumes appeared at a time when Soviet historians insisted, obviously for immediate political reasons, that the United States had always been behind all "anti-Soviet conspiracies," and intervention was simply a first act in a long series of wrongdoings. Kennan aimed to contradict these ideas, by showing that the intervention took place in the context of the World War.

After the American role in the intervention, it is the participation of the British that has been most thoroughly analyzed. On this topic the definitive work is Richard Ullman's three volume study *Anglo-Soviet Relations, 1917–1921* (Princeton, 1961–1972). Ullman, like Kennan, showed in his extremely detailed examination of British policies the ignorance of the British policy makers, and how the British committed one blunder after another.

There is nothing comparable on the important topic of French intervention. The most detailed work is Michael Carley's *Revolution and Intervention; The French Government and the Russian Civil War, 1917–1919* (Kingston, Ontario 1981). Carley's work suffers from extremely narrow concentration on the records of the French government. He considered French intervention in the Russian Civil War as something analogous to French nineteenth century colonial policies. His approach would have been closest to the views of Soviet historians before the age of *perestroika*. At the same time Carley, unlike Ullman and Kennan, had little interest and even less knowledge of the history of the Civil War. He had no clearer understanding of the situation in Russia than the French policy makers whose actions he so rightly criticized.

One of the best books on Allied intervention in the Russian Civil War is by George Brinkley *The Volunteer Army and Allied Intervention in South Russia, 1917–1921* (Notre Dame, 1966). What raises this study above the hundreds of others is the author's excellent knowledge of the confused Russian situation. Brinkley, unlike most other historians, looked at the intervention not only from the point of view of the foreign powers, but also from the point of view of those who were supposed to be helped by it.

Arguably it was not Allied intervention that made the greatest difference in the Russian Civil War, but the role Germany played in 1917 and 1918. The Germans had the best intelligence concerning what was happening in Russia and they had the simplest agenda: they were exclusively interested in the expansion of their own power and the weakening of the old Russian Empire. They pursued a clever policy of supporting the Bolsheviks at the center of the country and anti-Bolshevik forces on the peripheries. The best books on German policies in the East is Oleh Fedyshin's *Germany's Drive to the East and the Ukrainian Revolution* (New Brunswick, 1971); and Winfried Baumgart, *Deutsche Ostpolitik 1918: Von Brest-Litovsk bis zum Ende des Ersten Welkrieges* (Vienna, 1966). The important topic of Japanese intervention still awaits a competent historian.

The collapse of the Soviet system, the child of the Revolution, will undoubtedly profoundly influence historiography. For the first time scholars, foreigners, as well as Russians, can examine the rich collection of the so called Prague archives. (These are the documentary materials that the emigrés collected in the inter-war period and the Red Army captured in 1945.) But more important than an improved access to archives, historiography will change because historians will pose different questions. It is not self-evident why in the light of the present we should reexamine the past, nevertheless this is what historians usually do.

Chapter 17

SOVIET HISTORICAL SCHOLARSHIP OF THE 1920S AND 1930S IN THE LIGHT OF ANGLO–AMERICAN HISTORIOGRAPHY

George Enteen

Historiography as a field or subdiscipline of historical scholarship holds a less distinguished place in historical scholarship in the United States and Britain than it does in Russia and other European countries. Historians have, nevertheless, devoted a considerable amount of attention to the professional and political circumstances in which Soviet historians worked, and to their ideological guidance. Many of their writings have been journalistic in spirit even when they appear in scholarly journals. They often consist of efforts to observe the changing scene, to keep up, as it were, with current events. Few of them are scholarly in the sense of penetrating into the world of Soviet historians and reconstructing it on the basis of critically assembled and thoughtfully analyzed sources. Altogether the writings are numerous, and no attempt will be made in this essay to be exhaustive. I will provide references to most of the works but discuss only a few, chiefly those that form part of disputes and reveal trends, or those that touch upon controversies engaged in by Soviet historians.

The scholarly writings have a broad range and show considerable variety. They consist of studies of particular historians, such as Pokrovskii, Tarle,[1] Mints, and Nechkina.[2] Others trace the interpretations of Soviet scholars on

1. Ann E. Erickson, "E. V. Tarle: The Career of a Historian Under the Soviet Regime," *American Slavic and East European Review*, XIX (April 1960), 202–216.

2. Alan Kimball, "I. I. Mints and the Representation of Reality in History," *Slavic Review*, XXXV, no. 4 (December, 1976), 715–723; same author, "Militsa Vassilevna Nechkina," unpublished manuscript.

such specific questions as the formation of the Russian state, the life and work of Peter I,[3] the Russian revolution,[4] or the treaty of Brest–Litovsk.[5] A significant number of primary sources have been published in translation. These include Marin Pundeff's annotated collection of portions of forty documents.[6] The recent publication of Got'e's carefully and elaborately edited diary is an important source for many questions.[7] Numerous writings of Pokrovskii have appeared in English.[8] The quarterly journal, *Soviet Studies in History*, consists of translations of writings by Soviet historians. Many of these are studies of scholarship in the 1920s and 1930s. In addition, memoirs of Soviet historians written during the thaw and published in *Istoriia SSSR* have been translated in this journal. *The Communist*, a journal of the American Communist Party, contains some material pertinent to events on the historical front in the 1930s. Mention must be made of *The Modern Encyclopedia of Russian and Soviet History*, now fifty-four volumes published between 1976 and 1990. It contains numerous entries about Soviet historical scholarship in the 1920s and 1930s; some of them are biographical, some of them are about institutions such as Istpart and the Society of Marxist Historians, and some of them contain original findings. Larry Holmes, a historian at the University of Southern Alabama, has contributed more than a dozen articles, which constitutes in itself a body of findings and commentary.

---

3.   Nicholas V. Riasanovsky, *The Image of Peter the Great in Russian History and Thought* (New York, 1985).

4.   See below, p. 234.

5.   Raymond L. Garthoff, "The Stalinist Revision of History, the Case of Brest–Litovsk," *World Politics*, V, 1 (October, 1952), 66–87.

6.   *History in the U.S.S.R.: Selected Readings* (San Francisco, 1967).

7.   *Time of Troubles: the Diary of Iurii Vladimirovich Got'e, Moscow*, July 8, 1917 to July 23, 1922, ed. and trans,. by Terence Emmons (Princeton, 1988). The Russian language version that appeared in *Voprosy istorii* with a few changes was also edited in the United States.

8.   His *Brief History of Russia* was translated by D. S. Mirsky (London, 1933) and is held in numerous libraries. A major portion of his *Russian History from Earliest Times to the Rise of Commercial Capitalism* (New York, 1931) was translated by Jesse Clarkson, who conducted a correspondence with Pokrovskii in the course of his work on the manuscript. Roman Szporluk translated and published in a separate volume some of Pokrovskii's major writings, *Russia in World History: Selected Essays* (Ann Arbor, 1970). Some of Pokrovskii's political/methodological essays were published in the volume by Pundeff mentioned above and in a widely read collection entitled *Varieties of History: From Voltaire to the Present* (New York, 1956), Fritz Stern, ed.

Only two of the writings that appeared in Great Britain and the United States at the end of the 1920s and in the 1930s can properly be deemed scholarly. The others consist of bibliographical essays or informational reports. A scholar with long experience in Russia and one of the founding fathers of Russian studies in America, Samuel N. Harper, published some of the materials that grew out of the dispute the emigré historian Mikhail Rostovtsev created when he challenged the presence of the delegation of Soviet historians at the International Congress of Historians at Oslo in 1928. N.M. Lukin's account of the dispute, as published in *Pravda*, also appeared in Harper's note.[9] Michael Karpovich, an emigré historian with roots in the Kadet Party, produced a bibliographical essay about studies of the Russian Revolution.[10] It included observations about the circumstances under which Russian historians worked, and he drew attention to the growing politicization of historical scholarship.

The British journal *Slavonic and East European Review* was the main source of information about Soviet historiography. A. Florovsky published an important bibliographical article. It was well informed and penetrating, and quite remarkably passionate and fair-minded at the same time. Even as it called attention to the abuse of non-Marxist historians, it noted that scholarly activity continued. The author took note of the work of both Marxist and non-Marxist scholarship.[11] *The Slavonic and East European Review* published an obituary of Pokrovskii,[12] and in 1933 it published a note by a former Soviet scientist who had escaped to Finland from a Soviet concentration camp. It was written by V.N. Chernavin and entitled, "The Treatment of Scholars in the USSR." and conveyed information about the arrest, imprisonment and banishment of fourteen Russian and Ukrainian historians, among other scholars.[13]

An American historian, Stuart Tompkins, wrote an article for the *Slavonic and East European Review* about the evolution of Soviet historical scholarship.[14] His source base was meager, confined mostly to the journal *Istorik–*

9. "A communist View of Historical Studies," *Journal of Modern History*, I, 1929, 77–84.

10. "The Russian Revolution of 1917," *Journal of Modern History*, II, 1930, 258–280.

11. "Historical Studies in Soviet Russia," *Slavonic and East European Review*, XIII (1934–1935), 457–469. *The Slavonic and East European Review* published an obituary of Pokrovskii.

12. A. F. Dobbie–Bateman, XI (1932), 187–189.

13. XI (April, 1933), 710–714.

14. "Communist Historical Thought," XIII (1935), 294–319.

marksist, but, because he was not only accurate but provided an implicit periodization of his subject, the article should be deemed genuinely scholarly. He distinguished between the early and mid–1920's, when a form of pluralism prevailed among historians, and the years following that witnessed the forcible silencing of non–Marxist historians.

B.H. Sumner, a founder of modern Russian studies in Great Britain, published a distinctive two–part article.[15] It was distinctive in that the author did not seek the political determinants of historical constructions, even though he took note of the acquisition of a monopoly position by Marxist scholars and of the campaign against Pokrovskii as well. He took the work of Soviet scholars at face value and sought to assess the answers they provided for their own questions, 1) the question of the nature of socio–economic formations and the applicability of the concept to Russian history prior to 1870; 2) the existence of objective social laws; 3) the role of the individual in history.

After defining and discussing the concept of socioeconomic formations, Sumner summarized the efforts to apply it to specific historical problems. He emphasized the writings of B.D. Grekov who asserted that Russian feudalism emerged not from a slave-owning society but directly from a pre–class society. Grekov's interpretation implies that commerce never played a defining role in the Kievan period of history. This relegated the Varangians to a secondary role. He did not bring out the political importance of this finding. Grekov stressed the difficulties encountered "in periodising pre–capitalistic history in accordance with the method of historical materialism, particularly in the case of Russia," and he noted that Soviet historians are admittedly very far from having reached agreement on many of the most crucial problems.[16]

Affirmation of the existence of laws of development did not solve the problem of objectivity for Soviet historians, according to Sumner. Historians came to include an element of relativism in their theory of historical materialism. Without using the term 'partiinost', he presents its meaning and employs it to explain the intrusion of relativism.[17] As concerns the role of the individual and subjective factors as agencies of historical change,

---

15. "Soviet History," *Slavonic and East European Review*, XVI (1937–1938), 601–615; XVII (1938–1939), 151–161.

16. pp. 614–615.

17. p. 153.

18. pp. 159–161.

Sumner noted the impact of Stalin's words on these matters. He took note of two other tendencies that emerged in this connection. The first was the broadening of the range of studies beyond the boundaries of Russian history and the effort to write the histories of national minorities in the Soviet Union. The second tendency was the revival of Russian themes in connection with the promotion of Soviet patriotism. There was a direct effort to re–awaken pride in Russian national traditions.[18]

The appearance of five separate works in the 1950s and early 1960s revealed the presence of a new generation of scholars and indicated a new stage of Anglo-American scholarship. In 1956 an important sbornik edited by Cyril E. Black and entitled *Rewriting Russian History* appeared; in 1958, a revised edition of the textbook of the emigré historian Anatole G. Mazour, *Modern Russian Historiography* was published. At about the same time, Paul Aron, an American graduate student at Columbia University, produced two papers of considerable weight.[19] In 1962 the Ukrainian emigré historian, Konstantin Shteppa, published a wide-ranging study that constituted a sustained polemic and that serves as a reference work.[20] These works, taken together, formed the bedrock for the next generation of graduate students and young scholars.

Rewriting Russian History was the most important of these works and brought the study of Soviet scholarship to a higher level. It consists of two parts; the first, entitled 'The Evolution of Theory', consists of four essays. The first one, written by the editor C.E. Black, at the time a professor of Russian history at Princeton University, was entitled "History and Politics in the Soviet Union." Two essays follow written by an emigré historian using the name Leo Yaresh: "The Problem of Periodization," and "The Role of the Individual in History." An essay by the Ukrainian emigré historian Konstantin F. Shteppa concludes the section, "The 'Lesser Evil' Formula."[21] Section II consists of applications of theory to specific problems such as "The First Russian State" by Alexander Vucinich, "Byzantine Cultural Influences," by Ihor Sevcenko, "The Formation of the Great Russian State"

---

19. Aron presented the papers to the Russian Research Center of Harvard University. Neither provided footnote reference, and only one of them was ever published. On December 15, 1950, he spoke on the theme, 'Diversity and Uniformity in Soviet Historiography: A Case Study.' I believe at approximately the same time he spoke on the theme, 'M. N. Pokrovsky and the Impact of the First Five Year Plan on Soviet Historiography,' pp. 283–302 in *Essays in Russian and Soviet History in Honor of Geroid Tanquary Robinson*, ed. by John Shelton Curtiss (New York, 1963).

20. *Russian Historians and the Soviet State* (New Brunswick, 1962).

by Yaresh, "Ivan the Terrible and the Oprichnina" by Yaresh, "The Reforms of Peter the Great" by Black, "The Campaign of 1812" by Yaresh, "Bakunin and the Russian Jacobins and Blanquests" by Volodymyr Varlamov and "Allied and American Intervention in Russia, 1918–1921" by John M. Thompson. The second edition includes a translation of a long review of the book that was originally published in *Istoriia SSSR,* no. 6, 1959. Much of the writing relates to the 1940s and 1950s as well as the 1920s and 1930s.

The two most important essays are the introductory essay by Black and the essay by Yaresh on debates about periodization. Black's may be considered a deepening and broadening of the path opened by Tompkins, and Yaresh's may be deemed an enlargement and refinement of Sumner's study. Black's introductory paragraph conveys the major concerns that guided Anglo-American historiography at the time, the tendency to see historiography as a barometer of politics.

The relationship between historical writing and the Communist Party line offers some valuable insights into the workings of the Soviet system. It touches on the role of Marxism in Soviet policy, and on the question whether Marxism as a working philosophy can be said in fact to offer a guide to historical interpretation. This relationship also illustrates the nature of the controls exercised by the party and state over scholarship, and the uses to which history can be put in propaganda and education. Perhaps most significantly, it provides an example of the extent to which scholars can oppose, evade and counterbalance the massive power of party and state–the extent to which they can, in dealing with the authorities, use the bargaining power represented by their training and knowledge.[22]

Black briefly discusses the traditions and achievements of historians in Imperial Russia and then traces the fortunes of Soviet historians through the turmoil of the early Khruschev years when Pankratova and Burdzhalov suffered defeat in their efforts to de-Stalinize Soviet historiography. Black stresses the relationship between historians and the state, especially those historians employed in the Historical Department of the All-Union Academy of Sciences, and he raises a variety of interesting questions.

Drawing upon sociological concepts current at the time, Black attempts to construe the historical profession as an interest group. As a result he draws a very sharp line between historians and the Party. His analysis was

21. See also the opening chapters of Lowell Tillett, *The Great Friendship: Soviet Historians on the Non–Russian Nationalities* (Chapel Hill), 1969.

22. p. 3.

helpful, but perhaps it underestimated the subtlety and variety of party controls over historians and the degree to which historians had internalized the norms of the party even as they rejected some of its practices. The very methodology in which the historians were instructed, defining scholarship as an instrument of class warfare, inclined them to subordinate themselves to the leadership of the Party. Black is mistaken, I believe, in his estimation of Pokrovskii. He wrote that what "distinguished him most of all, and what ultimately led to his posthumous condemnation, was his relative independence from manipulation by the bureaucrats of the Central Committee apparatus."[23] These adverse criticisms of Black's work are not intended to denigrate it; it remains important to this day, and at the time it provided young investigators with a coherent picture of Soviet scholarship, upon which they could base their own research.

Black characterized the writings of Soviet scholars as follows:

> After 1934 the party stressed such historical themes as the repulsion of foreign invasions, the heroic efforts of Ivan the Terrible and Peter the Great in defending domestic enemies and in centralizing the government, and the territorial growth of Russia. These themes served to provide justification in Russian history for certain policies of the regime, and helped to base these policies on the common historical experience of the Russian people rather than on Marxist doctrine. These developments in the field of history in the 1930's were thus part of the general trend in Stalinist political thought away from the theoretical determinism of Marxism and in the direction of a voluntarism which as yet had an unclear theoretical basis.[24]

The writings of Shteppa and Mazour mentioned above are roughly in agreement with interpretations found in the volume edited by Black. In contrast, the writings of Aron provide a counterpoint. Constituting a rival synthesis, they must be presented in some detail.[25] Aron's summary of Pokrovskii's synthesis of Russian history draws heavily on the writings of his posthumous denigration. He presents Pokrovskii as a rigid determinist who gave no play to conscious forces in history. He does this by citing only Pokrovskii's early writing about the nature of the historical process, while ignoring Pokrovskii's efforts in the 1920s to free himself from his earlier views.

Aron's unpublished report on diversity and uniformity poses the ques-

23. p. 12.
24. pp. 23–24.
25. See above, note 19.

tion, Does uniformity of opinion exist in the Soviet Union? He proposes that a definitive answer can emerge only after the examination of many fields of study. Short of that he wishes to study a single field to provide a partial answer. The issue he chose "concerns the nature of the social structure of Kievan Russia from the 9th to the 12th centuries." His case study covers "the time span from the death of M.N. Pokrovskii in April 1932 to the German invasion of Russia in June 1941." He asserts that "in 1932 when M.N. Pokrovskii and his followers dominated the historical profession the range of permitted variation was insignificant." Against this background, B.D. Grekov made his report in December 1932 which asserted among other things that the society of Kievan Rus "developed directly from primitive communism to feudalism skipping the stage of slavery." Aron reports that Grekov "emerged triumphant from the discussion" and that between 1935 and 1938 "little difference of opinion on this issue was expressed." Then in 1939, on the basis of a passage in the *Short Course*, A.V. Shestakov "dropped an ideological bombshell" when he asserted that "Kiev Russia was a slaveholding society."

Aron concludes that:

> The historical profession had indeed come a long way since the days of Pokrovskii. Of course, this is only a case study and as such is but a stone in the complex mosaic of the Soviet ideological and institutional structure. Only further research can determine how representative the case study is.

The general picture that emerges from Aron's reports is remarkable and at odds with most depictions of Soviet reality. The years of the New Economic Policy, usually deemed pluralistic and given to wide-ranging disputes, are viewed as dictatorial and marked by uniformity. The 1930s, usually, deemed oppressive and fear-ridden owing to Stalin's growing predominance, are deemed a period of growing liberty and diversity. Despite the achievements of the nonMarxist historians, who were restored to the historical profession, there is something bizarre in Aron's implicit suggestion that growing freedom characterized Soviet historiography at this time.

In the 1960s, five Ph.D. dissertations about Pokrovskii were undertaken in the United States and one in Canada, and in 1972 a dissertation about Pokrovskii was completed in Great Britain. At about the same time John Barber in Britain produced a dissertation that had much to say about Pokrovskii even if it was not centered on him. It dealt with many of the same questions that were examined in the dissertations about Pokrovskii. Three articles about Pokrovskii's rehabilitation were also published. What

produced this sudden surge of interest and why did it center on Pokrovskii?
Part of the answer lies in the fact that the Anglo-American writings had
reached a level of maturity that provided a foundation for interested graduate students. Black's writings and Shteppa's somewhat unwieldy but large–
scale and argumentative study deserve special mention. Second, the beginning of direct contacts with Soviet scholars in the late 1950s provided further stimulus. If I may write in a personal vein, I spent the academic year
1959–1960 in Leningrad as a graduate exchange student and had numerous
opportunities to observe Soviet historians at work. I was favorably impressed
by their mastery and manifest love of the past and at the same time struck
and puzzled by what seemed to me to be their dogmatism and unwilling-
ness to ask certain questions. I was determined to understand the Stalinist
period of Soviet historiography. Very quickly I realized that this was an
inappropriate starting point, that I must retreat to the 1920s to get my bearings. A study of Pokrovskii seemed the only way to study the formative
period of Soviet historiography.

Szporluk published his first article about Pokrovskii while still a graduate student at Stanford University working under the supervision of Anatole
Mazour.[26] He stated the themes that would reappear in later writings. Of
interest is the fact that he placed himself directly in the context of Soviet
historiography. He did not respond to questions posed in the Anglo-American literature as much as to the assertions of Soviet historians in their campaign to repudiate Pokrovskii. The fact that Szporluk was born in the Ukraine
may have some bearing on his taking a position strongly in favor of
Pokrovskii. It is well known that Pokrovskii was a severe critic of the policies of the Imperial Russian government toward Ukraine and other national
minorities.

Szporluk provides a sensitive and sympathetic reading of Pokrovskii's
extensive corpus of writings. He explores the conception of merchant capitalism and concludes that Pokrovskii's usage was consistent with that of
both Marx and Lenin. Szporluk finds the concept valuable in its own right,
useful especially for explaining change in Russia during the sixteenth and
seventeenth centuries. Merchant capital was the designation for the process
and age of primary accumulation of capital. He praises Pokrovskii for successfully linking Russia to world history.[27] Szporluk defends Pokrovskii
against the charge of economic determinism and denies also that Pokrovskii's

26. Pokrovskii and Russian History, *Survey*, LIII (October, 1963), 107–118.

27. See above, note 8.

interpretation was schematic. Pokrovskii, he argues, gave due weight to the actions of individuals and political leaders in the historical process. Szporluk praises Pokrovskii's efforts as a teacher and as an administrator of the historical front, viewing his leadership as essentially constructive. He thus largely overlooks or greatly simplifies the stance Pokrovskii took and the policies he devised with respect to the representatives of non-Marxist scholarship, which most investigators and observers view as nihilistic. He depicts Pokrovskii as the bearer of the older norms of scholarship by overlooking the emphasis he placed on class warfare and on scholarship as an instrument of politics. This shortcoming in Szporluk's analysis results, I believe, from the fact that he gives too little attention to the evolution of Pokrovskii's ideas and policies. Against the background of Stalin's rise to power, Pokrovskii became more militant and less resistant to manipulative and intimidating actions.

Szporluk provides an original reading of Pokrovskii's interpretation of the Russian Revolution, weaving into a whole the concept of merchant capital and Pokrovskii's interpretation of intellectual history, especially his ideas about the evolution of the revolutionary movement.[28] This forms the explanatory backdrop of the October Revolution. Stated briefly, Pokrovskii proposed two explanations. The first was the conventional view that the contradictions of capitalism drove the workers into opposition and upheaval. The second explanation places more emphasis on the role of the Bolshevik Party. On the one hand Bolshevism was a normal response to capitalist development; on the other hand, it derived from specific traditions of the Russian intelligentsia that existed as far back as the Decembrists, some of whom perceived the ineffable connection between autocracy and serfdom. The doctrine, which the Bolsheviks inherited from the intellectuals, had not been inspired by the struggle of the workers. The intellectuals came before the masses; the "workers' party" existed in their minds before there was a working class. Pokrovskii, according to Szporluk, came close "to formulating a 'two-world' theory of the historical process and, accordingly, treated Russia as the first country of the 'second world,' the backward nations, to have entered a socialist path distinct from that destined for the West."[29] This interesting suggestion can be accepted only after further confirmation.

On the basis of this insight, Szporluk provides a suggestion about the

---

28. "Pokrovskii's View of the Russian Revolution," *Slavic Review*, XXVI, no. 1 (March, 1967), 70–84.

29. p. 79.

meaning of Pokrovskii's synthesis and a key to its subsequent demise. He
proposes a consistency, both logical and ideological, between merchant capitalism and Preobrazhanskii's theory of "primitive socialist accumulation."
This theory, Szporluk claims, was not only hostile toward the peasants, it
constituted a justification of Stalin's policy of collectivization of agriculture. Pokrovskii's concept thus pointed an accusing finger at Stalin and consequently had to be excised. Szporluk's assertion is original and interesting;
there may well be an affinity between the ideas he discusses. Confirmation
awaits, I believe, evidence that the ideas had this meaning for those who
participated in the discussion of Pokrovskii's synthesis.

In my own study of Pokrovskii, I was struck by the instability of his
synthesis, and I placed emphasis on its evolution in the 1920s and early
1930s.[30] I explained the changes in his interpretations with reference to
changes in Pokrovskii's political and professional milieu. I examined the
factional struggles that took place in such institutions as the Society of
Marxist Historians and the Institute of History of RANION. I took note of
Stalin's direct intervention into the struggles of historians such as in his
famous letter to the editors of the journal, *Proletarskaia revoliutsia,* and of
his indirect intervention through his manipulation of the factional struggle.
I understood factionalism somewhat differently from Aron, stressing that
the attacks on Pokrovskii indicated that his position was far from dictatorial. He was seeking to uphold his power in the face of an organized challenge led by E. Iaroslavskii, an important member of Stalin's circle. In the
face of this challenge Pokrovskii abandoned some of his most characteristic
ideas, and he modified his policies as a leader in a direction more acceptable to Stalin.

Pokrovskii's policies as leader of the historical front evolved radically as
well. Until 1928 he championed Lenin's policy of using non-communist hands
in the building of communism, that is, he helped create arrangements where
non-Marxist scholars could continue their work with a significant measure of
autonomy. In 1928, he drastically changed this policy and led the charge against
the representatives of the traditional intelligentsia. During the first stage, as
Pokrovskii propounded and justified his policies, he produced a theory which
legitimated the pluralistic arrangements that constituted the essence of the
NEP; after 1928, he propounded a new theory that came to justify in part
Stalin's and the Party's dictatorship over scholarship.

---

30. *The Soviet Scholar Bureaucrat: M. N. Pokrovskii and the Society of Marxist Historians*
   (University Park, PA, 1978).

I argued also that in 1927, Pokrovskii abandoned the interpretation of the October Revolution that he had hitherto upheld. He helped to devise a new account that would constitute the core of what I would now call the foundation myth of Soviet historiography. Pokrovskii sought to articulate systematically Lenin's assertions about the growing over of the bourgeois-democratic revolution into the socialist-proletarian revolution. It is important to note that he did so in Stalinist fashion: he banished from consideration (and hence falsified) Lenin's international perspective, the problem of the revolution in the West as a precondition for socialist revolution in Russia.[31]

In the course of the next five years, Party historians heatedly debated such matters as the revolutionary precursors of Bolshevism (especially Narodnaia volia), the Revolution of 1905, European imperialism and the development of Russian capitalism, German Social Democracy, and the theory of socio–economic formations. They repudiated the existing interpretations of these matters and produced an original and unified doctrine. This doctrine conformed to the premises of Pokrovskii's new interpretation of the October Revolution and in a broader sense conformed to Stalin's reinterpretation of Leninism and his theory of socialism in one country. This vast redrawing of the historiographical map brought into prominence the concept of feudalism and thus undermined the concept of merchant capitalism by rendering it superfluous.

In 1981, the English historian John Barber published an important study.[32] It covers much the same territory as my study mentioned above, but from a rather different perspective. The real subject of his book is the disputes mentioned in the paragraph above. Whereas I treat them as aspects of Pokrovskii's biography and as a context of his activity, he introduces Pokrovskii's ideas and policies as a context of the controversies and policies that he investigates. Of special interest in Barber's study is his introduction of a new explanatory schema which reflected political changes growing out of the war in Vietnam and methodological changes that in large measure demonstrated the impact of the Annales School of French historiography. In the 1970s a generation of revisionist historians had come upon the scene. Ideologically, they sought to rid the field of Soviet studies of the concept of totalitarianism; methodologically, they were drawn to the techniques of social history. They sought to depict Soviet society as seen from below, to demonstrate the autonomous existence of social groups and to show their effectiveness as agents of socio–political change. By showing the limitations of control from the center, they questioned a basic assump-

tion of the previous scholarship that had been influenced by the theory of
totalitarianism. Were the changes that swept Soviet historical scholarship during the first
five year plan initiated from above or from below? That is to say, in what
respects and to what degree did they derive from the policies of the Communist Party and its leadership? To what degree were they initiated and
propelled by the aspirations of rank and file historians and cultural bureaucrats? John Barber's study was an important statement in this discussion.
He represented the revisionist position among those studying Soviet historical scholarship. It was not just the ongoing discussions that shaped
Barber's position. There was an intellectual affinity with his distinguished
teacher, E.H. Carr.

Barber argued that despite considerable "influence on Soviet intellectual
life on the part of the political leadership," in the years of violent controversy from 1928 to 1931, the leadership did not enunciate a party line or
enforce orthodox interpretations in cultural and scientific questions... largely
because it saw no pressing need to do so. The largely spontaneous activity
of the militants was, after all, transforming the intellectual world in a highly
suitable manner. Bourgeois influence was being eliminated, oppositionist
ideology was being combated, and Marxist theories of questionable orthodoxy were being challenged. Then suddenly, in October 1931, Stalin intervened in an intellectual controversy, and in so doing changed the whole
relationship between the political leadership and the intellectuals.[33]

I entered into a polemic with Barber. While seeking to call attention to
the numerous virtues of his study, I questioned his basic argument about the
importance of initiatives taken by militants. There is some confusion as to
who are the militants; they would seem to include even Iaroslavskii. To
view him as someone distinct from the political authorities and to deem his
actions as constituting part of a movement from below was, I argued, mistaken.[34]

A considerable amount of information about Party historiography in the
1920's and 1930's has become available to Anglo-American readers thanks
largely to the publication of the *Modern Encyclopedia of Russian and So-*

31. I stated this idea in an article in *Voprosy istorii*, 7, 1989, "Spor o M. N. Pokrovskom
prodolzhaetsiia," 154–159.

32. *Soviet Historians in Crisis*, 1928–1932.

33. p. 11.

34. "More about Stalin and the Historians," *Soviet Studies* (July, 1982), 448–452.

viet History. In addition, a number of studies of Party historiography published as articles have appeared through the years. In combination they shed some light on Stalin's decisive intervention into historical scholarship with his "Letter to the Editors of the *Proletarsskaia revoliutsiia*"; other than that they do not form a whole; that is to say, the authors are not talking to each other and pursuing the same questions. They examine separate aspects of Party historiography.

Bertram Wolfe, a former communist who possessed formidable literary prowess and polemical skill, published an influential article in the journal *Foreign Affairs* in 1952.[35] He republished versions of it subsequently; he read his final formulation to a conference of Western specialists in Geneva in 1961, published in 1964 under the title *Contemporary History in the Soviet Mirror*. For Wolfe, Party histories are not merely slanted histories or works containing occasional distortions of fact; he deems Party historiography an enterprise that consists of systematic falsification. The more recent the history, the greater the falsification.

He finds the first principles of party historiography in Lenin's writings. Lenin "set the example of harnessing Clio to his chariot." In every polemic he turned to history for support of his position. His "abuse" of history, for example, was to present his movement as the legitimate heir of all that was admirable in populism.[36] He was always ready to show the stages of degeneration of his opponents and "their 'essential identity' with some movement he and they had previously denounced... ." Wolfe traces the habit of periodization to Lenin who "is tireless in his use of it as a device for demonstrating the progressive rise and magnification of his own movement and the progressive decline of opposing movements."[37] For Wolfe, the epitome of falsification was Stalin's *Short Course* which, "though virtually unreadable, could be memorized by the faithful, and indeed, as life insurance had to be."[38]

A different approach to Party historiography was taken by Jonathan Frankel, an English-born historian who teaches at Hebrew University in Jerusalem.[39] Frankel is more concerned with the substance of Party histori-

---

35. "Operation Rewrite: the Agony of Soviet Historians," XXXI, no. 1 (October), 39–57.

36. p. 44.

37. p. 45.

38. p. 51.

39. "Party Genealogy and the Soviet Historians (1920–1938)," *Slavic Review*, XXV, no. 4 (December, 1966), 563–603. See also Paul Avrich, "The Short Course and Soviet Historiography," *Political Science Quarterly*, LXXV, 4 (December, 1960), 539–553.

ography than is Wolfe, that is, with the ideas of historians, their clustering
into schools, and with patterns of changing ideas. Unlike Wolfe, Frankel is
not trying to prove anything about Party historiography at large. His work is
less polemical; he does not expose falsification but inquires as to the determination of ideas. He traces the histories of controversies and almost in
passing observes that in the course of the 1920s political authorities played
an increasingly important role in determining the outcome of disputes.

Larry Holmes and William Burgess produced an interesting study[40] that
dealt with the question of diversity of opinion among Party historians. They
examined the unfolding of scholarly norms in the course of disputes between Istpart on the one hand and the Lenin Institute on the other. The problem historians faced was the extent to which history "should be distinct
from propaganda." Holmes and Burgess argue that, "this rivalry of ideals,
aggravated by personality conflicts and opposing institutional loyalties,
determined to a significant extent the nature of historical literature in the
USSR during the 1920s and for years to come."[41] To a considerable extent
the struggle became a personal conflict between Ol'minskii and Kamenev.
The defeat of Istpart obliterated the distinction between scholarship and
propaganda. In 1930, confronting defeat, Ol'minskii sent a letter to the editors of *Proletarskaia revoliutsiia* (never published) which asserted "that while
propaganda could ignore such historical facts as the cooperation of
Mensheviks and Bolsheviks, a 'true Party history' had to mention them."
The reverse was leading to "castrated Leninism and a one-sided history of
the Party." The study is a good example of what could be learned even
without access to archives.

Robert Tucker in the second volume of his biography of Stalin[42] has done
much to clarify Stalin's interest in history and his interference with the writing of it; in a separate article he has done much to elucidate the circum-
stance of the appearance of Stalin's infamous letter to the Editors of
Proletarskaia revoliutsiia.[43] While stressing Stalin's need for ego gratifica-
tion, he unveils his subtle rhetorical strategy. He finds that Stalin "pursued
a tripartite purpose in cult-building...." First, "he arrogated to himself the

40. "Scholarly Voices or Political Echo? Soviet Party History in the 1920s," *Russian His-
    tory/Histoire Russe*, 9, Parts 2–3 (1982), 383–398.

41. p. 379.-Istpart: The Commission for the Study of the October Revolution and the CPUSSR.

42. *Stalin in Power: The Revolution from Above, 1928–1941* (New York), 1990.

43. "The Rise of Stalin's Personality Cult," *American Historical Review*, 84 (April, 1979).
    347–366.

position of premier party historian and arbiter of contentious issues.... Second,... Stalin followed the strategy of cult building via the assertion of Lenin's infallibility." In doing so he implicitly nominated himself, "the 'successor-vozhd', for similar treatment." Third, the task of historians was not to use archival documents to ascertain facts indiscriminately. They were to assert "higher truths," such as the "a priori" assertion "that Lenin, being a 'real Bolshevik,' could never have underestimated centrism or that Stalin, also a 'real Bolshevik,' could never have taken an unBolshevik position at any juncture."[44] John Barber, in the book cited above, devoted a chapter to Stalin's letter, and he published a separate article that provided an even more detailed analysis.[45] He started from a point diametrically opposed to that of Tucker, who stressed Stalin's personal ambitions. "If we accept the common portrayal of Stalin as a ruthless megalomaniac aiming to subordinate every sphere of Soviet life to his personal and absolute domination, the question why Stalin published the letter may appear naive."[46] Barber suggests, furthermore, that a better explanation may be found by viewing the government and Stalin as reacting to urgent situations rather than the "prompting of long-term aims."[47] "The wave of Leftism, politicization, 'Bolshevization'" that swept through the intellectual life, "resulted largely from the actions of militant intellectuals themselves, with the party leadership essentially standing aside, sometimes encouraging the militants, sometimes occupying a completely neutral position."[48]

Another part of Barber's explanation is that Stalin was reacting to the persistence of opposition in the Party even after the defeat of the Left and Right Oppositions. He asserts that Trotskyites continued to hold important positions in the intellectual apparatus. This may have been sufficient reason to silence "unorthodox views."[49] He then seeks to explain the timing of the letter: why the autumn of 1931? His answer is that the Party was deeply concerned about the declining quality of recruits. He cites a report delivered by Postyshev in the summer of 1931 that expressed this concern and points out that Stalin's letter reiterated some of the main themes of this

---

44. pp. 355–356.

45. "Stalin's Letter to the Editors of *Proletarskaya revoliutsiia*," *Soviet Studies*, XXVII no. 1 (January, 1976), 21–41.

46. p. 25.

47. p. 41.

48. p. 26.

49. p. 34.

report. "It seems highly likely that this concern with the political education
of party members...was the immediate political reason for Stalin's interven-
tion in the intellectual world."[50] The final part of Barber's explanation was his answer to the question,
why was history chosen to provide the example? Barber goes on to describe
the great turmoil in the world of historians. "Profound disarray" invited
Stalin's intervention. The immediate aim was "an ideology suitable for new
entrants into the party...." But events had a momentum of their own and
soon ran out of control. The passions were so great that finally Postyshev,
who had opened the campaign, stepped in to bring it to a close. The leadership had been surprised by the "intensity of the reaction."[51] Barber provides
an ironic perspective. The outcome does not mean that the letter "was intended to have the effect it had, or that it was conceived as the vital turning
point it was."[52] Barber's account demonstrates how different Soviet politics
look when one attempts to perceive it from below and assumes that the
leadership was reactive rather than pursuing ideological goals or perform-
ing a social experiment or enlarging and rendering secure their own power.
His interpretation is plausible but not confirmed by the evidence.

In my study of Pokrovskii, I shared Barber's perception of "profound
disarray" among Marxist historians. I concluded that the campaign con-
trived by Iaroslavskii had resulted in a stalemate. Effective work had ceased
on the historical front, and it was impossible even to send the journal *Istorik-
marksist* to press. I perceived that conflict entangled with a larger struggle
within the Politburo. It was evident that behind Iaroslavskii stood Kaganovich
who sought to heat up the atmosphere in the wake of Stalin's letter. His
purpose was to complete an overturn on the historical front similar to the
one that had taken place in the field of philosophy. Iaroslavskii was to replace Pokrovskii as the commander. Postyshev spoke up in a successful
effort to cool the atmosphere and he forestalled the overturn. I further specu-
lated that Stalin stood behind Kaganovich. In this respect the incident was a
temporary setback for Stalin in at least one respect. He postponed setting up
the arrangements he most desired in the field of history.[53] Under the influence of some observations by M. Ia. Gefter,[54] I reviewed

50. p. 36.

51. p. 40.

52. p. 41.

53. pp. 160–164.

54. See Roy A. Medvedev, *Let History Judge: The Origins and Consequences of Stalinism*
(New York, 1971), pp. 516–518.

the creation of what Soviet historians called the Leninist conception of Party history. This to me was a misnomer, and I entitled my article "The Stalinist Conception of Communist Party History."[55] Stalin's interpretation of Leninism decisively shaped how Party historians understood Lenin's writings. Party historians, most notably D. Ia. Kin, an associate of Iaroslavskii who did not survive the purges, created a model of Party history. By model I mean something more abstract than an interpretation. It is primarily a set of assumptions about how change occurs; it also implies a normative code. He conceived the Party as a self-contained feedback mechanism, and its mainspring was the struggle of factions.

The internal history of the Party consists of the overcoming of factions and the elimination of differences of opinion. For Kin, the emergence of factions was inherent in Party life. Differences of opinion that crystallized into factions had a class basis. "It does not suffice to show how the Leninist line was worked out within the Party; one must show that it was done through the overcoming of factions. It is through overcoming factions that the Party propels itself forward."

To an outsider it may appear that the free play of factions dominates Party history. It is of fundamental importance, however, to note that from Kin's perspective this is not so: one of the groups in contention represents the Party itself and embodies the correct line. All the other groups are mere factions.[56] How do we know which is the correct group, the Party itself? What signs mark it as possessing knowledge of the single correct path to the future? Kin does not pose, no less answer such questions. To do so would have revealed the metaphysical character of his assumptions.

The writings of Soviet historians about the February and October Revolutions has been the object of considerable attention. Anglo-American historians often comment on these writings in their own studies of the Revolution and a number of articles have been devoted to their analysis. Robert McNeal, a recently deceased American authority on Soviet history, reiterated the question raised by Anastas Mikoyan at the Twentieth Congress of the CPSU, why after almost forty years had historians failed to produce either a short or a comprehensive textbook on the history of the October Revolution? McNeal answered the question with respect to the political obstacles, most notably restrictions imposed by Stalin. In elaborating, he provided an account of the work of Istpart on the history of the Russian

55. *Studies in Soviet Thought*, 37, 1989, 259–274.

56. p. 268.

Revolution, the enterprise presumably initiated by Gorky.[57] This is an elegant account about the attribution to the Bolsheviks of a Menshevik authored document that played an important role in the Revolution of 1905. Soviet historians uncovered the truth, but some of them chose or were compelled to continue to misrepresent it.

After describing the vicissitudes imposed by the *Kratkii kurs*, McNeal judges that "it is probably to the credit of Soviet historians of the revolution that they did not fabricate more than they did." He credits them with the creation of three myths: that Stalin defended Lenin's views before the latter returned from Switzerland; that Stalin led the resistance to Kornilov; finally that Stalin was the head of the Party center that directed the seizure of power. With respect to interpretation, McNeal praises historians for elaborating the theory of growing–over (pererastanie). He judges the theory a successful means of explaining the complex processes that occurred in 1917. He judges them to have blundered in quoting Lenin to the effect that "the future of the proletarian revolution in Russia was hopeless without the support of a proletarian uprising in Europe."[58]

A different approach to the historiography of the Revolution was taken by Larry Holmes.[59] In Schliapnikov, Holmes found an illustration of "the interrelationship of politics and historical writing from the early 1920s until 1931."[60] He stresses Schliapnikov's resistance to the growing practice of using history to justify past and present policies. Holmes provides a moving account of Schliapnikov's ordeal that led to his death in the gulag.

James White, who teaches at the University of Glasgow, has produced one of the most striking and original works about Soviet historiography.[61] He seems to have been influenced by the study of semiotics. Although he accepts the prevalent assumption that works about the Revolution written after 1924 were shaped by political conflicts within the Communist Party,

---

57. "Soviet Historiography on the October Revolution: a Review of Forty Years," *Slavic and East European Review*, XVII (1958), 269–281. See also Herbert J. Ellison, "Soviet Historians and the Russian Revolution," Lyman Letgers, ed., *Russia, Essays in History and Literature* (Leiden, 1972). See also Robert M. Slusser, "The Forged Bolshevik Signature: A Problem in Soviet Historiography," *Slavic Review* (June 1994), 294–308.

58. p. 279. For a different interpretation of the theory of growing–over, see George M. Enteen, Tatiana Gorn and Cheryl Kern, *Soviet Historians and the Study of Russian Imperialism* (University Park, PA, 1979).

59. "Soviet Rewriting of 1917: the Case of A. G. Schliapnikov," *Slavic Review*, XXXVIII, no. 2 (June), 224–242.

60. p. 224.

he rejects the associated assumption that works written before that date were necessarily true and objective, that political and ideological considerations had not marked them. The first history of the October Revolution was written by Trotsky while he was conducting negotiations with the Germans at Brest-Litovsk. His study of German newspapers prompted him to reject charges that the Bolsheviks had come to power undemocratically and were seeking to establish a dictatorship. He thus stressed the groundswell of popular support for the Bolsheviks that arose in the wake of General Kornilov's unsuccessful putsch. The Party was on the road to electoral success when Kerensky intervened to disrupt the electoral process and to thwart the intentions of the masses. To defeat Kerensky's anti-democratic strivings, the Bolsheviks were compelled to organize an insurrection. The point is that no great emphasis is placed on the events of October 25. It does not mark the opening of a new era. Rather it stands in a continuum of events that led to Bolshevik efforts to form a coalition government with the Mensheviks and Socialist-Revolutionaries. These initiatives failed owing to the "intransigence and treachery" of these parties.[62] This very schema found embodiment in John Reed's famous book, *Ten Days that Shook the World*.

By 1920, when Lenin had produced a new interpretation with the publication of *Left-Wing Communism, an Infantile Disorder*, political requirements had changed. The Bolsheviks now sought to define the strategy and tactics of the Comintern parties. They thus imparted universal experience to their own revolution. In Lenin's account, October 25 acquires the central place, the moment when the proletariat in Russia came to power. Due weight is given to the organizing and planning of the insurrection. Coalition politics disappeared, "strictest centralization and iron discipline," which had arisen on the "granite theoretical foundation" of Marxism, which constituted the essence of Bolshevism had triumphed.[63]

White brings into focus still another political determinant: the ideas of A. A. Bogdanov, which found expression both in the Proletkult movement and in the Workers' Opposition. The ideas of both groups tended to create skepticism about the influence of the intelligentsia, they encouraged the view that it was a source of the degeneration of the revolution. Lenin en-

---

61. "Early Soviet Historical Interpretations of the Russian Revolution 1918–24," *Soviet Studies*, XXXVII, 3 (July 1985), 330–352.

62. p. 333.

63. p. 339.

listed Ia. A. Iakovlev to produce a history that would counter Bogdanovite ideas. Iakovlev did so by demonstrating that the workers were doomed to failure if they acted independently. The workers had brought down the Tsarist regime in February but proved incapable on their own of organizing a new power in its place. This awaited the efforts of the Bolsheviks in October.[64] In the course of his analysis, White takes the reader into the heart of Istpart.

Recently two studies have been completed that indicate a revival of interest in the formative years of Soviet scholarship. Robert F. Byrnes, a senior historian who has had ample opportunity to observe Soviet historians at work, is the author of a forthcoming biography of V. O. Kliuchevskii and approaches Soviet historiography through the eyes of Kliuchevskii's students. Michael F. Fox is a graduate student at Yale University who is studying communist institutions during the NEP and who has already done extensive research in Russia, where he has gained access to archives previously closed to foreign scholars.

"Creating the Soviet Historical Profession, 1917–1934" is the title of a report that Byrnes first presented to the 1989 Moscow Historians Conference.[65] His essay is broadly descriptive of individual historians and of institutions, both the traditional scholarly institutions, those created for the purpose of realizing Lenin's policy of using non–Marxist hands in the building of communism. Byrnes seeks to capture the spirit of the times. He sees the non-Marxist historians as accommodating to the regime, even passive. They provided excellent material for Lenin's policy of accommodation. His thesis is that Lenin's policy achieved success: both the Party and the historians got most of what they wanted from the bargain. Historical scholarship did not face a crisis in 1927.[66] He describes the turbulent years from 1927 to 1934 when the historical profession was transformed along Stalinist lines. His implied conclusion was that this upheaval was unnecessary and undesirable, hence irrational. Byrnes' essay is an excellent introduction to the subject that updates the work done earlier by Black.

Michael Fox, a graduate student at Yale University, has also studied at Moscow State University. His article, "Political Culture, Purges and Proletarianization at the Institute of Red Professors, 1921–1929,"[67] is a promising, even brilliant, study that in some respects marks a new stage in the study of the formative period of Soviet historical scholarship. The author's

---

64. pp. 346–347.

65. Subsequently in the *Slavic Review*, 50, no. 2 (Summer, 1991),297–308.

66. p. 304.

extensive use of archives makes him the envy of older colleagues who earlier had gained only limited access. He has penetrated deeply into the life of the Institute (IKP) and conveys a nuanced sense of its inner workings. He has, moreover, transcended some of the old categories of explanation and marked out a significantly new approach.

Fox relates the history of the IKP by presenting the main controversies that entangled it. How should students be recruited? Should preference be given to those with the best academic credentials or to those with proletarian origins, or those with the best political-party profile? Who should teach these future leaders? If the number of Marxist professors is inadequate, should bourgeois professors be invited? And what about Menshevik intellectuals as teachers? (Lenin himself was asked to decide this issue.) How much emphasis in the curriculum should be placed on questions of theory as opposed to practical tasks? How much practical work should be demanded of the students?

Purges figured prominently in the life of the IKP and Fox conveys the controversies that surrounded them and the principles that guided them. He is especially informative about the student purge of 1924 that rid the Institute and other VUZY of students sympathetic to Trotsky. This led to a major proletarianization of the student body. One of the most original aspects of the study is Fox's elucidation of the political culture of the students that was forged in the smithy of dispute, especially in the working out of the theory and practice of purges. It was this that produced the norms that guided the work and day-to-day behavior of the students. The proximity of IKP to the Central Committee gave the students a sense of power; the frequency of expulsions imparted a sense of vulnerability. Fox's most striking conclusion is that no significant Right Opposition existed in the IKP.

Fox calls into question the metaphor of change from below versus change from above as a category of explanation, which had, the reader will recall, entered the discussion in the 1970s. He also rejects the notion of "party control" as an independent explanatory category. He explains the emergence of the political culture as an outgrowth of the controversies he carefully delineated, and he explains much of the specific behavior by reference to the political culture. Perhaps he has gone a bit too far in excluding the personalities and goals of individuals from his explanatory model. If he had extended his account into 1930 he would certainly have had to take greater note of Stalin's actions.

The earliest writings about Soviet historical scholarship that appeared in

---

67. Scheduled for publication in the *Russian Review* sometime in 1992.

Great Britain and the United States consisted mostly of the experiences and insights of Russian emigrés. In the 1950s and 1960s under the influence of the concept of totalitarianism, Soviet historiography was viewed mainly as a political barometer. How much light did it shed on the accumulation and exercise of power? This was not the exclusive perspective; some investigators persisted with the question, how much light did it shed on the past? A wave of social history began to make itself felt in the 1970s as historians made the effort to view society from the perspective of those who were the objects of power and to highlight the structures that constrained leaders. This approach had limited but genuine influence on the study of Soviet historiography. It seems to me that the findings of Soviet historians in recent years have not strengthened this approach. The rebirth of national scholarship in the former Soviet Union is bound to create a variety of new perspectives.

Chapter 18

THE PUBLICATIONS OF EDWARD C. THADEN

Nick Ceh

Books:
Conservative Nationalism in Nineteenth–Century Russia. Seattle: The University of Washington Press, 1964.

Russia and the Balkan Alliance of 1912. University Park, PA: Pennsylvania State University Press, 1965.

Russia Since 1801: The Making of a New Society. New York: John Wiley, 1971.

Russification in the Baltic Provinces and Finland, 1855–1914, editor and coauthor with M. Haltzel, C.L. Lundin, A. Plakans, and T. Raun. Princeton: Princeton University Press, 1981.

The Western Borderlands of Russia, 1710–1870. With the collaboration of Marianna Forster Thaden. Princeton: Princeton University Press, 1984.

Finland and the Baltic Provinces in the Russian Empire, in *Journal of Baltic Studies (Special Issue),* coedited with Toivo Raun, 15, nos. 2/3 (1984): 87–227.

Interpreting History: Collected Essays on the Relations of Russia with Europe. Boulder: Social Science Monographs; distributed by Columbia University Press, New York, 1990.[1]

Forthcoming: *The Origins of Historicism in Russia.*

---

[1] The articles in this volume are listed separately when they first appeared and are marked by an asterisk.

Chapters in Books:

"'Skjaersommernatsdrømmen', by Bjørnstjerne Bjørnson." In *Shakespeare in Europe*,Translated by Edward Thaden, ed. O. LeWinter, 286–295. Cleveland: World Publishing Company, 1963.

"Liberals Versus Conservatives in Soviet Art and Literature." In *The Triangle of Power: Conflict and Accommodation*, ed. J. Prybyla, 53–60. University Park: Pennsylvania State University, 1967.

"Nationality Policy in the Western Borderlands of the Russian Empire, 1881–1914." In *American Contributions to the Seventh International Congress of Slavists*, vol. v., 3: History, ed. A. Cienciala, 71–80. The Hague: Mouton, 1973.*[2]

"Public Opinion and Russian Foreign Policy Toward Serbia, 1908–1914." In *Les grandes puissances et la Serbie à la veille de la première guerre mondiale: Recueil des travaux présentés aux assises scientifiques internationales de l'Académie Serbe des Sciences et des Arts qui ont eu lieu du 13–15 septembre 1974 à Belgrade*, 217–230. Beograd: Srpska Akademija Nauka i Umetnosti, 1976.*

"Diversity and Convergence in the Western Borderlands of the Russian Empire, 1762–1863." In *Comité International des Sciences Historiques, 15e Congrès International des Sciences Historiques, Grand thèmes et méthodologie*, 113–121. Bucharest: Editura Academiei, 1980.

"Deutsche Universitäten und die Agrar–und Sozialreform in den Ostseeprovinzen des russischen Reiches 1804–1866." In *Wegenetz europäischen Geistes, vol. 2*, ed. K. Mack and R. Plaschka, 225–240. Vienna: Österreichisches Ost–und Südosteropa-Institut, 1987.*

"V. N. Tatishchev and the Germanic Scholarly World." In *Gesellschaft und Kultur Mittel–,Ost–und Südosteuropas im 18. und beginnenden 19.Jahrhundert: Festschrift für Erich Donnert zum 65. Geburtstag*, ed. Helmut Reinalter(Bern: Peter Lang, 1994): 35–42.

---

[2] This article also appeared under the title "Russification," in *Major Problems in the History of Imperial Russia*, ed. James Cracraft (Lexington, MA: D.C. Heath, 1994): 403–409.

Journal Articles:

"The Beginning of Romantic Nationalism in Russia". *American Slavic and East European Review* 13 (1954): 500–521.*

"Charykov and Russian Foreign Policy at Constantinople in 1911." *Journal of Central European Affairs* 16 (1956): 25–55.*

"Natural Law and Historicism in the Social Sciences." *Social Science* 33 (1957): 32–38.*

"Encounters with Soviet Historians." *Historian* 20 (1957): 80–95.*

"Montenegro: Russia's Troublesome Ally, 1910–1912." *Journal of Central European Affairs* 18 (1958): 111–33.*

"N.A. Manasein." *Baltische Briefe* 21 (1968): 7.

"N.A. Manaseins Senatorenrevision in Livland und Kurland während der Zeit von 1882 bis 1883." *Jahrbücher für Geschichte Osteuropas* 17 (1969): 45–58.*

"Obituary for Oswald P. Backus III." *American Historical Review* 78 (1972): 197–198.

"Samarin's Okrainy Rossii and Official Policy in the Baltic Provinces." *Russian Review* 33 (1974): 405–415.*

"Soviet and 'Bourgeois' Historians on Modernization, Human Rights, and Nationalism." *Canadian Review of Studies in Nationalism* 6 (1979): 117–121.

"Privileged Elites in the Western Borderlands and the Russian Government, 1796–1830." *Proceedings of the American Historical Association* (1979): 1–13.

"The Western Borderlands of the Russian Empire, 1710–1870." *Occasional Papers of the Kennan Institute for Advanced Russian Studies* 120 (1980): 1–20.

"Estland, Livland, and the Ukraine: Reflections on Eighteenth-Century Autonomy." *Journal of Baltic Studies* 12 (1982): 311– 317.

"Finland and the Baltic Provinces: Elite Roles and Social and Economic Conditions and Structures." *Journal of Baltic Studies* 15 (1984): 216–227.

"Baltic National Movements During the Nineteenth Century." *Journal of Baltic Studies* 16 (1985): 411–421.

"Iurii Samarin and Baltic History." *Journal of Baltic Studies* 17 (1986): 321–328.

"V.N. Tatishchev, German Historians, and the St.Petersburg Academy of Sciences." *Russian History* 13 (1986): 367–398.*

"Ivan IV in Baltic German Historiography." *Russian History* 14 (1987): 377–394.*

"Otsenka amerikanskogo obschchestva Slavistiki v istoricheskom perspektive." *East European Quarterly* 22 (1988): 271–275.

"V.N. Tatishchev and the St. Petersburg Academy of Sciences." *Mezhdunarodnaia komissiia po istoriko–slavisticheskim issledovaniiam, Sobranie komissii 28–30 avgust 1985 g., Shtuttgart.* Moscow: IN-ION,(1988) 11–13.

"Reflections on Glasnost, Education, and Peace in Eastern Europe and Russia in the 20th Century." *Mezhdunardonaia komissiia po istoriko–slavisticheskim issledovaniiam, Simposium komissii Moskva,* 6–8 sentiabria 1988 g. Moscow: INION, (1989): 26–29.

"The Vocabulary of Russian Historicism." *Russian History* 17 (1990): 297–303.*

"Friedrich Meinecke und der frühe Historismus in Russland." *Wissenschaftliche Zeitschrift Martin–Luther–Universität Halle–Wittenberg* 40 (1991): 85–96.*

Encylopedia and Dictionary Articles

Modern Encyclopedia of Russian and Soviet History, edited by Joseph L. Wieczynski (Gulf Breeze,FL: Academic International Press):
"Bestuzhev–Riumin, Konstantin Nikolaevich (1829–1897)," 4 (1977): 96–98.

"Boltin, Ivan Nikitich (1735–1792)," 5 (1977): 100–102.

"Conservative Nationalism in Russia," 8 (1978): 14–19.*

"Fadeev, Rostislav Andreevich (1824–1883)," 11 (1979): 41–44.

"Granovski, Timofei Nikolaevich (1813–1855)," 13 (1979): 99–101.

"Karamzin, Nikolai Mikhailovich (1766–1826)," 16 (1980): 4–12.

"Moscow Slavic Benevolent Committee," 23 (1981): 110–111.

"Pogodin, Mikhail Petrovich (1800–1875)," 28 (1982): 153–156.

"Polevoi, Nikolai Alekseevich (1796–1846)," 28 (1982): 178–181

"Russification in Tsarist Russia," 32 (1983): 205–212.

"Samarin, Yurii Fedorovich (1819–1876)," 33 (1983): 56–61.

"Shakhovskoi, Sergei Vladimirovich (1852–1894)," 34 (1983): 140–142.

"Tatishchev, Vasilii Nikitich (1685–1750)," 38 (1984): 196–200.

"Western Borderlands of the Russian Empire," 43 (1986): 192–199.

"Zinov'ev, Mikhail Alekseevich (1838–1895)," 46 (1987): 104–105

"Strakhov, Nikolai Nikolaevich (1836–1896)," 53 (1990): 186–189.

Great Historians from Antiquity to 1800: An International Dictionary,
edited by Lucian Boia (New York: Greenwood Press, 1989):

"Henry of Livonia (Henricus de Lettis) (Saxony, c. 1178–Papendorf, Livonia, c. 1259)," 23–24.

"Russow, Balthasar (Reval, now Tallinn, c. 1535–Reval, 1600)," 24–25.

Great Historians of the Modern Age: An International Dictionary
edited by Lucian Boia (New York: Greenwood Press, 1991):

"Kruus, Hans (Tartu, 1891–Tallinn, 1976),"59–60.

"Samarin, Iurii Fedorovich (St. Petersburg, 1819–Berlin, 1876)," 61–62.

"Wittram, Reinhard (Bilderingshof near Riga, 1902–Meran, 1973)," 64–65.

"Zutis, Jānis (Kurland, 1893–Riga, 1962)," 65–66.

Book Reviews:

X. J. Eudin and R.C. North (eds.), *Soviet Russia and the East. Historian* 20 (1957): 96–97.

X. J. Eudin and H. H. Fisher (eds.), *Soviet Russia and the West. Historian* 20 (1957): 96–97

G. Guins, *Communism on the Decline. Historian* 20 (1957): 97–98.

H. Koht, *Education of an Historian. Indiana Journal of History* (1957): 444–445.

L. Gruliow (ed.), *Current Soviet Policies, II: The Documentary Record of the 20th Party Congress and Its Aftermath. Russian Review* 17 (1958): 73.

C. Black (ed.), *Rewriting Russian History: Soviet Interpretations of Russia's Past. Slavic and East European Journal* 16 (1958): 181–182.

E. Viefhaus, *Die Minderheitenfrage auf der Pariser Friedenskonferenz 1919. Slavic Review* 20 (1961): 709–710.

B. and C. Jëlavich (eds.), *The Education of a Russian Statesman: The Memoirs of N. K. Giers. Slavic Review* 22 (1963): 332–333.

A. Vucinich, *Science in Russian Culture to 1860. American Historical Review* 69 (1963): 1148–1149.

S. H. Baron, *Plekhanov: The Father of Russian Marxism. Slavic and East European Journal* 8 (1963): 476–477.

A. Dallin, *Russian Diplomacy and East Europe, 1914–1917. Balkan Studies* 6 (1965): 225–226.

R. A. Pierce (ed.), *Russia's Hawaiian Adventure. American Historical Review* 71 (1965): 114–115.

S. Pushkarev, *The Emergence of Modern Russia, 1801–1917. Slavic and East European Journal* 9 (1965): 226–227.

F. E. Manuel, *Shapes of Philosophical History. Journal of General Education* 18 (1966): 330–331.

E. Oberländer, *Tolstoj und die revolutionäre Bewegung. Jahrbücher für Geschichte Osteuropas* 13 (1966): 625–626.

N. Ia. Danilevskii, *Rossiia i Evropa*, ed. Iu. Ivask. *Slavic and East European Journal* 9 (1967): 502.

E. J. Brown, *Stankevich and His Circle. Russian Review* 26 (1967): 76–78.

M. Raeff, *Origins of the Russian Intelligentsia: The Eighteenth- Century Nobility. Russian Review* 26 (1967): 300–301.

M. Katz, *Mikhail N. Katkov: A Political Biography, 1818–1887. Russian Review* 27 (1968): 103–104.

N. M. Druzhinin, *Vospominaniia i mysli istorika. Jahrbücher für Geschichte Osteuropas* 17 (1969): 120–121.

R. E. MacMaster, *Danilevsky: A Russian Totalitarian Philosopher. Slavic Review* 28 (1969): 487–489.

Vneshniaia politika Rossii XIX i nachala XX veka, 1st series, vol. 6. *American Historical Review* 75 (1969) 170–171.

A. Walicki, *W kr,egu konserwatywnej utopii: Struktura prezmiany rossijskiego slowianofilstwa. Polish Review* 14 (1969) 116–117.

J. Bergamini, *The Tragic Dynasty: A History of the Romanovs. Russian Review* 29 (1970): 352–353.

M. Wolters, *Aussenpolitische Fragen vor der Vierten Duma: Ein Beitrag zur Geschichte des russischen Parteiwesens in der konstitutionellen Monarchie, insbesondere der Stellung zur Aussenpolitik während des Ersten Weltkrieges. American Historical Review* 76 (1971): 529.

I. N. Undzhiev, *Vasil Levski : Biografiia. American Historical Review* 76 (1971): 799.

D. Kalmykow, *Memoirs of a Russian Diplomat: Outposts of the Empire, 1839–1917. Slavic Review* 31 (1972): 670.

I. A. Fedosov et al., *Istochnikovedenie istorii SSSR XIX–nachala XX v. Slavic Review* 31 (1972): 683–684.

R.T. McNally, *Chaadayev and His Friends: An Intellectual History of Peter Chaadayev and His Russian Contemporaries. Russian Review* 32 (1973): 93–94.

A. D. Ferguson, R.T. Fisher, Jr., S. Pushkarev, A. Lossky, and G. Vernadsky, eds., *A Source Book for Russian History from Early Times to 1917. Russian Review* 32 (1973): 312.

M. Paléologue, *An Ambassador's Memoirs*, 3 vols. *Slavic Review* 32 (1973): 388–389.

B. Bonwetsch, *Kriegsallianz und Wirtschaftsinteressen: Russland in den Wirtschaftsplänen Englands und Frankreichs. Slavic Review* 33 (1974): 139.

E. P. Trani, *The Treaty of Portsmouth: An Adventure in American Diplomacy.* Slavic Review 33 (1974): 775.

H. Mehlinger and J. M. Thompson, *Count Witte and the Tsarist Government in the 1905 Revolution.* American Historical Review 79 (1974): 540–541.

O.R. Liess, *Sowjetische Nationalitätsstrategie als weltpolitisches Konzept.* Canadian Review of Studies in Nationalism 2 (1975): 201–202.

J. Zeldin (ed.), *Poems and Political Letters of F.I. Tyutchev.* Russian Review 34 (1975): 231–232.

M. F. Shabaeva (ed.), *Ocherki istorii i pedagogicheskoi mysli narodov SSR: XVIII v. i pervaia polovina XIX v.* American Historical Review 81 (1976): 184–185.

U. Liszkowski, *Zwischen Liberalismus und Imperialismus: Die zaristische Aussenpolitik vor dem Ersten Weltkrieg im Urteil Miljukovs und der Kadettenpartei 1904–1914.* Erasmus: Speculum Scientiarum 28 nos. 9–10, (1976): 299–301.

E. Birth, *Die Oktobristen (1905–1913): Zielvorstellungen und Struktur.* Erasmus: Speculum Scientiarum, 28, nos. 9–10, (1976): 301–302.

R. Fuhrmann, *Die orientalische Frage, das "Panslawistisch–Chauvinistische Lager" und das Zuwarten auf Krieg und Revolution: Die Osteuropaberichterstattung und Vorstellungen der "Deutschen Rundschau" 1874–1918.* Jahrbücher für Geschichte Osteuropas 25 (1976): 247–248.

A. Giesinger, *From Catherine to Khrushchev: The Story of Russia's Germans*, (with L. Schelbert). Slavic Review 35 (1976): 733.

D. Field, *Rebels in the Name of the Tsar.* Slavic Review 36 (1977): 115–6.

M. K. Bachstein, *Wenzel Jaksch und die sudetendeutsche Sozialdemokratie*, (with J. Vacek). Erasmus: Speculum Scientiarum 29 (1977): 816–818.

A. Vucinich, *Social Thought in Tsarist Russia: The Quest for a General Science of Society, 1861–1917.* Journal of Modern History 50 (1978): 183–184.

B. Kondis, *Greece and Albania, 1908–1914.* Slavic Review 38 (1979): 151–152.

J. Long, *The German Russians: A Bibliography of Russian Materials.* Slavic Review 38 (1979): 695.

V. S. Vardys and R. J, Misiunas (ed.), *The Baltic States in War and Peace.* *Slavic Review* 39 (1980): 331–332.

G. von Pistohlkors, *Ritterschaftliche Reformpolitik zwischen Russifizierung und Revolution: Historische Studien zum Problem der politischen Selbsteinschätzung der deutschen Oberschicht in den Ostseeprovinzen Russlands im Krisenjahr 1905. American Historical Review* 85 (1980): 436.

R. Schweitzer, *Autonomie und Autokratie: Die Stellung des Grossfürstentums Finnland in russischen Reich in der zweiten Hälfte des 19, Jahrhunderts (1863–1899). Slavic Review* 39 (1980): 679–680.

H. D. Löwe, *Antisemitismus und reaktionäre Utopie: Russischer Konservatismus im Kampf gegen den Wandel von Staat und Gesellschaft, 1890–1917. Slavic Review* 39 (1980): 684–685.

E. Amburger, *Ingermanland: Eine junge Provinz Russlands im Wirkungsbereich der Residenz und Weltstadt St. Petersburg–Leningrad,* 2 vols. *Journal of Baltic Studies* 12 (1981): 299– 300.

A. Attman, *The Struggle for Baltic Markets: Powers in Conflict, 1558–1618. Slavic Review* 40 (1981): 132.

A. Rossos, *Russia and the Balkans: Inter–Balkan Rivalries and Russian Foreign Policy, 1908–1914. American Historical Review* 87 (1982): 153– 156.

I. S. Dostian, *Russkaia obshchestvennaia mysl' i Balkanskie narody: Ot Radishcheva do dekabristov. American Historical Review* 87 (1982): 1429–1430.

D. von Mohrenschildt, *Toward a United States of Europe: Plans and Projects of Federal Reconstruction of Russia in the Nineteenth Century. Russian Review* 41 (1982): 325–326.

J. Borys, *The Sovietization of Ukraine: The Communist Doctrine and Practice of National Self–Determination. Canadian Review of Studies in Nationalism* 9 (1982): 338–339.

M. Engman, *St. Petersburg och Finland: Migration och influens 1703–1917,* (with C. Nokkentved). *Jahrbücher für Geschichte Osteuropas* 15 (1984): 69–71.

H. D. von Engelhardt and H. Neuschäffer, *Die Livländische Gemeinnützige und Oekonomische Sozietät (1792–1939). Jahrbücher für Geschichte Osteuropas* 15 (1984): 71–72.

H. G. Linke, *Das zaristische Russland und der Erste Weltkrieg. American Historical Review* 89 (1984): 814–815.

U. Haustein (ed.), *Ostmitteleuropa: Berichte und Forschungen. Jahrbücher für Geschichte Osteuropas* 32 (1984): 116–117.

A. Henriksson, *The Tsar's Loyal Germans–The Riga German Community: Social Change and the Nationality Question 1885–1905. Canadian Journal of History* 29 (1984): 138–140.

A. Ezergailis, *The Latvian Impact on the Bolshevik Revolution: The First Phase, September 1917 to April 1918. Nationality Papers* 12 (1984): 287–288.

N. Tumarkin, *Lenin Lives! The Lenin Cult in Soviet Russia. Canadian Review of Studies in Nationalism* 11 (1984): 164–165.

S. L. Chernov, *Rossiia na zavershaiushchem etape vostochnogo krizisa, 1875–1878. American Historical Review* 90 (1985): 723.

M. G. Müller, *Polen zwischen Preussen und Russland: Souveränitätskrise und Reformpolitik 1736–1752. Slavic Review* 44 (1985): 561–562.

M. Behnen, *Rüstung, Bündnis, Sicherheit: Dreibund und informeller Imperialismus, 1900–1908. American Historical Review* 91 (1986): 686–687.

E. Judge, *Plehve: Repression and Reform in Imperial Russia, 1902– 1904. Journal of Modern History* 58 (1986): 380–381.

G. Hamburg, *Politics of the Russian Nobility, 1881–1895. Journal of Modern History* 58 (1986): 996–997.

E. Donnert, *Neue Wege im russischen Geschichtsdenken des 18. Jahrhunderts. Slavic Review* 45 (1986): 322–323.

P. Ramet (ed.), *Religion and Nationalism in Soviet and East European Politics. Canadian Review of Studies in Nationalism* 13 (1986): 304–305.

P. Luntinen, *F. A. Seyn: A Political Biography of a Tsarist Imperialist as Administrator of Finland. American Historical Review* 92 (1987): 692.

W. Wawrykowa, *"Für eure und unsere Freiheit": Studentenschaft und junge Intelligenz Ost–und Mitteleuropas in der ersten Hälfte des 19. Jahrhunderts. Slavic Review* 46 (1987): 329–330.

S.M. Solov'ev, *History of Russia. Journal of Baltic Studies* 18 (1987): 107.

I. Fleischhauer, *Die Deutschen im Zarenreich: Zwei Jarhunderte deutsch–russische Kulturgemeinschaft,* (with L. Schelbert). *American Historical Review* 93 (1988): 194.

I. Fleischhauer and B. Pinkus, *The Soviet Germans,* (with L. Schelbert). *American Historical Review* 93 (1988): 194–195.

T. Raun, *Estonia and the Estonians. Journal of Baltic Studies* 19 (1988): 178–179.

P. Potichnyi and H. Aster (eds.), *Ukrainian–Jewish Relations in Historical Perspective. Canadian Slavonic Papers* 30 (1988): 523–524.

G. von Rauch (ed.), *Geschichte der deutschbaltischen Geschichtsschreibung. Jahrbuch des baltischen Deutschtums* (1989): 190–192.

D. Lee, *The People's Universities of the USSR. Journal of Baltic Studies* 20 (1989): 198.

G. von Pistohlkors (ed.), *Die Universitäten Dorpat/Tartu, Riga und Wilna/ Wilnius, 1579–1979: Beiträge zu ihrer Geschichte und ihrer Wirkung im Grenzbereich zwischen West und Ost. Slavic Review* 48 (1989): 526–527.

E. Donnert, *Peter der Grosse: Der Veränderer Russlands. Slavic Review* 48 (1989): 653.

Z. Kohut, *Russian Centralism and Ukrainian Autonomy: Imperial Absorption of the Hetmanate 1760s–1830s. Journal of Ukrainian Studies* 1 (1990): 78–81.

J. Long, *From Privileged to Dispossessed: The Volga Germans, 1862–1917. Russian Review* 49 (1990): 200–201.

R. Pipes, *Russia Observed: Collected Essays on Russian and Soviet History. Russian History* 17 (1990): 227–228.

T. Polvinen, *Riket och Gränsmarken: N. I. Bobrikov, Finlands Generalguvernör. Slavic Review* 49 (1990): 297–298.

J. Alexander, *Catherine the Great: Life and Legend. Journal of Modern History* 63 (1991): 614–616.

G. Simon, *Nationalismus und Nationalitätenpolitik in der Sowjetunion: Von der totalitären Diktatur zur nachstalinischen Gesellschaft. Canadian Review of Studies in Nationalism* 18 (1991): 268–269.

M. Bruchis, *The USSR: Language and Realities. Canadian Review of Studies in Nationalism* 18 (1991): 272–273.

A. Alexander, Frank Kämpfer, and A. Kappeler (eds.), *Kleine Völker in der Geschichte Osteuropas: Festschrift für Günther Stökl zum 75. Geburtstag. Slavic Review* 51 (1992): 608–609.

N.I., Tsimbaev, *Sergei Solov'ev. Russian Review* 52 (1993): 129– 130.

B. Jelavich, *Russia's Balkan Entanglements 1806–1914* (with N. Ceh). *Canadian Review of Studies in Nationalism*, XX, 1–2 (1993): 147–148.

A. Kappeler, *Russland als Vielvölkerreich: Entstehung, Geschichte, Zerfall*. *Russian Review* 52 (1993): 573–574.

E. Donnert, *Das russische Zarenreich: Aufstieg und Untergang einer Weltmacht*. *Russian Review* 53 (1994): 576–577.

Forthcoming

"K. Leon'tev, Iu. Samarin, N.Strakhov." *West–östliche Spiegelungen*, Bd. 4–B, ed. Lev Kopelev. Munich: Wilhelm Fink Verlag.

"Traditional Elites, Religion, and Nation–Building in Finland the Baltic Provinces and Lithuania, 1700–1914." In *Poland, Finland and the Russian Empire*. London: School of Slavonic and East European Studies.

"Der sowjetische Historismus und Ostmitteleuropa nach 1939." *Jahrbuch des Instituts für ostdeutsche Kultur und Geschichte*.

O. Subtelny. *Ukraine: A History* in *Nationalities Papers*.

List of Contributors

John A. Armstrong, Professor Emeritus
University of Wisconsin, Madison
40 Water Street
St. Augustine, FL 32084

Nick Ceh, Ph.D. Candidate
Department of History
University of Illinois at Chicago
851 S. Morgan Street
Chicago, IL 60607-7049

James Cracraft, Professor
Department of History
University of Illinois at Chicago
851 S. Morgan Street
Chicago, IL 60607-7049

Rudolph Daniels, Professor
Department of History
Morningside College
1501 Morningside Avenue
Sioux City, IA 51106-1751

Erich Donnert, Professor Emeritus
Universität Halle
Eschenweg 4
D-06099 Halle, Germany

George Enteen, Professor
Department of History
Pennsylvania State University
University Park, PA 16802-6211

Stephen Fischer-Galati, Professor
East European Quarterly, Editor
P.O. Box 10039
Bradenton, FL 34282-0039

Eva-Maria Hartenstein, Professor
Hochschule für Kunst und Design
Theodor-Storm-Strasse 1
D-06099 Halle, Germany

Robert E. Jones, Professor
Department of History
University of Massachusetts
Amherst, MA 01003

Osmo Jussila, Professor
Department of Political History
University of Helsinki
Kuusiniemi 9b4
02710 Espoo 71, Finland

Peter Kenez, Professor
Department of History
University of California
Santa Cruz, CA 95064

John Kulczycki, Professor
Department of History
University of Illinois at
Chicago
851 S. Morgan
Chicago, IL 60607-7049

Bernard Michel, Professeur
Institut Pierre Renouvin
U.F.R. d'histoire
Panthéon—Sorbonne
14, rue Cujas 75231
Paris Cedex 5, France

Dominic Pacyga, Professor
Department of Liberal
Education
Columbia College
600 S. Michigan Avenue
Chicago, IL 60605

Andrejs Plakans, Professor
Department of History
Iowa State University
Ames, IA 50011-1202

Leo Schelbert, Professor
Department of History
University of Illinois at
Chicago
851 S. Morgan Street
Chicago, IL 60607-7049

Lech Trzeciakowski, Professor
Instytut Historii Uniwersytetu im.
A. Mickiewicza, Sw. Marcin 78
61-809 Poznan, Poland

Zdenko Zlatar, Senior Lecturer
Department of History
University of Sydney
N.S.W. 2006 Sydney, Australia

George Yaney, Professor
Department of History
University of Maryland
2115 Francis Scott Key Hall
College Park, MD 20742-7315